About Island Press

Since 1984, the nonprofit organization Island Press has been stimulating, shaping, and communicating ideas that are essential for solving environmental problems worldwide. With more than 1,000 titles in print and some 30 new releases each year, we are the nation's leading publisher on environmental issues. We identify innovative thinkers and emerging trends in the environmental field. We work with world-renowned experts and authors to develop cross-disciplinary solutions to environmental challenges.

Island Press designs and executes educational campaigns in conjunction with our authors to communicate their critical messages in print, in person, and online using the latest technologies, innovative programs, and the media. Our goal is to reach targeted audiences—scientists, policymakers, environmental advocates, urban planners, the media, and concerned citizens—with information that can be used to create the framework for long-term ecological health and human well-being.

Island Press gratefully acknowledges major support of our work by The Agua Fund, The Andrew W. Mellon Foundation, The Bobolink Foundation, The Curtis and Edith Munson Foundation, Forrest C. and Frances H. Lattner Foundation, The JPB Foundation, The Kresge Foundation, The Oram Foundation, Inc., The Overbrook Foundation, The S.D. Bechtel, Jr. Foundation, The Summit Charitable Foundation, Inc., and many other generous supporters.

The opinions expressed in this book are those of the author(s) and do not necessarily reflect the views of our supporters.

Resilient Cities

OVERCOMING FOSSIL FUEL DEPENDENCE

Resilient Cities

OVERCOMING FOSSIL FUEL DEPENDENCE

Second Edition

Peter Newman, Timothy Beatley, and Heather Boyer

Washington | Covelo | London

Library of Congress Control Number: 2016961434

✪ Printed on recycled, acid-free paper

Manufactured in the United States of America
10 9 8 7 6 5 4 3 2 1

Keywords: automobile dependence, autonomous vehicles, biofuels, climate change, environmental health, fossil fuel use, green architecture, green infrastructure, housing affordability, regenerative urbanism, renewable energy, social equity, solar energy, urban planning, urban policy, wind energy

Contents

Preface

When we put the first edition of this book together in the early part of the century, we were very hopeful that the agenda on resilience in cities would begin to include how to overcome fossil fuel dependence. This has undoubtedly happened, although we face new political challenges today. Yet this book remains one of hope for cities.

How did I get into this?
—Peter Newman

My involvement in these issues goes back to the first oil crisis in 1973, when I was a postdoctoral student at Stanford University in California. For the first time an external force had been imposed on the supply chain for gasoline. The OPEC-induced physical reductions in supply caused real panic in the community as people stayed at home or queued for hours for diminishing supplies. Social disarray began to be displayed as some people stole fuel; across society there were myths about giant caverns of oil being stored by greedy oil companies, and environmentalists were being accused of causing the decline. What stayed with me from this time was how suddenly a city can flip into a state of fear. It seemed to paralyze the city and lead to behavior you would never expect in normal times.

M. King Hubbert, by then age seventy, gloated to a rapidly convened energy course at Stanford that he had predicted this crisis in 1956. However, he said, though the crisis in 1973 seemed hard, the real test would be in the early part of the twenty-first century, when global oil would peak. This would be, he believed, the biggest challenge that our oil-based civilization had ever faced. The glue would begin to come unstuck. Climate change was something that we were all beginning to understand, but its impacts seemed a long way off. Together they challenged us to see that reducing fossil fuels was the agenda we must face up to sooner or later—especially in our cities.

I have spent the past thirty years trying to create awareness of this issue and to help prepare our cities and rural regions for the new constraint. I have been in and out of politics as an elected councilor and advisor to politicians for these past thirty years. Resilience for politicians is about getting reelected; for me it was about ensuring that cities like my own had a chance at a better future by being prepared for long-term underlying issues such as fossil fuel dependence. But I tried to see how both kinds of resilience could be achieved and indeed could be merged.

My main achievements have been in getting electric rail systems built, as they represented to me not only a better way to make a city work without oil but also a market-oriented way to restructure the city in its land use patterns to be less car dependent. Most of all, these rail systems seemed to generate a sense of hope in a city. The politicians loved it and won elections on the rail decisions.

I mostly learned that whenever politicians made decisions based on fear, they ended up regretting it. Polls and political advice might have suggested a certain policy direction to satisfy the fearmongers, but deep down they knew it wouldn't last and wasn't right. So I came to see that the resilience of cities is built on hope, not fear, and that the way we would cope with fossil fuel reductions and climate change would depend on whether the politics of hope or fear dominated in our cities. This book summarizes that journey.

How did I get into this too . . . ?
—Tim Beatley

The oil crisis of the early 1970s had a personal and profound impact on me as a newly licensed teenage driver. Growing up in an excessively car-dependent American society, that driver's license translated into long-anticipated freedom and independence. The sudden (and incomprehensible to my young mind) appearance of hours-long (and miles-long) lines at the gas pumps virtually ended my car-mobility before it started. For at least a while I rediscovered my feet and the ability to function quite well without a car. But the notion that there might actually be finite limits to something that I assumed was limitless was a profound revelation, and the lines at the pump, and the chaos and anxiety that ensued, remain vivid memories of my youth.

These events have certainly helped to shape my own sense of need to be less reliant on oil, less dependent on any single resource, especially one with such serious environmental and social costs.

Many years later, the opportunity of living in the Netherlands reawakened me to the virtues and possibilities of a life without a car, to the enriching possibilities of a life based on walking, bicycling, and public transit. Much of my professional and academic career has been focused on finding creative ways to plan and design highly livable urban environments less dependent on cars (and oil): places that at once strengthen our human connections and connectedness and our bonds to the natural systems and landscapes that ultimately sustain us. Often we have gotten it wrong, of course, and my work on coastal policy and environmental planning has shown the dangers of hubris and carelessness in our treatment of natural systems and of our failure to understand the profound interconnectedness of urban and natural systems—can we continue to fill coastal wetlands, modify natural river systems, and ultimately alter planetary climate itself without severe impacts in cities like New Orleans? I have also had the great fortune of studying and analyzing cities that are beginning to get it right, cities such as London and New York and Stockholm, that are finally recognizing the practical and moral necessity of confronting climate change, taking steps to wean themselves off fossil fuels, and in the process forging hopeful, indeed exciting, urban futures.

For more than twenty years I have had the privilege of teaching a form of urban planning that blends an appreciation of local places with a sense of global responsibility. Fossil fuel dependence presents the field of planning with an unprecedented opportunity to help shape a more sustainable, healthy, and just urban future. These are challenging times for planners, to be sure, but the chance to make a difference has never been greater.

And me . . . ?

—Heather Boyer

The themes running through this book are fear and hope, and these are ever present in the books I edit that earnestly detail the dangers of continuing with our current patterns of development and then provide plans, best practices, and examples of how we can create more livable, sustainable, resilient communities. On my journey I have experienced many different types of urban (and some suburban) living in Green Bay, Wisconsin; Minneapolis–St. Paul, Minnesota; Washington, DC; Boulder, Colorado; Cambridge, Massachusetts; and Brooklyn, New York. The city seen as the most sustainable—Boulder—is in fact a lovely, green oasis. But I found that once I left the inner-greenbelt bike paths (which are, gloriously, plowed immediately after a snow), getting around in most places required a car (or a bus that was likely to be sitting in the same traffic). But there is much to be hopeful for in Colorado, with its new transit system (and planned transit-oriented developments) for the Denver region.

After one year in Cambridge as a Loeb Fellow at the Harvard Graduate School of Design, I ended up in Brooklyn. From here I continue to work on books on urban resilience and see resilience efforts firsthand post–Hurricane Sandy. I am raising two kids in a city that we can navigate without a car. A city that is gritty, beautiful, diverse, amazing, and flawed. It is a model for some ecological resilience efforts while starkly showing the need to broaden the definition of "resilience" to include citizens regardless of race, income, beliefs, or ethnicity.

In the first edition of this book I wrote that I was hopeful that the federal government would implement policies that would help to further urban resilience. As the dust settles from the most recent U.S. election, I no longer have that hope. Yet, given the emerging power and innovation of cities to drive change in spite of unfriendly federal policy, I am hopeful that cities will continue to strive for greater resilience, inclusion, understanding, and tolerance. As Jane Jacobs wrote in *The Death and Life of Great American Cities*, "This is what a city is, bits and pieces that supplement each other and support each other."

Acknowledgments

The first edition of this book had a long gestation. As described in the preface, Tim and Peter began to note an emerging serious issue with cities and their oil dependence in the 1970s. We were not alone in that concern, and we have had a lot of help in putting our fears and hopes on paper.

Families have been especially important to all of us, as our lives in cities are primarily lived out through our families. Each of us owes a debt to our parents, partners, and children, who have been there to help us as we tried to reduce our footprints while improving our urban lifestyle opportunities. In particular, we would like to thank Jan, Sam, Anneke, Carolena, Jadie, Doug, Barb, Bob (who set an example by riding his bike year-round in Wisconsin), Elijah, and Alice.

Communities give context to our work. Fremantle, Charlottesville, Boulder, and New York have each provided opportunities for us to practice our policies and learn how hard it is to generate hope for a more resilient city. In drawing inspiration for our book, we have worked more recently in many other cities, including Christchurch, Singapore, Copenhagen, Pune, Bangalore, Shanghai, Beijing, and all the cities in Tim's Biophilic Cities Network.

Institutions have enabled us to pursue our ideas. Our universities, Curtin, Virginia, and Harvard, have given us the priceless opportunity to research and to teach about resilient cities. The Australian-American

Fulbright Commission provided a Senior Scholarship to Peter so that he could focus on the book, and the School of Architecture at the University of Virginia provided the Harry W. Porter Jr. Visiting Professorship, which enabled us to complete the first edition.

Particular thanks to colleagues who have contributed at various times should include Jeff Kenworthy, Anthony Perl, Randy Salzman, and Jeanne Liedtka initially and, more recently, Josh Byrne, Giles Thomson, Jemma Green, Evan Jones, Rohit Sharma, Sebastian Davies-Slate, Jana Söderlund, Mariela Zingoni de Baro, Kate Meyer, Yuan Gao, Vanessa Rauland, and Phil Webster.

Urban Resilience: Cities of Fear and Hope

*Look at the world around you. It may seem like an immovable,
implacable place. It is not. With the slightest push—in just the right
place—it can be tipped.* —Malcolm Gladwell, *The Tipping Point*

Resilience in our personal lives is about lasting, about making it through
crises, about inner strength and strong physical constitution. Resilience is
destroyed by fear, which causes us to panic, reduces our inner resolve, and
eventually debilitates our bodies. Resilience is built on hope, which gives us
confidence and strength. Hope is not blind to the possibility of everything
getting worse, but it is a choice we can make when faced with challenges.
Hope brings health to our souls and bodies.

"Resilience" is a term used in disciplines ranging from ecology to psychology. It became very popular to apply the term to cities after natural
disasters such as Hurricane Sandy in the New York region in 2012. Cities
too need to last, to respond to crises, and to adapt; cities require an inner
strength, a resolve, as well as a strong physical infrastructure and built
environment.

Fear undermines the resilience of cities. The near or total collapse of
many cities has been rooted in fear: health threats like the plague and yel-
low fever have struck cities and emptied them of those with the resources
to escape, leaving only the poor behind. Invading armies have destroyed

cities by sowing fear before an arrow or shot was fired. The racial fears of a generation in American cities decanted millions to the suburbs and beyond. Perhaps the biggest fear today in many cities is terrorism. In New York after 9/11, fear stopped people from congregating on streets or using the subway and sent many urban dwellers scurrying for the suburbs, but the city proved to be resilient and resisted collapse. Immediately after the terrorist bombings in Paris in 2015, city officials urged residents to stay indoors. And in the digital age the community responded with the Twitter hashtag #portesouvertes (open doors), to offer shelter to those unable to travel home immediately after the attacks. The city steeled itself to return to normal, to resolve to go to work and resume gathering in public spaces. At one of the target locations, the café La Bonne Bière, a sign was hung at the reopening: *Je suis en terrasse* (I am on the terrace).

As we complete the final draft of this book, the world is confronted by the U.S. election of Donald Trump as president. This appears to be a very significant and high-profile setback for overcoming fossil fuel dependence, since the president-elect has espoused skepticism about climate change and support for reviving coal in America's heartland economies. What does this mean for cities of fear and hope? This book will continue to set out the agenda for hope in global cities. The phasing out of fossil fuels on a global stage is now well under way, and a new administration will find it difficult, if not impossible, to prevent business and civil society from continuing this process. Cities have been leading this charge and will continue to do so. Indeed, the change at the top in the United States is likely to induce a powerful response from cities to ensure they do not lose their economic competitiveness because of nostalgia about a fossil fuel era that is ending.

Cities are working to address the threat of excessive dependence on fossil fuels in an age of carbon constraint. The past decade has seen the climate agenda taking a higher and higher profile, which has inevitably left cities saying: How do we do this? Is it possible? Networks such as the C40 Cities Climate Leadership Group were formed to help global cities address climate change; C40 now has ninety of the world's biggest cities closely involved in leading the way for the world to decarbonize more quickly. The Rockefeller Foundation launched its 100 Resilient Cities (100RC) network to help "cities around the world become more resilient to the physical, social and economic challenges that are a growing part of the 21st century."[1]

FIGURE I.1: Rather than retreat from public spaces after the terrorist attacks in Paris in 2015, people came together in a show of strength and support. (Credit: Citron/CC-BY-SA-3.0)

These networks and other groups, such as ICLEI—Local Governments for Sustainability, are likely to grow in their significance and focus.

When we were writing the first edition of this book in 2008, oil depletion had reached a point where cheap oil peaked globally and the price rose to $140 per barrel. As we set out in the first edition, this was a major factor in triggering the global financial crash as outer suburban mortgages could not be paid and whole land developments burst their bubbles. Cities were left with choices as to how they should now invest, and many began the journey away from coal, with its obvious damage to the climate and air quality, and oil, with its huge vulnerability to booms and busts. Many cities have shown that this movement away from coal and oil is not only possible but also preferable. They have said yes to options from new markets; new approaches to energy, water, waste, housing, infrastructure, and landscaping; and associated new governance approaches. They are delivering hope for the future of their cities.

National governments of the world have only just signed off on the Paris Agreement on climate change, while cities are mostly well down the track of adapting and innovating to cope with carbon constraint.[2] Adoptions of phase-out strategies for coal and oil have reached the stage where cities are now dealing with stranded assets—coal and oil assets that either are unnecessary as a result of renewable options or are unusable because of new policies and regulations. The International Energy Agency (IEA) has suggested that at least $300 billion in fossil fuel investments is likely to be stranded as the world takes climate policy more seriously. Peabody Energy, the largest coal miner in the world, has filed for bankruptcy. In Perth, Western Australia, you can buy a newly refurbished coal-fired power station for $1. Oil exploration companies are declaring bankruptcy on a daily basis. We will help to explain this and see how we can assist the adoption of non–fossil fuel innovations in an appropriate and timely way to avoid stranding assets.[3]

Resilient cities will become less dependent on fossil fuels as these energy sources become increasingly subject to three major forces:

- *Market forces.* Innovative markets are rapidly finding more effective alternatives, thus leaving fossil fuel suppliers to significant economic dislocation as their assets become stranded. Prices for fossil fuels will be volatile and vulnerable to rapid change rather than being the basis of good investment. Renewable energy prices continue to decline in a predictable way as mass production mainstreams the new technology.
- *Regulatory forces.* The Paris Agreement, which was adopted by the world's nations in December 2015 and came into force in November 2016, commits us all to phasing out fossil fuels. Increasingly, cities and nations will be regulating to enable this process. It is now inevitable that governments will intervene to push the market process; some will be very heavy-handed, and others will hold back. In the end, the use of fossil fuels will be transitioned into history.
- *Civil society forces.* The driving force behind long-term change is always the ethical, cultural, and political force best described as civil society—the combination of nongovernmental organizations, universities, scientific organizations, media, and religious institutions—which frames the visions and values driving change. The Intergovernmental Panel on Climate Change is in fact part of civil society, as it is a voluntary group of thousands of scientists who get together to write about climate change on the basis of their expertise and their shared

concerns. It is quite clear now that global civil society has won this agenda, and now it is just a question of delivering it in a time when some governments are looking backward rather than forward. While much of the agenda will take time, the early steps by urban leaders in community, government, business, and practice are well under way, as we show in this book.

Together these forces are part of a global process. Those who say that we cannot change and must hold on to the old fossil fuel economy at all costs will be undermining their cities and making them less resilient. They will drive cities into economic decline, and communities and local businesses will inevitably move to options better than fossil fuels.

This book is not about introducing a new fear; it is about understanding the implications of our actions and finding hope in the steps that can be taken to create resilient cities in the face of carbon constraint in both coal and oil. To do this, global cities need to reduce dependence on large-scale coal-based power and on oil-based automobile transport. Some cities exude hope as they grow and confront the future; some can even start to see a future in which the city is regenerating its local and global environment. Other cities reek of fear as the processes of decline set in and the pain of change causes distrust and despair. Most cities have a combination of the two. For example, Los Angeles is a city with some of the nation's worst traffic congestion (eighty-one hours of delay annually per traveler in 2015)[4] and rapidly growing urban sprawl. While it is experiencing areas of abandonment as a result of urban or suburban decline, its inner city continues to grow, reclaiming old areas once abandoned and reversing the decline of generations. Recent investments in walkable communities and mass transportation offer new hope for a more resilient L.A. As a *New York Times* writer observed, "Downtown is bustling with development, filled with people who make a life without cars, relying on walking, bicycles and mass transit."[5] One of the bright spots in the recent U.S. election was the passing of Measure M in Los Angeles, in which residents overwhelmingly voted yes on a permanent sales tax increase to fund a $140 billion expansion of their transit system.

Denver is another U.S. city that in the 1980s and 1990s had minimal transit and a declining central city. The city's FasTracks Program has

FIGURE I.2: A Metro Red Line train at North Hollywood Station. In 2016, voters in Los Angeles approved a sales tax increase to fund a major expansion of the county's public transit system. (By HanSangYoon via Wikimedia Commons)

built new urban rail across the city and helped to revive the downtown, as demonstrated by this book's cover photograph showing a popular children's water fountain play area in front of the newly restored Union Station.

Cities of fear make decisions based on short-term, even panicked, responses, while cities of hope plan for the long term, with each decision building toward that vision in hope that some of the steps will be tipping points that lead to fundamental change. Cities of fear engage in competition as their only driving force, while cities of hope build consensus around cooperation and partnership. Cities of fear see threats everywhere, while cities of hope see in every crisis opportunities to improve.

This book focuses on the challenges our metropolitan areas face in responding to their carbon footprint—their dependence on fossil fuels—and how this impacts our irreplaceable natural resources. Jared Diamond's book *Collapse* looks at how some settlements and regions have collapsed as a result of their inability to adapt, leading to an undermining of the natural resource base on which they depended. A characteristic of those societies appears to be that they became fixated by their fear of the future or were so stuck in their ways that they could not adapt to the future as changing conditions undermined their very existence. On the other hand, Diamond outlines examples of societies facing the same pressures that were able to adapt—they turned their hope into resilience.[6]

The Oxford University philosopher Nick Bostrom has expressed a new way of understanding this threat to the future by calling it an "existential threat." He writes, "Existential risks are those that threaten the entire future of humanity. Many theories of value imply that even relatively small reductions in net existential risk have enormous expected value. Despite their importance, issues surrounding human-extinction risks and related hazards remain poorly understood." Bostrom suggests that the main existential risks threatening the very possibility of human life on the planet are all anthropogenic—caused by human activities: greenhouse gas emissions, biotechnology and nanotechnology, artificial intelligence, and nuclear weapons stockpiling.[7] He suggests that "because of accelerating technological progress, humankind may be rapidly approaching a critical phase in its career,"[8] and he outlines a series of approaches to understanding how we must address these issues.

The key message of our book is that we must adapt our cities to lessen our dependence on coal and petroleum. This is no small task, as the use of coal and oil grew in every city in the world each year during most of the twentieth century. Yet it is within our reach to turn this trend around in the twenty-first century, and the process is already well under way without harm to our economies. Global governance is recognizing the implications of climate change and the impact of cities, and there is a powerful movement to require all nations and cities to reduce fossil fuel use each year. This is no longer a speculative plea to cities; it is becoming an economic and legal necessity. But how do we do it?

Few would suggest that creating resilient cities is possible with technological advances alone, and most would agree that it must involve change in our cultures, our economies, and our lifestyles. It is the human capacity of our cities that is ultimately being tested by these challenges.

Bostrom's approach focuses not on cities but on humankind. Diamond specifically focuses on cities. He suggests that there are many lessons to be learned from the history of cities and that we can apply them to today's biggest threat: climate change. He suggests that climate change and resource degradation threaten our cities and regions today in similar ways to threats in ancient times. These threats appear to be slow-moving phenomena, but they undermine the continued growth of cities. Our book takes this potential of urban collapse seriously but is focused on how we can adapt to our present crises, how we can make our cities more resilient for the future in ways that are socially and economically acceptable and feasible. As the quotation at the start of this introduction suggests, a positive tipping point can accelerate change toward resilience, just as a negative one can rapidly lead to decline.

Why Concentrate on Cities?

Cities have grown rapidly in the age of coal and oil; they now consume 75 percent of the world's energy and emit 80 percent of the world's greenhouse gases.[9] Cities are growing globally at a rate of 2 percent per year (more than 3 percent in less developed regions and 0.7 percent in more developed regions), while rural areas have leveled out and are in many places declining. Half of humanity lives in cities, and it is estimated that by 2030 the number of city dwellers will reach 5 billion, or 60 percent of the world's population.[10]

Urbanization has been taking place since the Neolithic Revolution, when agriculture enabled food surpluses to create a division of labor in settlements. The unlocking of human ingenuity to work on technology, trade, and urban culture has created ever-expanding opportunities in cities. However, while some cities took advantage of these new opportunities, many remained little more than rural trading posts. Urban opportunities accelerated with the Industrial Revolution and more recently with the globalization of the economy. But again, not every city has taken advantage of these opportunities. Some cities, such as Liverpool, Philadelphia, and Pittsburgh, have struggled to adapt to the new opportunities and have relied for too long on outmoded methods of industrial production. Yet other cities, such as Manchester and New York, have made the transition and are thriving.

Peter Hall, who has examined why some cities adapt more rapidly than others, suggests that the desire to experiment and innovate is found in the heart of the city's culture. Robert Friedel calls it the "culture of improvement," Lewis Mumford refers to this instinct in a city as a "collective work of art," and Tim Gorringe calls it "creative spirituality."[11] Whatever it is called, the ability to experiment and innovate is the tissue of hope and the core of resilience.

Overcoming the fear of change today must involve new experiments in green urbanism and climate entrepreneurship as cities seek to improve themselves in ways that fit their culture while they decarbonize. Which cities will respond to the new set of opportunities opening up around urban resilience? Rethinking how we create our built environment is critical in lessening our dependence on oil and minimizing our carbon footprint. Buildings produce 43 percent of the world's carbon dioxide emissions and consume 48 percent of the energy produced. It is projected that by shifting 60 percent of new growth to compact patterns, the United States will save 85 million metric tons of carbon dioxide annually by 2030.[12] We believe that the change, when dealing with global issues such as carbon constraint, needs to come from cities.

Nations can do a lot to help or hinder these efforts, but the really important initiatives have to begin at the city level because in any nation there is great variation in the way cities cope with challenges. Great leadership and innovation can be found in cities. For example, during the period when the United States was yet to ratify the Kyoto Protocol, more than 825 mayors of U.S. cities signed onto the U.S. Conference of Mayors Climate Protection Agreement to commit their cities to reaching the goals of the Protocol. The initiative, which was spearheaded by Seattle mayor Greg Nickels, set out to meet these goals through leadership and action advanced by a network of forward-thinking cities large and small. Since then, numerous city networks and organizations have formed, such as C40, mentioned earlier; Rockefeller's 100 Resilient Cities; the Carbon Neutral Cities Alliance, a project of the Urban Sustainability Directors Network; and ICLEI's Resilient Cities Network, which tends to work with small cities and local governments. Such power in cities is the real force for overcoming fossil fuel dependence. Places that turn their back on this global agenda will now find they are left out of urban best practice and left behind in a competitive economy.

The president and chief executive officer of the World Resources Institute, Andrew Steer, says that "if you want to win the climate change battle, it will be fought in the cities of the world."[13] An IEA study has shown that cities represent 70 percent of the cost-effective emissions reduction opportunities between now and 2050. Cities played a significant role in helping the world to accept the need for climate change as set out in the Paris Agreement in 2015, and they will continue to lead in the mainstreaming of coal and oil replacement. Bruce Katz of the Brookings Institution writes: "Centralized, hyper-specialized, one-size-fits-all approaches are fundamentally ill-suited for today's challenges. 21st century problems demand rapid, locally-tailored solutions that take a holistic approach to problem solving— approaches that deploy the expertise, capacity, and resources of the public, private, and civic sectors in collaboration."[14] Although this book's focus is on American cities, where perhaps so much more is needed, many of the examples will come from elsewhere in the world.

What Are Resilient Cities?

Since Hurricane Katrina, which devastated many Gulf Coast cities in 2005, the Haiti earthquake of 2010, which affected 3 million people, and Hurricane Sandy in the New York region in 2012, resilient cities have most often been discussed in relation to a city's ability to "bounce back" from a natural disaster. (Port-au-Prince still has not recovered from the 2010 earthquake.) We believe that a resilient city should be able to anticipate, plan for, and mitigate the risks, and seize the opportunities, associated with economic, environmental, and social change. It needs to "bounce forward," not just bounce back.[15]

Given the complexity of cities and resilience, we came up with six principles of urban resilience and organized this edition around them. A resilient city will do the following:

1. Invest in renewable and distributed energy.
2. Create sustainable mobility systems.
3. Foster inclusive and healthy cities.
4. Shape disaster recovery for the future.
5. Build biophilic urbanism in the city and its bioregion.
6. Produce a more cyclical and regenerative metabolism.

All of these will help remove fossil fuels from cities. The countries that signed on to the Paris Agreement strive to be 100 percent free of carbon emissions by 2100 and up to 80 percent by 2050. This goal would keep global warming below an increase of 2°C. Many scientists now say we

FIGURE I.3: In Mississippi, a man waits in line in the heat to get a gallon of gas. In the aftermath of Hurricane Katrina, gasoline was very scarce in the area, with some lines a mile long. Overcoming fossil fuel dependence in cities will contribute to resilience to natural disasters. (Photo by: Liz Roll, from the FEMA Photo Library via Wikimedia Commons)

should keep the increase below 1.5°C, as this is the safest strategy. We are already seeing significant climate change after just a 1°C rise.[16]

Resilient cities have built-in systems that can adapt to change, such as a diversity of transport and land use systems and multiple sources of renewable power that will allow a city to survive shortages in fuel. Brian Walker, David Salt, and Walter Reid have summarized the academic area of "resilience thinking," which has emerged as a way of managing ecosystems, such as coral reefs, or farming systems and other complex social-economic-ecological systems. Their principles of resilience are applicable to cities. They write: "Resilience is the capacity of a system to absorb disturbance and still retain its basic function and structure." Tabatha Wallington, Richard Hobbs, and Susan Moore say that ecological resilience "may be measured by the magnitude of disturbance the system can tolerate and still persist."[17] This book attempts to apply this concept to the complex social-economic-ecological systems of cities, to show how cities can move beyond bouncing back and can bounce forward, even becoming regenerative.

Sustainable Cities, Resilient Cities, and Regenerative Cities

Throughout urban history there have been attempts at re-visioning cities— the Garden City, City Beautiful, Broadacre City, Radiant City. More recently we have had the sustainable city and the resilient city and the emerging regenerative city. In Peter's 1999 book *Sustainability and Cities*, the sustainable city was defined as one that is reducing its environmental footprint (resource consumption and associated wastes) while improving its livability (economy, health, and community).

Just as garden cities were a reaction to industrial smog and overcrowded housing, the concepts of sustainable, resilient, and regenerative cities are a reaction to the exploitive city, with its multiple negative impacts of excessive resource consumption and associated footprint. The sustainable cities concept was created to help us reduce the impact of our cities from fossil fuels, water, materials, land, and waste and to ease the loss of biodiversity while maintaining or improving livability. The resilient cities idea was created in response to disasters but also to the looming disaster of climate change associated with excessive fossil fuel use. This calls for a more aggressive reduction in fossil fuel use and greenhouse gas emissions, in the order of an 80 percent reduction in carbon dioxide (CO_2) emissions by 2050 and a 100 percent reduction in CO_2 by 2100.

In a resilient city that is committed to reducing its fossil fuel dependence, every step of the city's development and redevelopment will make it more sustainable: it will reduce its environmental footprint (consumption of land, water, materials, and energy, especially the coal and oil so critical to their economies, and the output of waste and emissions) while simultaneously improving its quality of life (environment, health, housing, employment, community) so that it can better fit within the capacities of local, regional, and global ecosystems. Resilience needs to be applied to all the natural resources on which cities rely.[18]

In resilience thinking, the more sustainable a city is, the more it will be able to cope with reductions in the resources used to make the city work.

Sustainability recognizes there are limits in the local, regional, and global systems within which cities fit, and when those limits are breached the city can rapidly decline. The more that a city can minimize its dependence on resources such as fossil fuels in a period when there are global constraints on supply and global demand is increasing, the more resilient it will be. Atlanta needs 782 gallons of gasoline per person each year for its urban system to work, but Barcelona needs just 64 gallons. Carbon constraints will seriously confront Atlanta, but Barcelona will be likely to cope with ease. Both cities will still need to have plans in place to help their citizens cope with such a disturbance.[19]

Resilient cities are also sustainable cities, though they take the reduction of footprint, especially from fossil fuels, much further. So what is beyond this vision of future cities?

Figure I.4 sets out a process of change that has been emerging over the past decade in how we seek to frame the kind of cities we want in the future.

All of these recent city visions are about *reducing* impact or environmental footprint. They start by showing that cities are growing fast, they are a big part of the global planetary problem, and they need to reduce a range of associated impacts. Many examples in the first edition of this book (and in many other books)[20] show where this is now under way in cities as technology, planning regulations, governance, and financing have combined to reduce impact while improving livability.

Regenerative urbanism steps in here and pushes us further. Is it possible

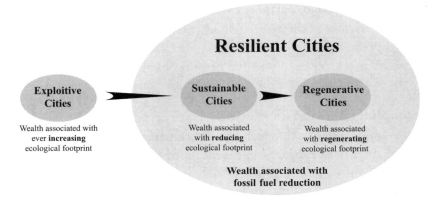

FIGURE I.4: The transition from exploitive cities to sustainable and then regenerative cities provides the framework for resilient cities.

for us to go beyond the reduction in impact to a new vision of how cities can operate in a way that is regenerative in terms of energy, water, waste, food, and biodiversity while continuing to improve livability? Can cities restore their local and global impacts rather than exploiting them? Can they be a major part of the planetary solution instead of part of the problem?

Landscape architect John Tillman Lyle was the first to extensively use the term "regenerative design" in the 1980s to describe the design of human settlements to mimic natural systems.[21] The increasing urgency for system redesign as various planetary boundaries have been, or are in danger of being, exceeded has led to a recent resurgence in the popularity of the regenerative design concept.[22]

In this book we are focused on resilient cities, for which we can show actual progress and examples. But throughout the book we will examine areas where there is potential for the next phase—regenerative cities. We will ask the questions that could get us closer to the regenerative city:

• How can we create cities that are like living ecosystems, repairing and restoring themselves as a part of the bioregional and biospheric cycles of carbon, nitrogen, phosphorus, water, and minerals?
• Is it possible for a city or region to create more renewable energy than it consumes, using the surplus to enable its productive functions (industries, buildings, and surrounding agriculture) to grow and thrive?
• Is it possible for a city's biodiversity to play a major role in enabling regional biodiversity to be improved rather than depleted? Can a city create more ecological niches, not fewer?
• Is it possible at the same time as regenerating local and planetary cycles to regenerate communities and economies so that cities are more livable and continue to provide the growth opportunities that have been cities' historical role?

Decoupling: A Cause for Hope?

Some commentators on the challenge of decarbonizing our cities have suggested that we must reduce wealth as measured by gross domestic product (GDP) or gross national income (GNI)[23] because they cannot see how an economy can be created that truly breaks free from fossil fuels and other damaging global impacts. Decoupling, a notion from the United Nations Environment Programme, posits that wealth and greenhouse gas (GHG)

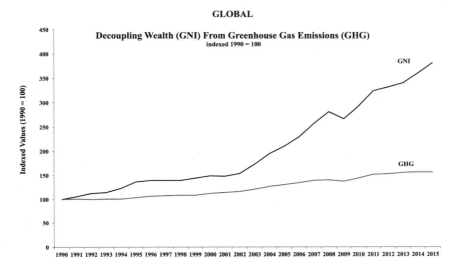

FIGURE I.5: Global decoupling of wealth (gross national income, or GNI) from greenhouse gas (GHG) emissions. The separation between growth in wealth and growth in GHG emissions set in globally around 2001 and has continued ever since. On this trajectory, GHG emissions will eventually decline. What can be seen by closely examining particular countries is that absolute decoupling is indeed happening. (Sources: International Energy Agency, 2015; World Bank, 2013)

emissions can be unlocked and even decoupled by a factor of five.[24] However, Tim Jackson, in his highly acclaimed book *Prosperity without Growth*, suggests that decoupling will always be only relative and not absolute—that is, GHG emissions will continue to rise even as the economy becomes relatively more efficient per unit of GDP.[25] As figure I.5 shows, worldwide GHG emissions are certainly now relatively decoupling from GDP (or GNI). The point where we actually declined in absolute terms may have been in 2015, and possibly earlier in most developed economies.

Figure I.6*A–E* shows how Denmark, the United States, Australia, China, and India are decoupling (some in absolute terms) from the two main fossil fuels, coal and oil. Denmark (*A*), as a typical European country, began to reduce its use of coal and oil back in the 1990s and struggled to grow in GNI, but during this century it has begun to thrive economically while rapidly phasing out coal and oil—both are decoupling absolutely. The United States (*B*) has been decoupling relatively since the 1990s but since

FIGURE I.6A

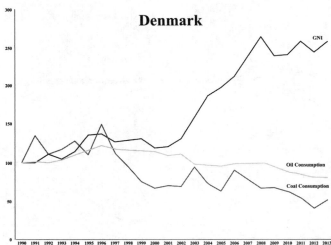

FIGURE I.6B

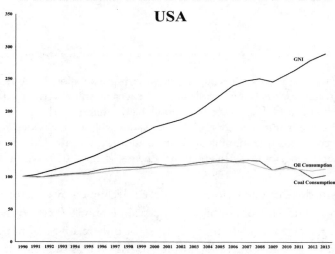

FIGURE I.6C

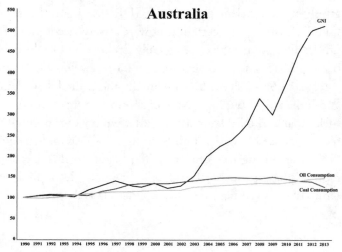

FIGURE I.6D · 17

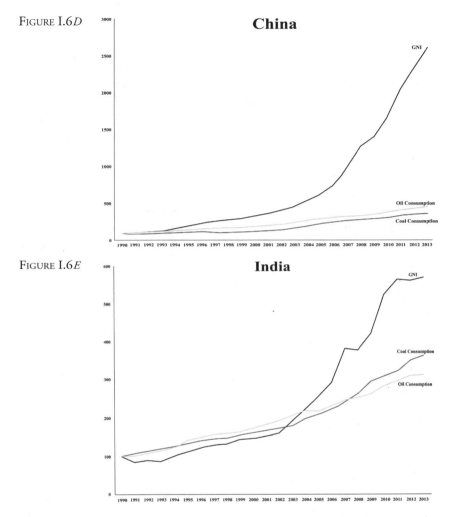

FIGURE I.6: Regional examples of decoupling showing gross national income (GNI) versus coal and oil consumption, 1990–2013. *A*, Denmark; *B*, United States; *C*, Australia; *D*, China; *E*, India. (Sources: International Energy Agency, 2015; World Bank, 2013)

2006 has been decoupling absolutely in both coal and oil. Australia (*C*) has a very similar trajectory, with very strong growth in GNI while coal began declining around 2006 and oil plateauing. China (*D*) has decoupled with dramatic growth in wealth while fossil fuels have plateaued and coal has begun to decline. India (*E*) has decoupled relatively but is still growing in coal and oil, as is the case with most developing nations and cities.

In the rest of this book, we shall see a pattern that these figures have shown us: Europe is leading the world in overcoming fossil fuel dependence; wealthy but recalcitrant places such as America and Australia are on the same trajectory as Europe but moving more slowly; China is setting the pattern for how the emerging world can lead in this process; and all parts of the developing world can leapfrog into the future of fossil fuel removal as they redirect their growth to global best practice, as seen in the graph of household energy use in the United Kingdom (see figure I.7). In all parts of the world, it is the cities that are decoupling their national economies from fossil fuels.

We can say with some confidence that as the economy grows, GHG emissions are unlikely to grow and economic growth will not suffer as the world overcomes its fossil fuel dependence. This is very important in easing extreme poverty, as committed to by all the world in September 2015 as part of the United Nations' Sustainable Development Goals. Decoupling remains a necessary global vision, along with removing fossil fuels from economic activity.[26]

It is also important to see that the rapid decline in extreme poverty (from more than 40 percent to less than 15 percent)[27] has mostly occurred within cities and that the extremely rapid urbanization in China (and now in India and Africa) is what fuels this dramatic change.[28] It is also clear that there was not as much concern for achieving GHG reductions during the rapid urbanization in the emerging world's cities over the period of the United Nations' Millennium Development Goals (2000–2015); these emerging cities have been focusing on ending poverty. But the new trend in China, where decoupling is under way, provides great hope that the process will spread to the whole emerging world. China will probably show the way to decouple rapidly: it not only led the world in recent energy efficiency gains but also is investing heavily in renewables ($90 billion in renewables in 2015, more than 60 percent of its energy investment). Much of China's continuing growth will be based on solar and wind energy, in contrast with the fossil fuel–based economic growth of the past fifteen years.

Although few would say that the battle is over, there is no doubt that the era of fossil fuel dependence is ending. This movement obviously needs to keep going and achieve exponential decline. Our book is written to help with that momentum through the powerful forces of change that are potentially available in our cities.

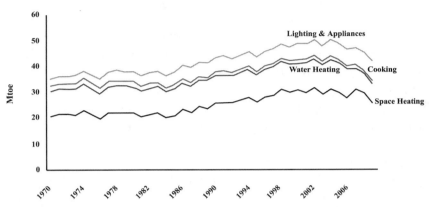

FIGURE I.7: Household energy use in the United Kingdom, 1970–2009, showing gains in household building and appliance efficiency. (Source: Intergovernmental Panel on Climate Change, 2014)

Map of the Book

The overcoming of fossil fuel dependence in our cities will consist of direct and indirect approaches to achieving this goal. These are set out in the six chapters that make up the body of this book, followed by a conclusion.

Direct approaches to fossil fuel removal consist of policies and practices that take fossil fuels out of power production (mostly coal and gas) and out of transportation (mostly oil). These are examined through the first two chapters.

Chapter 1, "Invest in Renewable and Distributed Energy," examines what is happening in renewable energy and what more is required. These changes are dramatically disrupting the energy sector.

In chapter 2, "Create Sustainable Mobility Systems," we focus on transportation and renewable options for powering it, as well as alternative transportation modes. We show that there are different urban fabrics for which different strategies for overcoming fossil fuel dependence will need to be adapted.

Indirect ways of taking fossil fuels out of our cities can achieve certain co-benefits in our cities. These indirect strategies are part of other urban agendas and processes that make our cities more resilient and more regenerative. They are examined in the next four chapters.

Chapter 3, "Foster Inclusive and Healthy Cities," looks at how to create greater equity and health for all urban citizens. Almost all the processes that lead to more inclusive and healthy places are simultaneously removing fossil fuels. A city cannot be resilient if it is resilient for only some of its citizens.

Chapter 4, "Shape Disaster Recovery for the Future," explores the resilience agenda of bouncing back and bouncing forward in the face of disaster. Creating a city with less dependence on fossil fuels is fundamental to good emergency and recovery planning.

Chapter 5, "Build Biophilic Urbanism in the City and Its Bioregion," examines how cities can use more natural systems in their buildings and regional infrastructure. Biophilic processes enable us to live better and with less need for fossil fuels.

Chapter 6, "Produce a More Cyclical and Regenerative Metabolism," is more visionary, whereas the previous chapters show trends already well under way. A new awareness of how planetary boundaries are pushing limits on our cities and regions suggests that more radical approaches are needed. Fossil fuels are embedded in all the processes threatening planetary limits, and cities can lead the way in urban geoengineering that reduces metabolism and then regenerates to minimize local and global impacts, including climate change.

Finally, in the conclusion, "Growing Regeneratively," we draw together these themes by returning to how we look at the future of cities in terms of their growth. We discuss the conflicting approaches of agglomeration benefits and anxiety costs, which need to be resolved in order to achieve a more resilient future with fossil fuels phased out. We suggest that the vision of a more regenerative city can help with this agenda and is the next goal beyond resilience. We end with a brief outline of how this can happen.

Conclusion

The introduction to the World Economic Forum's 2015 "Top Ten Urban Innovations" report states: "If the future of cities cannot be one of unsustainable expansion, it should rather be one of tireless innovation."[29] The innovations in this book that enable fossil fuel reductions require mainstreaming into all cities. For this to occur, rapid urbanization will need to be seen as an opportunity, as it concentrates human activity to create a tightly defined locus for action. Rather than being seen as a threat to future survival, cities will need to be seen as the solution as long as they adopt this historic task. This is the premise behind the United Nations' Sustainable Development Goal 11, "Make cities inclusive, safe, resilient and sustainable," which was adopted by 193 nations in 2015.

We see the response to climate change as the impetus for the next burst of innovation. This book looks at those innovative cities that have begun to grasp this new agenda and have moved (often timidly) down the track toward change. There is so much happening in the world's cities that we cannot possibly keep up with every innovative story and case study. We have tried to select the best new ones and relate them to the six principles for a resilient city. It is our belief that those cities that begin this transition first will manage better socially and economically in a world where the constraints on coal and oil will be pressing.

Although no one can predict the future of cities, we can visualize where we use coal-based power, gasoline, diesel, heating oil, and natural gas and then try to imagine home, neighborhood, industry, and region without them. Many of the case studies in this book can help us in this process of imagining our own transition. How might our cities look and feel if these resources were not available, or at least were in decline? With this in mind, each next step in development or redevelopment can show us how to wean ourselves from these resources. Can we imagine a city where we are largely tapping power from the sun for our buildings and transportation? Can we see how this involves radically reducing the energy we use and the amount of driving we do? This is not a set of abstract arguments about the fate of the planet; it has relevance to and is potentially understandable by everyone in terms of the places where we live. We can then imagine a future that involves alternative energy sources for power as well as funding for the design of transit and bicycling systems and the creation or redevelopment of vehicles, buildings, communities, cities, and regions based on the need for less coal and petroleum fuel.

Fear paralyzes us when we can't see a viable next step. Our book is about overcoming fear and generating hope in our cities. Only hope can deal with the resurgent fascist tendencies evident across our world that deny our planetary limits and try to overcome despair with violence led by divisive politics. Cities will need to claim a different future that helps us regenerate the whole planet.

We want to inspire and enable urban dwellers, planners, designers, and policy makers to learn from innovations and stories in other cities to see that there is not only know-how but also momentum and hope for creating more resilient cities.

This will require new partnerships among three segments of society:

- *Business*, based on new markets that require new technologies and new partnership schemes;
- *Government*, based on new demonstrations, regulations, educational and behavior change projects, and informed leadership; and
- *Community*, based on its ability to frame a viable future that overcomes fossil fuel dependence through direct and indirect means.

CHAPTER 1

Invest in Renewable and Distributed Energy

The global shift to renewable energy will fundamentally change the nature of energy economics and trade. Nations [and cities] with abundant low cost renewable energy will be the powerhouses of the renewable energy era and the natural home of energy intensive industry.

—Gerard Drew, in "Zero Carbon Australia: Renewable Energy Superpower"

In the first edition of this book, we wrote about a group of cities showing how to experiment with solar energy and wind power. They were proudly and bravely stepping into a largely unknown world, passionate about starting a journey that had to be embarked on no matter what it cost. These included Masdar City in the United Arab Emirates; Freiburg and Kronsberg in Germany; Malmö in Sweden; Perth, Adelaide, Melbourne, and Sydney in Australia; Cape Town in South Africa; Daegu in South Korea; Barcelona in Spain; London in the United Kingdom; Toronto in Canada; and Seattle, Chicago, San Francisco, Sacramento, Austin, Atlanta, and Honolulu in the United States. Today most of these cities are ramping up their commitments and countless others are joining them, as doing so is no longer an economic burden but an economic necessity. This chapter is about the rise of renewable energy and how it is providing new opportunities for resilient cities.

The major driving force behind this transition has been *investment* in renewable energy and distributed energy systems. Bloomberg New Energy

Table 1.1: Countries with high renewables transitions.

Country	Renewables in Power, 2015	Goal
Spain	47%	70% by 2030
Denmark	40%	100% by 2035
Germany	32%	40% by 2020
United Kingdom	24%	30% by 2020

Source: Bloomberg New Energy Finance, 2015

Finance (BNEF) has documented this trend toward investment in renewable energy.[1] BNEF's data show that the world's financiers are investing in renewable energy at twice the rate they are investing in coal- and gas-fired power systems. Many nations are well down the track of providing renewable power to their citizens, driven by a combination of policies, business, and community pressure through their cities. Some cities, such as Vancouver, British Columbia, and Christchurch, New Zealand, and countries such as Norway have had high renewables for decades, given their investments in hydropower. To replace fossil fuels with renewables globally, solar and wind power will be needed, in addition to a few other new kinds of renewables. In particular the rapid growth is in rooftop solar power, which is creating a whole new distributed energy system in our cities with multiple benefits for sustainable and resilient cities.[2]

With non-hydro renewables as the guide, Spain, Denmark, Germany, and the United Kingdom appear to be the world leaders in the renewable cities transition, as set out in table 1.1.

As explained in the introduction, Denmark's growth in wealth decoupled from growth in fossil fuels as the nation struggled to establish this new approach to the economy. In 2015, with its economic growth based on renewables, Denmark was able to produce 40 percent of its power from renewables, and its goal is to reach 100 percent in the power sector by 2035, with 100 percent renewable energy in all sectors by 2050. On one day in July 2015 when the wind was blowing strongly, Denmark produced 116 percent of its power from renewables at peak time and 140 percent during off-peak hours; the excess was shared with Germany and Norway, which have hydroelectric storage that can take excess power.

The European Union has a target of 75 percent renewables across all energy sectors by 2050, with 15 percent by 2020. There is little doubt that the renewables transition is under way in Europe, and it is driving not just the global political agenda but also the global economic agenda there. The decoupling of gross domestic product (GDP) from greenhouse gas (GHG) emissions has been driven mostly by European cities, and this is likely to continue to drive the global agenda to decarbonize our cities and regions.

This chapter will address the following questions:

1. What is happening with renewables across the world?
2. What will happen to the power grid in cities as they transition to renewables? Will it still be needed if solar and storage become commonplace?
3. What will drive industry toward renewables?
4. What about city initiatives, buildings, and urban development? How can renewables be incorporated?

What Is Happening with Renewables Across the World?

BNEF has made a detailed assessment of the trends across the world and by region.[3] Its assessment is that in the twenty-five years from 2015 to 2040, renewables will become the dominant power source in the world. Wind and solar will account for 64 percent of the new generating capacity, and globally there will be 60 percent zero-carbon power, replacing coal and gas, which will decline from 57 percent to 31 percent. See figure 1.1, which is based on trends under way now and indicates we are likely to reach the target of 80 percent by 2050 for all GHG emissions, though power is in fact likely to be ahead of other sectors.

These goals will be achieved because the cost of solar power will come down by 60 percent and wind power by 41 percent, becoming the cheapest energy options across most of the world. In some places and cities this is already the case. Prices for fossil fuels, especially oil and gas, have been very volatile over the past few decades and investors can now see a more reliable option in renewables, given their price decline certainty, universality, and political compatibility as the world becomes increasingly committed to phasing out fossil fuels.

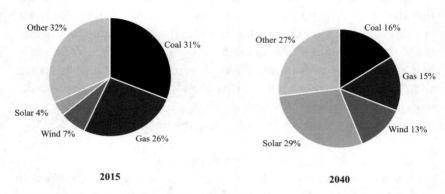

Global Installed Energy Capacity by Technology Type (%)
2015 Vs 2040

2015

2040

FIGURE 1.1: Global installed energy capacity by technology type, 2015 versus 2040, showing projected growth in renewables at the expense of coal and gas. (Source: Bloomberg New Energy Finance, 2016)

In the United States, wind power supplies approximately 5 percent of the electric power grid. The U.S. Department of Energy reported that by 2050 wind could power approximately 35 percent of the electric grid in the United States (increasing to 10 percent in 2020 and 20 percent in 2030).[4] It also reported that wind energy is getting less expensive every year as a result of policy changes and advances in technology: "Since the 1980s, the cost of deploying wind energy has dropped by 90 percent."[5]

However, the United States is one place where natural gas is seen by the Bloomberg report to be significantly cheaper than renewables because of cheap fuel (see figure 1.2*A–D*). Natural gas will likely account for around half of the growth in power investment, given the need to replace aging coal-fired power stations. The other half will more than likely come from small-scale rooftop solar power, which is estimated to increase from 0.8 percent of total installed capacity in 2014 to 40 percent in 2040. As outlined below, the United States has largely been distracted from enabling solar energy as a good business opportunity, as compared with places such as Australia, perhaps because of the political and popular fight between coal and gas, as well as the differences in economic growth between the two places; however, if this changes, the costs of small-scale solar could become cheaper than gas much more quickly.

The big growth in renewables is expected to be in rooftop solar because it fits into a very popular niche and provides new opportunities for consumers (see the Perth example that follows). Thus, the next phase in most cities will be managing the switch to distributed power systems—smaller, localized systems—based on solar or wind energy. For rooftop solar, the cost of battery storage is reducing dramatically.[6] This, along with system services such as demand response, control systems, and blockchain software (the software used to enable Bitcoin to be exchanged in a trustworthy way across the Internet), can create "citizen utilities," as outlined in this chapter.[7] Distributed power is the vanguard of innovation in the energy sector and is likely to lead to a renewal of economic activity in those places that can enable it.

The rapid adoption of rooftop solar across the world is what is now called a "disruptive" process that will be driven by cities.[8] This is a demand-led process with significant impact on the system within which the innovation happens, in this case the energy grid. Rooftop solar is disruptive because it is being driven by demand and it is disrupting the grid, in no small part due to the continuing decline in the cost of storage batteries as they follow the trajectory of rooftop solar. In Australia in 2016 the price of batteries dropped from A$2,000 per kilowatt-hour (kWh) to A$500, making the solar plus storage option truly competitive in most cities.[9] If this use of rooftops for solar power gathers political and popular momentum in the United States, driven by cities with a commitment to decarbonize their future, then it is possible that the growth in natural gas in the United States will be slowed, as is inevitably happening in most of the rest of the world. Without this change from natural gas to solar, U.S. cities will miss out on the many disruptive innovations and opportunities associated with distributed power generation.

Bloomberg expects to see global growth in the use of rooftop solar, particularly in regions such as the Middle East, Africa, and the Asia Pacific. It estimates that between 2015 and 2040, solar photovoltaic (PV) power will account for most of the growth in the power sector, with 3,429 gigawatts (GW) of capacity coming online, around half of it in utility-scale and half in small-scale PV.

Wind and solar capacity are of course variable in their geography, so the story will vary across the planet as to which will be dominant, as shown in figure 1.3. The cost of wind and solar comes down rapidly when they are in good supply.

FIGURE 1.2*A*

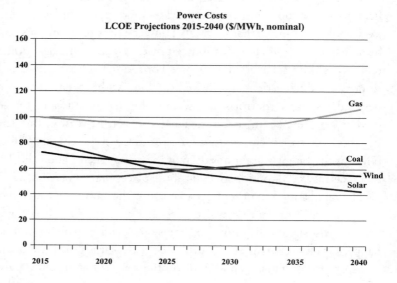

FIGURE 1.2*B*

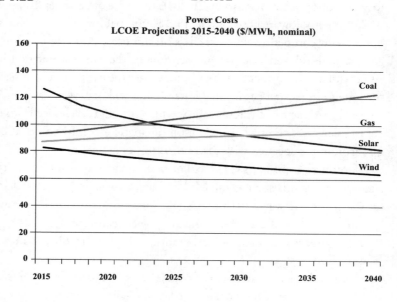

FIGURE 1.2: Projected costs of power, using levelized cost of electricity (LCOE) in nominal cost per megawatt-hour (MWh), 2015–2040: *A*, China;

FIGURE 1.2*C*

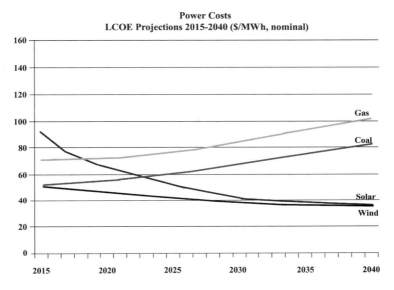

FIGURE 1.2*D*

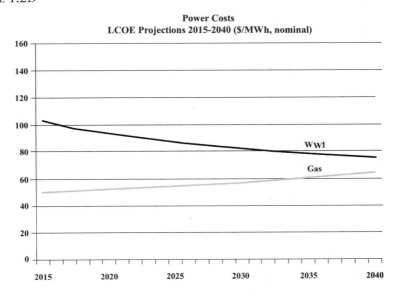

B, Europe; *C*, India; *D*, United States. (Source: Bloomberg New Energy Finance, 2015)

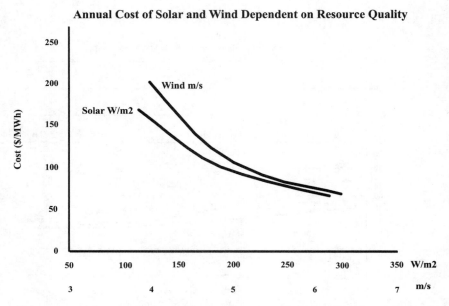

FIGURE 1.3: The annual costs of solar power and wind power depend on the quality of the resource. Here, solar power is measured in watts per square meter (W/m²); wind power, in meters per second (m/s); cost, in dollars per megawatt-hour ($/MWh). (Source: Drew, 2015)

The costs of power options are not just technological costs, however. There is a whole system of costs associated with each type of power source. Figure 1.4 shows that the costs of solar power in Australia are half what they are in the United States, which is why the cities of Australia are now having the highest uptake of rooftop solar in the world. The difference is partly in the cost of panels and inverters, which come mostly from China, but the major difference is in the business costs of permitting, marketing, and financing rooftop solar, which were mainstreamed much more quickly in Australia in the past five years.[10]

Cities need to capitalize on the new economy that will come from their natural advantages, just as the energy cities of the past were based on coal, oil, and gas resources nearby. Cities can assist this process through setting targets for renewables, creating business opportunities by facilitating establishment of innovative renewables-based companies, reducing the costs of permitting, and enabling residents to invest in renewable energy for their households.

USA vs Australia Costs of Rooftop Solar ($/W)

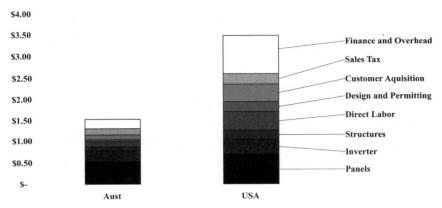

FIGURE 1.4: Installation cost of a 5 kW rooftop solar photovoltaic system, Australia versus United States. (Source: Jarnason, 2016)

The majority of new power will be in the developing world, and it is here that some fossil fuel plants will continue to be built just to keep up with demand for power, using countries' own fossil fuel resources, as in India and to some extent China. In these emerging nations the ability of solar PV installations to fit into cities is even more obvious, as they can provide immediate power, and with batteries there is potential to leapfrog into the future. Thus it is possible that the emerging cities of the world will proceed faster in the transition to renewables than predicted by Bloomberg.[11]

Three countries will dominate the new power capacity in Europe between 2015 and 2040, and each country will have a major influence on global trends because of its symbolic and political significance. They are as follows:

1. Germany will have the highest renewables power capacity, with 74 percent by 2040. It will be the first country in the Organization for Economic Cooperation and Development to demonstrate how to balance variable energy flows with flexible flows across its network. Battery capacity is likely to grow fastest here.
2. France has been the dominant nuclear power nation, with over 50 percent of its power from nuclear energy; but a 19 GW reduction resulting from retirements of nuclear plants will bring this to less than

20 percent by 2040. Small-scale rooftop solar will be the main source of replacement, growing to 30 percent of the power supply.

3. The United Kingdom has been building very large offshore wind power installations, but the new conservative government has begun to phase down the subsidy on this. Conservative governments will try to stop the renewables transition. Nevertheless, the growth of solar has begun to take over and will probably be unstoppable; Bloomberg expects it to grow to 44 percent of installed capacity by 2040 (31 percent from rooftop solar). Fossil fuel power will shrink from 60 percent to 15 percent, and the last coal-fired power station in the United Kingdom (which invented the technology two hundred years ago) will be turned off in 2032.

What Will Happen to Our Cities' Power Grids in the Transition to Renewables?

Solar power is not just coming, it is here. But what does that mean for our centralized grids? Will it mean we won't need a grid? Will we be able to live in splendid self-sufficiency with our own power? We now have an unlikely emerging demonstration city, Perth, Western Australia, that is enabling us to learn something about distributed rather than centralized generation and in particular to see a new phenomenon we have called "citizen utilities."[12] In this future grid, based on solar PV and battery storage, consumers are likely to create their own way of managing their local electricity needs and determine how they dispose of their excess electricity.[13]

Moving toward Distributed Energy

In global cities built around fossil fuels, the belief developed through the twentieth century that the most effective and efficient approach to providing energy was through large centralized production facilities and extensive distribution systems that transport energy over relatively long distances. These systems have proven to be vulnerable, yet many utilities and cities are fearful of the growth in renewables because of grid stability and energy security. As the cost of small-scale rooftop solar has become a major driver of future energy provision, it is necessary to create more local, distributed microgrid systems with smart grid control technologies and batteries for stability. This distributed energy offers a number of benefits, including energy savings through the ability to better control power production, lower vulnerability, and greater resilience in the face of natural and human-caused disaster, including terrorist attacks.[14] The same idea is being used for water and waste.[15]

The cost of providing the infrastructure necessary for distributed power, water, and waste systems is not a significant issue. For example, in Hopetoun, a remote settlement in Western Australia, a mining company and the state government had to assess how best to build the town's infrastructure to support a large influx of people for a new mining venture. They assessed three options: centralized, distributed, and decentralized (household based). The results showed that the distributed option was half the cost of the others and would save $0.5 billion in 2008. However, the utilities were not keen to try this unfamiliar approach.[16] In more recent times the cost of small-scale, integrated energy, water, and waste systems for remote and rural settlements has become much more established.[17]

In Perth, the number of households with rooftop solar PV is now around 25 percent, with more than 200,000 systems having been installed since 2010, translating into 550 megawatts (MW) of generating capacity, the largest power station in Western Australia. The purchase of solar PV in Perth is continuing to grow at more than 30 percent per annum. The entire process was not facilitated by any government program. It was simply a new market that was taken up by many households during the recent economic boom in Perth. Australia in general has been growing rapidly in its adoption of solar PV, with 1.5 million households with rooftop solar PV panels, which are likely to produce over 18,000 MW of power by 2031.[18]

The adoption of solar PV has been mostly a feature of middle-income households in Australian cities, as most are being purchased in the less wealthy outer suburbs, where people have large houses and high electricity bills in proportion to their income.[19] Some suburbs already have more than 50 percent of houses with solar PV. The growth rates are likely to continue.

The next step in distributed energy is the adoption of solar storage with lithium-ion (Li-ion) battery systems. The price of these batteries is declining as a result of their mass production for use in computers, mobile phones, and now electric vehicles. Solar storage based on Li-ion batteries has become so cheap that this combination reached grid parity in Perth sometime in 2017. These conditions in Perth make the city an ideal case study for evaluating the emergence of solar and storage as a mainstream power system technology and its impact on the grid.

Josh Byrne, a television personality from *Gardening Australia* and a research fellow at Curtin University, has built an affordable house that is fully monitored (it has seventy channels of information displayed on a public Web site) to test these questions as part of a project funded by the Cooperative Research Centre for Low Carbon Living. His household, consisting of two adults and two children, is a solar design with 3 kilowatts (kW) of solar PV and a battery storage system having 8 kilowatt-hours (kWh) of usable storage.[20] The results of some of this monitoring help us to understand the role of the grid when high levels of solar and storage are available.

The house is highly energy efficient—no mechanical heating or cooling is needed—and it is therefore making 75 percent more renewable power than it is consuming, even though it has a small PV system. However, despite producing more solar electricity than the family uses, Josh's household still uses most of its power in the evening and hence still pays an electricity bill. The price of peak power in the evening is around $0.26 per kWh, compared with the $0.07 per kWh the household receives back from the utility for the excess solar electricity it sells during daylight hours.

The incorporation of a battery system significantly reduced this highly energy-efficient household's reliance on the grid. From being around 55 percent self-sufficient before the battery system was installed, the house became more than 90 percent self-sufficient, while still uploading a large surplus of electricity to the grid. The 90 percent self-sufficiency results from the fact that the household still needs to draw energy from the grid during the few periods of consecutive cloudy days in winter, and this would be a significant cost if a much bigger storage system were required.

So, in the case of Josh's house, solar PV and a lithium-ion battery system facilitated a massive reduction in dependence on the grid, but the grid is still needed. For Josh's house to achieve 100 percent self-sufficiency the solar system would have to go from 3 kW to 5 kW, a 66 percent increase, and the battery would have to be substantially increased, from 8 kWh to 14 kWh, a 75 percent increase in capacity, just to ensure that power could be maintained for a few days a year. This is not good economics.

FIGURE 1.5: Model solar house in Perth, Western Australia, that is demonstrating zero-carbon outcomes. (Source: Josh Byrne)

The first key conclusion from this is that the electric power grid is unlikely to be abandoned by most household consumers when they have solar PV and battery storage. The solar storage system cannot carry the household throughout the year even in highly sunny Perth, as the costs increase exponentially between 90 percent and 100 percent self-sufficiency. However, this may not apply if we move to using solar and batteries on a shared precinct basis. Single household self-sufficiency will always be difficult when it comes to energy, water, food, waste management, or social matters such as health and education. However, if a few hundred households get together, the scale of opportunity increases substantially. What if suburbs began to reorganize themselves so they could share PV and batteries with a local electricity supply system that could afford a bit more storage for those days with little sun? It seems that the grid would still be needed because energy would flow in two ways. The technology and grid management systems for this is likely to be developed over the next ten years as cities experiment in managing these two-way flows.

Such a project is an exercise funded by the Australian Renewable Energy

Agency, an independent agency of the Australian federal government, at White Gum Valley (WGV)—a suburb of Fremantle, Western Australia—where 120 houses are being built on a LandCorp site with solar power and battery storage across the whole precinct.[21] The strata title companies associated with each of the project's three main developments will be managing the power. Early data suggest that the WGV precinct will still need the grid for some times of the day and year, but mostly it will produce more power than needed after filling the battery storage systems. A follow-up development that is ten times as big as WGV is being planned with a large-flow battery that can become a community storage demonstration to enable a cheap way for whole communities to utilize battery storage from their rooftop solar. The utility associated with this project, Western Power, is watching with great interest, as the grid could develop a new role of providing for two-way flows of energy.

For many reasons, the grid is likely to continue after solar and batteries are mainstreamed in all parts of our cities.

The grid is needed for resilience. Grids do go out when their main lines are disrupted by extreme weather, fires, and earthquakes, and in the new world of solar power and battery storage the impacts of these breaks will be lessened, but a grid can enable those parts impacted to be quickly restored as adjacent unaffected parts feed into the area from their storage. Grids and battery storage can work together in good times and bad. The grid is also needed to enable households to feed back their excess solar generation into helping cities to become regenerative. For example, Josh Byrne was uploading 75 percent of his household's surplus electricity to the grid, generating green power to the system and making money for the family.

So the grid is needed, but it will take a very different form in the future. From this Perth case study it is clear that there will be no further growth in the centralized grid and no more power stations should be anticipated. Solar power is taking hold very quickly, and it enables energy to be produced where it is consumed. Big regional grids are likely to become a series of smaller grids, and cities will have multiple microgrids linked together.

Most utilities experiencing this disruption in the way they work will need to adjust their commercial plans. Perth's dramatic growth in solar PV was a market that was not anticipated. The boom time in Perth was predicted to rapidly increase the need for peak power from the centralized

FIGURE 1.6: At White Gum Valley (WGV), a suburb of Fremantle, Western Australia, 120 houses are being built on a LandCorp site with solar power and battery storage throughout. (Source: LandCorp)

system, and hence an old coal-fired power station was recommissioned, at a cost of $400 million, to service the grid. However, it was never needed. The households' solar PV production reduced the demand on the grid so effectively that the minister for energy concluded that the grid would never again need a new power station. He predicted that the growth of solar PV will mean that 70 percent of households will have rooftop solar by 2025. The market for solar power made this inevitable. Similar responses to rapid growth in solar can be expected from cities across the world.

The evidence for these bottom-up responses to solar storage is that technology platforms are already being invented to sell excess local electricity generated by households using blockchain software. Microgrids will be feasible to both move electricity and payments associated with it. Blockchain software is a distributed community-based infrastructure facilitating trust between power producers and consumers. Using blockchain software, microgrids create a commonly used database for managing transactions. This can be used for electricity management (checking to see whether some users have more power use than they want) and financial payments associated with it.[22] Trials at WGV and at Busselton, Western Australia, by the local firm Power Ledger are designed to show how this trustworthy ledger system can enable the grid to be used to transfer solar-derived electrons but be managed through an Internet link. Citywide utilities that own networks can charge for these transfers and thus pay for their "poles and wires" systems. Trials of blockchain software for power management have begun in New York, though this new technology will not be enabled if the United States chooses to move from coal to natural gas rather than solar power.[23]

Distributed power through microgrids will start with group housing, where residential building managers can act as the utility, generating a new profession of local energy managers as in the WGV project. Similar exercises are being developed for lifestyle villages and industrial estates like those around airports, where the owner can become a local utility. It is not hard to see this spreading to associations of households linked only through the Internet.[24] We are entering the era of the citizen utility. Box 1.1 gives an example of how communities can create citizen utilities to ensure equity in the transition to a more resilient and sustainable city.

As we seek to build smart, inclusive, and sustainable solar cities, we would do well to ensure that they are cities that still work together.

What about Industry?

Industry needs power, and it needs process heat, which is usually provided by natural gas. What will provide the renewable technology to replace this? We see a combination of technologies emerging to assist in this.

1. *Rooftop solar for small-scale industries.* Commercial operations will rapidly take up rooftop solar and batteries as these become the cheapest option, especially if there is a substantial amount of rooftop space available. For example, an airport in Western Australia is facing expansion and has examined the options for its future. By far the most cost-effective option is to use solar PV on the airport's many large rooftops and use batteries to stabilize the system and create a market for all users. This will save hundreds of millions of dollars, and it need not be seen as "green" or even innovative; it is simply by far the best business proposition.[25]

2. *Business-owned renewable energy utilities.* Businesses are also becoming their own utilities, as shown by high-tech companies such as Apple becoming energy "prosumers," making solar power and selling

Box 1.1: Solar Gardens

A new idea for advancing solar energy is emerging in several western U.S. states. "Solar gardens" were the brainchild of a renewable energy activist in Boulder, Colorado, born of the realization that many urban residents want to support solar energy but don't have the financial resources or even a physical rooftop to do so. A solar garden addresses these obstacles in several creative ways: it allows a resident to buy a share in a solar garden, as little as a kilowatt of production, joining with others to share in the overall cost of the system. And because this is a community-based solar project the actual installation takes place somewhere else—on the roof of a nearby business, say, or on a vacant lot, or a nearby farm or orchard. Once a share has been purchased, the resident is entitled to benefit from a share of the solar production, which is delivered in the form of an energy credit on the resident's monthly energy bill. Joining a solar garden, moreover, allows participants to realize a share of the state and federal tax credits. The idea of solar gardens bridges the gap between an individual rooftop system and a utility-scale solar energy system and dramatically expands the potential number of city residents who can directly participate in and invest in solar energy. While the law was first amended in Colorado to allow solar gardens, Minnesota has followed suit and California is considering similar legislation. And the idea is gaining some popularity. A recent newspaper article predicted that solar gardens are "about to flood across the Twin Cities."[a] There is even a Solar Gardens Institute, based in Colorado, helping to promote and advance this idea (see www.solargardens.org).

---

[a]Bob Shaw, "Solar Gardens Are About to Flood across the Twin Cities—Here's Why," *Twin Cities Pioneer Press*, March 11, 2016.

excess back to the grid along with grid services. The twenty-four largest current buyers of renewable power—a group that includes Google, Amazon, Microsoft, Ikea, Equinix, Mars, Dow, Walmart, and Facebook—have bought 3.6 GW of renewable energy since the beginning of 2015, enough to power about half the state of Connecticut.[26]

3. *Utility-scale solar with multiple PV systems and interconnected grids using high-voltage direct current (HVDC) technology.* Bloomberg does not predict much development in solar thermal power because its costs have not declined as expected. Large-scale PV can, however, be highly competitive and does not have the risks associated with

high-temperature molten salt storage. Links to grids are expected to increasingly use HVDC, enabling areas with high insolation to be connected to areas without. Plans for such HVDC cables, underground and undersea, linking cities to regions with high insolation are well developed in Europe, Asia, and Australia.[27]

4. *Renewable natural gas.* Industrial heat can be produced from electricity, but it is more likely to be provided by renewable natural gas from biological or chemical sources. Methane (CH_4) has been biologically derived for many years from anaerobic digestion of organic material. This can be scaled up, and plans for producing methane from seaweed have been developed by Gunter Pauli, as described in *The Blue Economy*.[28] Chemically derived methane can be created from the sun and carbon dioxide (CO_2) using a technique called the Sabatier process, which is similar to photosynthesis but needs a catalyst to enable the process to work. The Sabatier process has not yet been commercialized; a series of catalysts are still being tested. However, when this happens it could be the simplest solution to decarbonizing the use of natural gas.[29]

An Australian think tank, Beyond Zero Emissions, has addressed these issues across Australia. In a global context it has made recommendations about how a city, region, or nation can become a "renewable energy superpower" by not only solving these problems for its own industries but also exporting its surplus into growing markets eager to use green energy (see this chapter's opening quotation).[30]

What about City Initiatives, Buildings, and Urban Development?

The shift toward renewable cities through buildings and urban development can occur through many actions taken. The following are some examples:

- Demonstration solar or low-energy homes created to show architects, developers, and citizens that green can be appealing (e.g., as in Chicago and Freiburg).
- Procurement actions that source regionally produced wind and other

renewable energy to power municipal lights and buildings (e.g., as in Santa Monica).

- Green building standards, which at the highest level require renewable energy for all new public and private buildings. Many cities, such as Seattle and Chicago, now mandate minimum Leadership in Energy and Environmental Design (LEED) green building certification for new public structures, and some cities, such as New York, have adopted higher-performance building standards in order to reach renewable energy targets.

- Precinct-scale development accreditation systems that require integrated energy and water systems with low- or zero-carbon and low- or zero-mains water outcomes. An example is WGV (White Gum Valley in Perth, discussed earlier in the chapter), which uses the One Planet Living accreditation system. Similar stretch target approaches are required by the Living Building Challenge and by EcoDistricts, which came out of innovations in Portland, Oregon, in 2009 and has been adopted by the Clinton Global Initiative in ten precincts in eight North American cities to guide their governance and procurement processes.[31]

Few cities have been as active in seeking and nurturing a reputation as a renewable city as Freiburg.[32] Known to many as the "ecological capital of Europe," Freiburg has adopted an impressive and wide-ranging set of environmental planning and sustainability initiatives, many focused on renewable energy. Through its SolarRegion Freiburg program, the city has actively supported solar energy as an important element of its economic base, including the promotion of it as a form of local tourism. A series of "solar tours" have been organized, for instance, as a way to view and learn about the innovative solar energy projects in the city. And there are many such projects, from dramatic individual residences (e.g., Rolf Disch's Heliotropic House) to prototype experimental homes (e.g., the Freiburg zero-energy house) to business structures (e.g., the zero-emissions Solar Fabrik, the Solar Tower, high-rise office building) and public buildings and installations. The city has also become home to an impressive number of scientific and educational organizations, including the Fraunhofer Institute for Solar Energy Systems and the International Solar Energy Society (ISES), among others. Freiburg has supported these organizations in different ways, including offering ISES subsidized rent for the historic city-owned structure that became its headquarters. Freiburg is one of the few cities to recognize that the attraction of modern renewable energy businesses and expertise will give it an economic edge.

Freiburg has, moreover, incorporated renewable energy in all major new development areas, including Rieselfeld and Vauban, which are compact green areas of the city that employ both active and passive solar techniques. The city also mandates a fairly stringent energy standard for all new homes. In Vauban, all homes are very low-energy, many incorporating solar panels. Vauban also boasts an area of plus-energy homes that produce more power than they need, as well as a solar office complex and two solar parking garages. The combined heat and power plant for Vauban uses waste wood.

The Hotel Victoria, in the center of Freiburg, markets itself as the world's first zero-emissions hotel, boasting that all its energy needs are satisfied through renewable energy sources, including solar. A host of other environmental features are available to guests, including free passes for the city's exemplary public transit system.

There are also impressive examples in the United States of cities promoting and supporting (some through financial incentives) the installation of solar and renewable energy technology. Austin, Texas, for instance, set a target of 15 MW of solar energy production by 2007; by 2014 this was 23 percent renewable and by 2016 it was 37 percent, mostly from wind. Austin's next goal is to develop utility-scale solar power, and the city has contracts to provide around 13 percent of its power by 2017.[33]

California gets around 30 percent of its electricity from renewables, and this is planned to increase to 50 percent by 2030. In Sacramento, new PV systems are being placed on car-parking structures, on nature center rooftops, and on a structure in the Sacramento Zoo. Through the Community Solar program of the Sacramento Municipal Utility District (SMUD), customers contribute to these installations through a modest rate premium (one cent per kilowatt-hour above current rates). Sacramento has also taken many steps to reduce energy consumption in public buildings and facilities (e.g., converting traffic lights to LED, upgrading lighting in public buildings).[34]

San Francisco became California's first large city to mandate installation of solar panels on rooftops. These requirements, adopted in April 2016, mandate that all new buildings under ten stories install rooftop solar, either in the form of PVs or solar thermal. The city has also set the target of satisfying 100 percent of its electricity needs by renewable energy by 2030. California has been a leader in addressing renewable energy and climate change, and many of the positive steps taken by cities such as San Francisco are encouraged and reinforced at the state level. The California Global Warming Solutions Act of 2006 (AB 32) set in motion a remarkable process of planning for transition toward renewables. The state has established a cap-and-trade program that has generated significant funding for a variety of climate and energy investments, from public transit to urban tree planting. It has established renewable standards for new construction, such as the requirement that all new housing developments over a certain size must be designed to be "solar ready." And cities must now develop climate action plans, many of them setting ambitious renewable energy and climate change targets. San Diego's is one of the most impressive, establishing the goal, like San Francisco's, of 100 percent renewable energy, and setting the target of cutting by half its greenhouse gas emissions by 2035—and these are legally enforceable targets! It is also adjusting its land use planning to ensure that at least half of all commuters in the city live within a half mile of a transit station.

The city of Adelaide envisions itself as a solar city as part of its larger green city initiative. Spearheaded by the Adelaide Capital City Committee, efforts have already resulted in a carbon neutral strategy and a number of solar projects, including designation of the North Terrace Solar Precinct and installation of PVs on the rooftops of four government buildings: the South Australian Museum, the Art Gallery of South Australia, the State Library of South Australia, and Parliament House. The city's solar initiative was first funded by a federal grant from the Solar Cities program. The city and state have been collaborating on a solar schools initiative, with the goal of 250 solar schools (schools that have rooftop installations and incorporate solar and renewable energy into their educational curricula). This idea has since been taken up by the Australian federal government to be applied to every school in the country. And, most creatively, Adelaide has been installing grid-connected PV street lamps that produce some six times the energy needed for the lighting. These new lights are designed in the distinctive shape of a mallee tree, a eucalyptus tree native to the area, and are referred to as "solar mallees." This is one of the few examples of solar art or solar "place" projects.[35]

Along with incentives (financial and otherwise), renewable cities recognize the need to set minimum regulatory standards. Barcelona has a solar ordinance that requires new buildings and substantial retrofits of existing buildings to obtain a minimum of 60 percent of hot water needs from solar power. This has already led to a significant growth in that city in the number of solar thermal installations.[36]

Sydney has mandated that new homes must be designed to produce 40 percent lower greenhouse gas emissions than a standard house (after initially requiring 20 percent and finding that was relatively easy to achieve). New homes are also required to use 40 percent less water. While many mayors have committed to reducing their city's carbon footprint, it is a complicated task to implement policy that will reduce carbon beyond the single building level. But again, there are hopeful examples. LEED for Neighborhood Development and the STAR Community Rating System are used in the United States. One Planet Living has been used in many countries since the development of BedZED—the Beddington Zero Energy Development—the first carbon neutral eco-community in the United Kingdom. Here, a new neighborhood of green apartments and live-work units in the London borough of Sutton demonstrates a new kind of "solar urbanism"—it is also next to a train station. This is not an agenda of sacrifice at all, and once one sees the apartments awash in sunlight, the unusual rooftop gardens (sky gardens), and the other impressive elements of this neighborhood, such as its social housing arrangements, one imagines that sustainable living would be a relatively easy sell; comfort and quality of life are maximized, not sacrificed, through such a zero-energy, carbon neutral vision. Estimates suggest that residents are able to reduce their environmental footprint by one-third (and live with a footprint less than half of that of an American) simply by moving into BedZED.[37]

The U.K. government began a process of seeking zero carbon after seeing that BedZED worked so well. Each local government in the United Kingdom was asked to produce a carbon neutral strategy to show how it would create a carbon-reduced future. These have been set aside for some more modest outcomes, as the program was probably a decade ahead of its time. The One Planet Living system, developed from BedZED, was used to enable Perth's WGV project, mentioned earlier in the chapter.

In Sweden, Malmö has stated that it has already become a carbon neutral city and Växjö has declared its intention to become a fossil fuel–free city; Newcastle, in the United Kingdom, and Adelaide, South Australia, also aspire to be carbon neutral. Each has taken important steps in the direction of renewable energy consistent with the renewable city vision articulated in this chapter. In all Australian cities, the carbon and GHG emissions associated with many municipal motor pools are being offset through innovative tree-planting initiatives and organizations such as Greenfleet, which has planted more than 8.7 million native trees in Australia. Transportation companies such as airlines offer carbon neutral service, and local governments including the City of Fremantle, schools such as South Fremantle Senior High School, and many businesses, such as News Corp Australia, are committed to being carbon neutral. The carbon offsetting, accredited through a government initiative called Greenhouse Friendly, provides a strong legal backing to ensure that plantations are real, are related to the money committed, and are guaranteed for at least seventy years as required by the Kyoto Protocol. Much of the revenue from the carbon offsetting programs goes to biodiversity plantations that regenerate the bioregional ecology around the cities (e.g., Gondwana Link in Western Australia).[38]

In the Western Harbour district in Malmö, the goal was to achieve 100 percent renewable energy produced from local sources. This has been realized by incorporating into the fabric of this new urban neighborhood a mix of renewable energy production ideas and technologies, including a wind turbine and facade-mounted solar hot water collectors. The solar panels are a visible feature of this delightful urban district, which boasts other sustainability initiatives including innovative storm water management, habitat and biotope restoration, and green courtyards and green rooftops.[39]

In addition to helping to sequester carbon, trees help to naturally cool buildings and homes and can reduce the use of energy for artificial cooling. Initiatives in the United States to provide greater tree coverage include the tree-planting program of the Sacramento Municipal Utility District. SMUD has been actively promoting tree planting as a way of reducing energy consumption and addressing the problem of urban heat islands. Since 1990, this program, which provides residents with free shade trees, has re-

FIGURE 1.7: The Bo01 City of Tomorrow, located in the Western Harbour in Malmö, Sweden, is a mixed-use development that uses renewable power and creative storm water management. This former industrial site is now a model of resilience.

sulted in the planting of more than 500,000 trees.[40] The program could be expanded to provide residents and businesses with carbon neutral options.

While many sense that renewable energy techniques and technologies are potentially quite useful, others argue that they are for the most part not suited to urban settings, where significant numbers of people live and where development patterns may be quite dense. Part of the paradigm shift will involve refuting or moving beyond this aversion to urban settings as sites for production. Large solar production projects, for instance, or wind energy farms, it is commonly thought, require relatively remote sites (in part to minimize perceived conflicts with residents and communities). But today there are rooftop PV installations, microturbine wind systems on roof ridges and building edges, geothermal power and air-conditioning from shallow hot water, and small-wave power technologies that can feed directly into coastal cities. Integrating renewable energy sources into urban areas is not only necessary for resilience but also makes energy, and solar energy in particular, a visible part of communities. There are many ways that small-scale solar projects can be incorporated into urban areas, and an increasing number of good case studies show the possibilities.

A 2015 study at Stanford University showed the potential to use solar power in existing built-out urban areas. The study focused on California—the state leading the United States in solar energy production (apart from Hawaii). According to the study, there is enough solar power potential in California's developed areas to meet the state's electricity demand more than three times over (producing more than 20,000 terawatt-hours of power annually).[41]

Islands that until now have used diesel have the most to gain by switching to renewables. Honolulu has a goal of 100 percent renewables by 2030 and is ranked the least carbon-emitting city in the United States. The Spanish island El Hierro has become something of a renewables sensation, with 100 percent renewable energy use. Its wind farm creates sufficient power, with intermittency issues overcome by a pumped storage system that creates a steady power supply based on hydroelectricity when the wind is not blowing. When the wind is blowing, the power goes to homes and industries before pumping water uphill to a dam. This 100 percent green island has reversed its population loss and created a series of local food-based industries and a big tourism industry.[42]

In North America, few metropolitan areas are making as much progress in harnessing solar energy as Toronto, Ontario, spurred on by a combination of grassroots interest and activism and some new and impressive economic incentives. In 2006 a law was passed mandating that all of Ontario's ninety utilities must purchase renewable energy from small producers at premium prices. The law requires utilities to pay forty-two cents per kilowatt-hour for solar power, the most generous production subsidy available in North America. Predating the Ontario law, neighborhoods in Toronto had been organizing and forming solar buying cooperatives in which they pooled their buying power to negotiate special reduced prices from local PV companies. It all began in Toronto's East End, where residents of the Riverdale neighborhood formed the first of these solar buying clubs. A new neighborhood organization was created—the Riverdale Initiative for Solar Energy, or RISE—and eventually about seventy-five residents joined together to purchase rooftop PV systems, resulting in about a 15 percent savings in their purchase cost. The Toronto (and Ontario province) example suggests the merits of combining bottom-up neighborhood solar activism with top-down incentives and encouragement. As other neighborhoods embrace solar energy, Toronto will likely emerge as a successful model of how to stimulate the transition to a distributed city.[43]

In Kronsberg, an ecological urban district in the German city of Hannover, a number of low-energy and renewable energy ideas have been integrated into this compact, walkable community. Three relatively large wind turbines (the largest a 1.8 MW turbine) have been sited just a few hundred meters from some residences, and many of the apartments are supplied by a centralized solar water heating system. District heating and two small combined heat and power stations (one in the basement of a residential building) provide the neighborhood's remaining hot water needs and produce electricity. The use of district heating, and combined heat and power plants, has become a standard design feature in new European developments and is a much more efficient and sustainable way to heat and power communities.[44]

Perhaps Vauban is the best available model, especially as it was planned and built around a community-based model by Forum Vauban. This public-community partnership model is how the switch to distributed systems is likely to be driven. Other communities are following this model, including WGV in Perth, with a citizen utility for energy and water and an expanding role for shared electric vehicles and bikes.

To move the implementation of distributed infrastructure beyond these few cities, utilities will need to develop models with city planners of how they can do local energy planning with community-based approaches. They will need to coordinate with local government to ensure that the best features of renewable energy and water management are integrated in a way that is coherent, community based, and technically acceptable.[45] Reducing energy use will be central to this agenda. All of the clever technologies of "big data," in which sensors in buildings and streets can manage energy far more efficiently, will be needed, as well as the incorporation of biophilic urbanism into buildings and streets to air condition the city naturally (see chapter 5).

Conclusion

In this chapter, we have shown how trends in energy markets are already moving to phase out fossil fuels. We have used Bloomberg projections, but they are not the most radical. The Carbon Tracker Initiative goes beyond Bloomberg projections and suggests that low-carbon technologies will be highly disruptive to fossil fuel markets. The Carbon Tracker Initiative suggests the following:

- Solar photovoltaics, with associated energy storage costs included, could supply 23 percent of global power generation in 2040 and 29 percent by 2050, entirely phasing out coal and leaving natural gas with just a 1 percent market share. ExxonMobil, on the other hand, sees all renewables supplying just 11 percent of global power generation by 2040.
- Electric vehicles (as outlined in the next chapter) could account for approximately 35 percent of the road transport market by 2035, yet BP put this figure at just 6 percent in its 2017 energy outlook. By 2050, electric vehicles could account for more than two-thirds of the road transport market, severely disrupting oil markets. This growth trajectory sees electric vehicles displacing approximately 2 million barrels of oil per day (mbd) in 2025 and 25 mbd in 2050. To put these figures in context, the 2014–2015 oil price collapse was the result of a 2 mbd (2 percent) shift in the supply-demand balance.[46]

Thus, exponential growth of solar storage and electric transport (that is powered by renewables) will fundamentally change our cities and make them far less fossil fuel dependent.

In each area of society—business, government, and community— change will be needed to adapt to the dramatic transition to renewables now well under way.

Business

The world's markets are moving quickly toward a renewable energy future. Businesses either will recognize this and commit to seeking a role in this transition or will find themselves dealing with stranded assets and contributing little to the expanding world of employment opportunities based on efficient and sustainable energy. Businesses will also need to show governments that there are barriers, and subsidies to the old order of fossil fuels, that need to be removed. Business associations can create partnerships with governments and communities to ensure their cities are leaders, not laggards, in the renewables transition.

Government

Governments at all levels, including the city level, need to set renewable energy targets and strategies, including exposing where renewable energy markets are impeded by old systems of governance, hidden and blatant subsidies, and lack of information about emerging markets. City governments need to send signals that green buildings and green precinct developments will receive priority and extra bonuses if they include substantial energy efficiency and renewable energy components. Infrastructure for electric vehicles, electric bikes, and electric transit needs to be provided to enable solar-based public recharging and special bonuses in urban development if facilitated.

The recent dramatic political changes at the national level in the United States underscore the importance of progress in renewable energy at state and local levels and especially, we believe, at the city scale. Innovative government programs such as tax incentives and feed-in tariffs are now phasing out around the world as renewable power mainstreams in the marketplace, but government will still need to facilitate the shift to distributed power systems and not put up barriers based on the nostalgia of coal or the idea that centralized power is the only way cities can work.

Community

Nongovernmental organizations and community associations need to constantly lobby their government representatives to inform them that the renewables transition is well under way and needs to be facilitated much faster. Householders need to ensure that their household is energy efficient and uses renewable energy. Residents of new developments and old suburban regeneration projects need to look at how they can start a citizen utility to create markets for solar energy in their area.

CHAPTER 2

Create Sustainable Mobility Systems

Sustainable mobility provides an alternative paradigm within which to investigate the complexity of cities, and to strengthen the links between land use and transport. —David Banister, in "The Sustainable Mobility Paradigm"

Most of the oil consumed in the world is for transport. But transport can phase out oil rapidly, just as power systems are phasing out fossil fuels, as shown in chapter 1. As with power systems, this change will be driven by the world's cities through advances in technology and strategic changes in the way cities are designed, planned, and operated. A new system of sustainable mobility is already emerging rapidly, as we show in this chapter.

We begin by looking at how renewable fuels may be moving into the transport sector, and then we look at another new technology—autonomous vehicles—to see if they are likely to be as transformative as they are being touted. We examine why and how our cities are changing to encourage declines in car use and how we can further encourage sustainable mobility through urban planning based on the theory of urban fabrics. This system of sustainable mobility must reduce the need for energy as well as provide new renewable fuels, just as energy efficiency is a critical part of new renewable power systems.

This chapter will address the following questions:

1. Is transport transitioning to renewable fuels?
2. Will autonomous vehicles transform our cities? Will they help make them more resilient? What role could they play in sustainable mobility?
3. What is happening to reduce car use? How does it relate to the different types of urban fabric in cities? How can it be facilitated to ensure sustainable mobility?
4. Can we reduce car use 50 percent and oil use 80 percent by 2050 and 100 percent by 2100?

Is Transport Transitioning to Renewable Fuels?

Transport remains the biggest challenge in decarbonizing cities, but there is great opportunity to transition to renewable fuels and sustainable mobility. The dominance of motorized transport demands carbon-free fuels. The two obvious ways ahead are electric vehicles (which can tap into the growing use of solar power) and renewable fuels.

Electric Vehicles

Electric mobility will need to be the basis of solar-based transport and will be important for most types of vehicles: cars, trains, buses, and bikes.

Electric vehicles (EVs) are growing globally at more than 40 percent per year and are expected to reach 25 percent of the vehicle fleet by 2040. This will be part of the larger transition, as EVs are able to plug into household solar systems. Most of this growth is in China (see figure 2.1), which is likely to mean cheaper exports.[1]

The growth in the United States is just 19 percent. The trend in electricity becoming more dominated by renewables means that growth in solar-powered EVs is likely to be driven by demand similar to that for rooftop solar. EVs are already being used to fit cleverly into home photovoltaic (PV) and battery systems, with a high potential for V2G— "vehicle to grid"—transfers of power to enable extra storage options in the grid. Signs that this transition to electric transport is under way are appearing in demonstration projects such as those in Boulder, Colorado, and Austin, Texas, and in Google's 1.6 megawatt (MW) solar campus in California with 100 plug-in electric vehicles (PEVs); we are also seeing oil companies acquire electric utilities.[2]

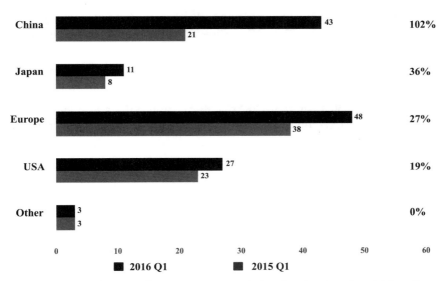

Volume of Plug-in Electric Vehicles and % Growth 2015-2016

FIGURE 2.1: Volume and percentage growth in plug-in electric vehicles, first quarter 2015 to first quarter 2016. (Source: Carlin, Rader, and Rucks, 2015)

According to one study, the integration of PEVs with the electric power grid could reduce gasoline consumption by 85 billion gallons per year in the United States. That's equal to the following:

- 27 percent reduction in total U.S. greenhouse gases
- 52 percent reduction in oil imports
- $270 billion not spent on gasoline[3]

Many other vehicle types are becoming electrified and linked into the solar grid, such as electric buses, bikes, scooters, and three- and four-wheeled mobility scooters (e.g., Gophers in Australia). China has more than 120 million electric bikes, which enable significant reductions in car use, as they go beyond walking and cycling distances. With their extra speed, they are quite competitive with cars, so fewer high-energy vehicles are needed.[4]

California has taken many steps to promote and support electric vehicles and has set the ambitious goal of having 1.5 million zero-emissions vehicles on the road by 2025. To support this kind of target will require a significant ramping up of vehicle recharging stations, and cities will need to invest in new infrastructure to support electric vehicles. A range of start-up companies offer products designed to address a world of electric vehicles. One company, Totem Power, has designed an innovative platform for charging electric vehicles—a solar-powered streetlight that also serves as a recharging station. The system collects solar energy during the day and stores it in a battery for use at night or whenever an EV requires it.[5] The system would probably be drained quite quickly by a car's electricity needs, but it would be ideal for local electric bikes to recharge as part of an urban trip. This is made more relevant to urban cyclists, as the streetlight system also provides a WiFi and 4G communication station.

A similar community-based project in Fremantle, Western Australia, has converted a parking space, as part of city policy, into a "solar parklet" with chairs, tables, free WiFi, and free power provided by a solar collector and storage battery on the neighboring property.[6] These distributed systems will also help address resilience, as they will be fully functional in the event of central power grid failure.

Electric trains have been around for more than a century and are now mainstreamed, unlike electric cars. Transit is likely to continue to electrify and become zero carbon as we move to renewables, especially as light rail is converted to no-catenary systems using lithium-ion batteries that can be recharged quickly at stations. Light and heavy rail station precincts can be converted to rooftop solar as part of the role of transit and provide an immediate and cheap source of power similar to that used by households and offices.[7] Electric buses are now on the market as well.

Renewable Fuels

Two types of renewable fuels are being developed: biofuels and renewable gas.

Biofuels

Biofuels have promised a lot, but they have been criticized for their impact on food prices when used to convert grain to fuel.[8] However, they still have a potentially significant role in some areas where there is a crop surplus and, eventually, when the technology improves to make them from cellulose materials (agricultural and forestry waste), from seaweed, and from blue-

FIGURE 2.2: Solar parklet, Wray Avenue, Fremantle, Western Australia. (Source: Jean Paul Horré)

green algae. It is likely that biofuels will be used as a do-it-yourself fuel on farms.[9] Thus biofuels may have a role in agricultural regions as a fuel to assist farmers. However, as a widespread fuel for cities, they are not an option that can yet be taken seriously. The option of electric vehicles has proven to be much more promising.

Aircraft are the hardest to imagine in low-carbon mobility. They can reduce their fuel intake by a range of efficiency measures, though the Intergovernmental Panel on Climate Change believes that only biofuels appear suitable as a replacement for oil.[10] However, the cost of biofuels for aviation appears to make them prohibitive at this stage. Canadians Richard Gilbert and Anthony Perl suggest a few ways in which air travel will adapt, but mostly they see little potential other than regional high-speed rail and a return to ship travel.[11]

Perhaps another regional transport technology that could make a comeback is the airship. These are able to fly at low altitudes at speeds of 150–200 kilometers per hour (kph) and carry large loads with one-tenth of the fuel of aircraft technology.[12] They are already being used to carry large mining loads to remote areas and to take groups of two hundred or so on ecotourism ventures, similar to a cruise ship. Perhaps this is a possible use for biofuels, as they will be a much smaller part of the regional cost of travel than present-day aviation.

There is some hope in aviation with the development of an electric plane by Airbus. This plane makes use of Li-ion batteries, which have five times the energy density of older batteries. Its range is just 80 to 200 kilometers, depending on the passenger load, but like EVs on the ground, the electric plane is likely to increase its range over the next decade.[13]

Overall, it does not seem that a commercial option is yet available for aviation to replace oil with a renewable resource in the way that cities are rapidly adapting to solar electric mobility.

Renewable Gas for Freight

What do we do with freight transport and regional transport outside of cities, where electric power grids are not so easily used with vehicles? Can they also go oil free?

Freight is a highly contested area for the future. There are potential reductions in freight as the economy dematerializes (an example of which is that mobile phones now contain more than twenty functions, replacing twenty other devices).[14] Food miles (the distance traveled by your food before it reaches your plate) are also likely to reduce as local food cultures grow.[15] But freight trucks, ships, and trains and regional transport will still go on.

Various futures are predicted for freight, including the use of electric trucks powered through batteries or overhead catenaries, though this is unlikely given the extent of the infrastructure required. The transitional stage for larger vehicles, industry, and regional transport is to switch to greater use of natural gas supplemented by some biofuels. Trucks, trains, and boats can use compressed natural gas or liquefied natural gas in their diesel engines, with payoff times of just a few years, especially with high diesel costs. Cars for regional transport can be switched over as well, particularly if the manufacturer standardizes the use of natural gas, as occurred in Sweden when the government committed to natural gas cars for its vehicle fleet. The attraction is that natural gas is already in place in terms of infrastructure, covering almost 80 percent of the population in most developed nations.[16]

As mentioned in the previous chapter, Bloomberg's predictions show that natural gas will go into decline not long after coal in terms of its use for power. So natural gas can be only a small part of the transition to renewables unless it is made renewably. It will, however, be an obvious way to ease the pressure on diesel supplies and will be a great advantage to low-carbon cities (natural gas buses have already shown their big advantages over diesel buses in air quality) as well as energy security by taking pressure off the need for oil production in dangerous places.[17]

The benefit of the transition to natural gas has always been seen as an enabler of the long-term transition to hydrogen. However, hydrogen is not a good carrier of energy, as it requires a whole new system of storage. Natural gas pipelines cannot take hydrogen because of embrittlement. There may be niche value in hydrogen fuel cells; however, widespread use of hydrogen as a fuel is unlikely. The idea of a "hydrogen economy" should be abandoned. The use of renewable natural gas has much greater potential. Biogas can be created from biomass via gasification, and this could play a bigger role in the future, though at present it is mostly used in villages in developing countries.[18] However, the Sabatier process, which facilitates the joining of carbon dioxide (CO_2) and water (H_2O) into methane (CH_4) and oxygen (O_2), has more potential in moving us toward an oil-free future. Around the world a range of research labs are vying to develop this process into a commercially successful system using different catalysts.[19]

Thus if there can be a development in the hydrogenation of CO_2 using renewable energy, natural gas can itself become a renewable fuel, which can be fed into the present natural gas grids and even be an export item as liquefied natural gas. There is large potential in this process, considerably more than in "clean coal," as a totally new infrastructure will not be required for its distribution. Most coalfields (and hence coal-fired power) are long distances away from the deep caverns that can act to absorb CO_2. In the interim years, as coal-fired power stations are being phased out, they can have renewable natural gas production facilities attached to them. Eventually CO_2 can be extracted from the atmosphere and used as a renewable fuel.

Freight, industry, and regional transport are likely to continue to expand into natural gas and transition into the use of renewable natural gas. Thus natural gas can be given a long-term future and can be part of the renewables transition through transport rather than power.

Will Autonomous Vehicles Transform Our Cities?

Autonomous vehicles (AVs) have been called a disruptive innovation that will transform our cities because they will reduce road accidents, save time, and save fuel.[20] But will they?

Disruptive innovations find niche applications and then disrupt the whole system they are in because of their superior qualities. We described this in the previous chapter with solar PV and battery storage, which are moving rapidly from a niche to disrupting the whole centralized utility model. Will AVs do the same thing in our cities? We don't think so.

AVs are mostly being touted as the solution to peak hour congestion, which will bring economic benefits as well as benefits to community and human health (less time in traffic, lower stress, and reduced road accidents). The attraction is that they will save time and lives. But will they be significant improvements or just be facilitating an ongoing car dependence that is a bigger problem? Do they actually disrupt the transport system into a much better set of outcomes?

Time Savings

A few numbers will help put perspective on this. Table 2.1 shows the number of people who can be accommodated in a lane of road space using various modes of transit.

Where do AVs fit? If they were 1 meter apart and traveling at 100 kph (an aim that has been stated as the ultimate hope), they could take around 25,000 people per hour down a freeway lane. This is impressive movement capacity, though only half as good as a train, which can usually go faster and carry a lot more people than any other mode. However, to get this capacity means that 100 percent of the vehicles must be under control of the guidance system and no one chooses to take over their controls. As soon as one driver did this, the whole system would slow down considerably, as is found on freeways now.

To avoid this would require removing people's ability to take over their vehicles and imposing a total ban on driver freedom. Is this likely? Without this ban on human control the freeway would become not much better than a present-day freeway, where at peak times cars crawl along with gaps of around 2 meters between them or travel at higher speeds with larger spaces between them. This does not save much time; the reality is that cars

Table 2.1: Spatial efficiency of travel modes in the same single lane of road space.

Mode	Number of People Carried in the Space of One Road Lane per Kilometer per Hour
Car in normal street lane	800
Car in freeway lane	2,500
Bus in normal street lane	5,000
Bus in freeway lane	15,000
Tram on street	10,000
Light rail on separate right-of-way	20,000
Heavy rail on separate right-of-way	50,000

Source: Newman and Kenworthy, 2015

are inherently spatially inefficient compared with public transport, especially trains, which are twenty times as spatially efficient.

A further difficulty with the freeway of AVs is that a car must slow down when it takes an off-ramp. Most off-ramps would need to be extended considerably to prevent major traffic pile-ups extending back into the freeway flow. Off-ramp extensions would be politically and financially difficult, as they would take up a lot of extra land. In the end we are unlikely to have many examples of long troops of AVs doing 100 kph with 1 meter spacings, offering disruptive time savings.

Altogether this would mean little more than 2,000 people per hour, perhaps 4,000 if there were a higher number of passengers per vehicle, though this is hard to imagine. Almost no incentive scheme to increase vehicle occupancy has worked anywhere in the world, apart from some signs that UberPool may be working well in some parts of some cities.[21] Cars are essentially a very private mode of travel. Even with more demand-based opportunities, they are limited by the need to match origins and destinations. Where land use and urban fabric are scattered, it will always be hard to increase vehicle occupancy. No matter how much traffic engineering models make AVs into small buses, they will not compete with individual mobility on the one hand and transit-based mobility on the other.

The incredible technology that could, however, travel down a freeway at 100 kph only 1 meter apart is a bus that could immediately turn a freeway lane into a driverless bus rapid transit (BRT) system (like Adelaide's O-Bahn) with a much higher capacity than is presently available for buses. Trains too can use the technology to upgrade their signaling systems and move much faster and closer together than anything yet seen in our cities. Perhaps this could lead to capacities of around 100,000 people per hour being taken down a rail line. That would be disruptive! One train line would be able to carry fifty times what a present freeway lane carries. It would mean that cities reaching limits on the capacity of their train lines could manage significantly higher numbers on these lines without having to double the tracks.

Like the dream of all freeways and automobile lobbies, AVs will in reality remain stuck in traffic at peak times, with or without their autonomous qualities, as they will be victims of their urban fabric (see the discussion of urban fabrics later in this chapter).

Safety

The common good outcome from AVs is that they are hoped to be safer. Many human lives will be saved. But is this likely? What is the evidence so far, and what are the prospects for a fail-safe technology?

The record so far is not encouraging. Testing has certainly not been fail-safe, with the conclusion that "human error is perhaps the most problematic issue facing autonomous cars. That applies not only to drivers but other road users. Roads are hardly isolated places, nor are they restricted to car use,"[22] and it is other road users, such as pedestrians and cyclists, who need considerable care in any new transport system, especially a sustainable mobility system. Autonomous trains have been around for thirty years and have a very good track record because they don't involve humans being able to intervene suddenly, nor do they have a chance of harming others, as they are isolated on separate tracks. But AVs have both these problems.

Unless the possibility of human intervention is removed, a troop of cars doing 100 kph with 1 meter spacing will constantly be interrupted by those wanting to take over control to get out of the column or through some preference or panic. The potential for immense car accidents would be very high at this speed and spacing as long as humans are given the right to take the wheel when they want.

When AVs leave the freeway, they will be in a much less predictable space shared with other vehicles, cyclists, and pedestrians that are not under any kind of control system. The likelihood of accidents in this space is high unless AVs are tuned to react beyond anything yet imagined. Design engineers are promising this, but that will work against the time savings in any mixed-use street. Highly sensitive AVs would crawl along, reacting to every little movement. Drivers would be likely to go into override mode frequently in response. Is this the kind of "transformative system" we want in our future cities?

What are we left with? Not much, really. In terms of time savings and safety, AVs will not be disruptive to urban transport systems. Added to this is the fact that highly automated door-to-door mobility systems would mean that people would walk even less, only adding to the health problems outlined in chapter 3. Cities based on AVs would essentially create more car dependence. So what potential use is there for AVs?

The new urban economics, outlined later in this chapter, is showing that cities can save time and reduce road accidents if they spend their precious infrastructure resources on fast rail that can go around, under, or over traffic and on highly walkable, pedestrian-friendly city centers and subcenters.[23] It means that new rail lines and new centers need to be built deep into car-based suburbs struggling to find a truly disruptive transport system. This means that we need to think about how AVs can help in this transition.

AVs will need to be banned from city centers and other features of the walking city urban fabric that prioritize pedestrians. They will be completely inappropriate for the kind of urban space that needs to build on its car-free qualities, not be given over to moronic cars looking for people. Walking cities across the world are likely to ban AVs, just as all vehicles are now banned in places such as Times Square.

In the transit urban fabric, where quality transit runs quickly down corridors linking transit-oriented developments (TODs), the role of AVs is also hard to see. They will be just as much of a nuisance in the areas around stations, where walkability is the core feature sought by local governments, business investors, and communities. As long as issues of access equity are covered for the elderly and people with disabilities in the corridor—and this is easily done with taxis, small buses, and UberPool systems—what advantage is there to having AVs cluttering up the area? Perhaps they can join this group of supplementary services creating local links, but this is not transformative, and indeed it may be less effective in crowded station precincts.

However, out in the car-based suburbs there will be a need to provide new, fast transit with a mix of new TODs, and because of the automobile-based fabric they are serving they will need car-accessible stations. Increasing numbers of people will need help getting to the nearest train station so they can travel quickly across the city, past all the vehicles stuck on the freeway (autonomous or other), and then at the other end they will need help with the short distance to a destination. This is the "last-mile" or "first-mile" issue in public transport planning, and solutions have involved buses, bikes, and car drop-offs. Now it could include AVs. As suburbs age and people increasingly do not want to own vehicles, AV "taxis" could find an important niche with their demand-responsive systems. There will be fewer conflicts with pedestrians and more value in time savings if there is a seamless link to fast urban rail corridors.

Thus AVs could be an important part of how we adapt automobile urban fabric to be more sustainable in its mobility. Such AVs could be electric, along with the trains, helping make an oil-free, equitable, and efficient system. Such a system in the highly car-dependent suburbs could be disruptive. It would be part of a sustainable mobility system but only within the car-based suburbs. In walking and transit-based urban fabrics, AVs will be a nuisance and an economic waste and will probably continue to be part of the problem, not part of the solution. AVs are probably mostly hype, like that coming from big coal. The vehicle industry is trying desperately to hold onto market share when it should probably be looking at the decline and stranding of mobility assets due to peak car use, or reduced car use per person.

One more positive approach to AVs is their use as light-duty vehicles, as summarized in figure 2.3.[24] Automated mobility service vehicles are a combination of AVs with demand-responsive mobility services from the likes of taxis, UberPool, and small buses. The reduction in demand is a result of the growing phenomenon of "peak car."

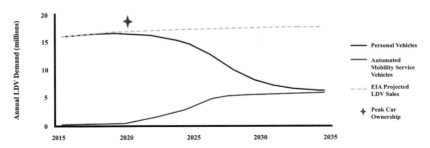

FIGURE 2.3: Peak car ownership versus projected light duty vehicle (LDV) demand. The graph indicates declining car ownership due to a combination of reduced personal demand and increased use of automated mobility service vehicles. (Source: Carlin, Rader, and Rucks, 2015)

What Is Happening to Cause Peak Car?

There have been two big positive changes since we wrote the first edition of this book; the first is the rise of renewable energy, and the second is the fall of private car use.

The peak in car use per capita probably shouldn't have surprised us, as the trend started back in the 1980s and 1990s, but it did cause a big stir because cars are so dominant in the world's cities and traffic always seems to be getting worse. However, these are the trends that are set out in detail in Peter Newman and Jeffrey Kenworthy's 2015 book *The End of Automobile Dependence.*

Per capita car use has declined in all the world's developed cities for most of the twenty-first century. In emerging cities such as those in eastern Europe, Latin America, and Asia there is a clear slowing down that will turn into a decline quickly. Shanghai and Beijing have entered a period of decline in car use modal share relative to growth in transit. Although there are some signs that the decline in car use per capita may have slowed or reversed in U.S. cities because of very low fuel prices, the trend is not clear in other cities around the world. This is because the causes of the decline are structural, with slowing traffic speeds relative to transit and with knowledge economy jobs drawing younger and wealthier people into more central locations. Thus it is possible that the reduction of car use per capita will become a part of the global processes that are helping cities to decouple

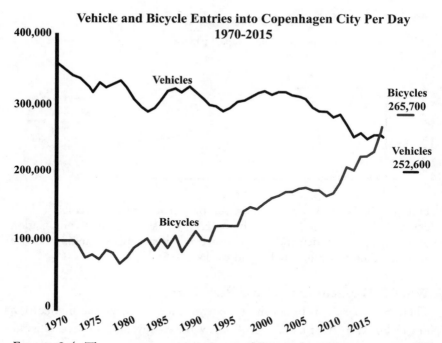

FIGURE 2.4: The great crossover: trips on bikes replace trips in cars as the biggest mode entering Copenhagen. (Source: City of Copenhagen)

economic growth from greenhouse gas emissions. These trends are outlined later in the chapter and detailed in other work.[25]

Transit growth has entered a huge global spurt based mostly on a "second rail revolution." Urban rail went into a hiatus during the expansion of the car-based city and the freeway era. However, starting in the 1990s and accelerating in this century there has been a dramatic increase in urban rail.[26] The rapid growth of urban rail can be seen in the traditional transit cities of Europe and in the recent automobile cities of North America and Australia, as well as in the emerging cities in the Middle East, Asia, and Latin America. In our Global Cities Database the growth rates in transit passenger-kilometers between 1995 and 2005 were as follows: European cities 22 percent, Asian cities 20 percent, Australian cities 11 percent, Canadian cities 12 percent, and American cities 16 percent.[27] Such growth rates have not been seen for many decades; indeed, they have mostly been falling.

Walking and cycling have also increased. Data on this are hard to collect, on the same basis as the previous data on car use and transit use, but overview studies such as that by John Pucher and Ralph Buehler suggest a significant increase in walking and cycling, especially in the old walking urban fabric of many European cities,[28] with recent positive trends in the United States and Australia.[29] Few cities can claim the growth in cycling demonstrated in figure 2.4 in Copenhagen, where cycling trips to the city have now outstripped car trips.[30]

Pucher and Buehler have also shown (see table 2.2) that there are dramatic growth rates in many U.S. cities following the building of a cycle network.

Table 2.2: Growth in cycling in U.S. cities in relation to growth in cycle network and safety impacts.

City	Years	Growth in Bicycle Network (%)	Growth in Bicycle Trips (%)	Change in Crashes per 100,000 Trips (%)	Change in Fatalities and Severe Injuries per 100,000 Trips (%)
Portland, OR	2000–2015	53	391	−62	−72
Washington, DC	2000–2015	101	384	−46	−50
New York, NY	2000–2015	381	207	N/A	−72
Minneapolis, MN	2000–2015	113	203	−75	−79
San Francisco, CA	2000–2015	172	167	−36	N/A
Cambridge, MA	2000–2015	27	134	−57	N/A
Chicago, IL	2005–2015	135	167	−54	−60
Seattle, WA	2005–2015	236	123	−25	−53
Los Angeles, CA	2005–2015	130	114	N/A	−43
Philadelphia, PA	2008–2015	17	51	N/A	−49

Source: Pucher and Buehler, 2016

Why is this move to a more sustainable mobility system happening?

Several overlapping factors seem to be behind these trends: urban regeneration is competing with urban sprawl; transit is competing with cars in time and cost; and the knowledge economy and a more urban culture are driving business and community.

Urban Regeneration Is Competing with Urban Sprawl

Cities are structured by transport. There is a universal travel time budget of a little over one hour on average per person per day, that is, around thirty minutes on average for the journey to work. This travel time budget has been found to apply in every city studied; we found it holds true in all one hundred or so cities in our Global Cities Database as well as in data on U.K. cities for 600 years.[31] This travel time budget has led to three types of urban fabric, as outlined in figure 2.5 and table 2.3: walking city, transit city, and automobile city urban fabrics. Most cities today have a mixture of all three.

Cities built mostly in the automobile era have primarily a low-density automobile city fabric and are heavily oil dependent, as shown in figure 2.6. There is an exponential link between urban density and transit fuel use.

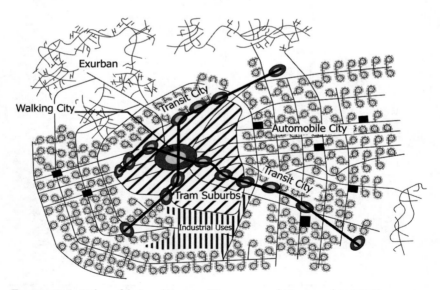

FIGURE 2.5: Urban fabrics. (Source: Newman and Kenworthy, 2015)

Table 2.3: Urban fabric characteristics.

Urban Fabric	Function Years	Transport Priority	Speed (Kilometers per Hour)	City Radius (Kilometers)	Land Use Pattern
Walking city	8,000 years ago to 1850s	Walking	3–4	2	Dense (over 100 persons/hectare) and mixed land use
Train-based transit city (outer areas)	1820s–1850s	Train, fast metro, or fast light rail	20–40	10–20	Less dense (around 50 persons/hectare) and mixed land use along rail lines Walking-based nodal centers
Tram-based transit city (inner areas)	1890s–1950s	Tram or light rail	10–20	5–10	Linear medium-density development along tram routes Regular grid or strip streets
Automobile city	1950s onward	Automobiles	50–80	20–40	Low density (less than 20 persons/hectare and 35 persons/hectare maximum) Dispersed and decentralized Automobile-reliant suburbs

Source: Newman, Kosonen, and Kenworthy, 2016

A new world is emerging in this fundamental structuring of cities: reurbanization. Cities had been reducing in density over the past one hundred years as the benefits of faster movement rebuilt urban development opportunities around mechanized transport, first rail based and then road based. In figure 2.6, data from the Global Cities Database

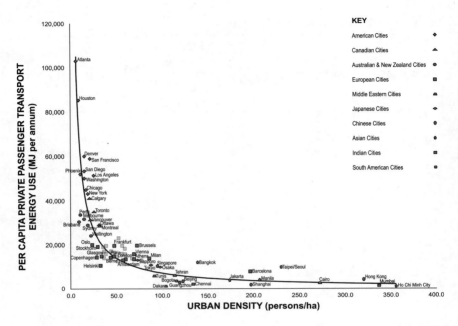

FIGURE 2.6: Urban density and transport fuel use. (Source: Newman and Kenworthy, 2015)

show how cities stopped declining in density, plateaued, and now are becoming more dense.

If a city increases in density, then in structural terms it will reduce its car use and fuel use. In fact, it will reduce it exponentially. Reurbanization is a structural move supporting low-carbon mobility and can explain the peak car and transit growth phenomenon. But why is this happening?

In figure 2.7 the growth in the travel time budget in cities of Australia and New Zealand as a result of urban sprawl and traffic congestion is very evident. All of these cities are now structurally dysfunctional, as they have gone beyond the thirty-minute average travel time for the journey to work.

The increase in travel times despite decreases in per capita car use is probably a result of cities becoming more focused in centers for the growing knowledge economy and its services. Hence travel is more peaky than if it were just general travel with less focus on office times. It is not hard to see why cities would respond to such increases in travel time and urban focus by enabling reurbanization so that people can live closer to their work

Urban Density Trend in 23 Cities in the USA, Australia, Canada and Europe, 1960-2005

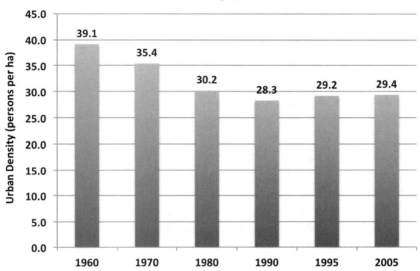

FIGURE 2.7: Urban density trend in twenty-three cities in the United States, Australia, Canada, and Europe, 1960–2005. The graph shows a reversal of density declines in the world's cities. (Source: Newman and Kenworthy, 2015)

and save commuting time and also by investing in rail projects that can go around, over, or under the traffic and generate some real travel time savings. This is evident in the data that follow.

Transit Is Competing with Cars in Time and Cost

Transit growth has been based on massive new investment. In Europe 65 cities added light rail to their transit systems, and now a total of 160 cities recognize that light rail can bring transit city urban fabric back to life. Expanded heavy rail and dramatic growth in high-speed rail across Europe have also been features of the rapid growth in transit. The dense emerging cities of the Middle East, Asia, and Latin America are seeing even more investment in new transit. Most Middle East cities, even in Saudi Arabia, are now building fast citywide metro systems. In China, 81 cities are building metros, as are 52 cities in India after Prime Minister Narendra Modi announced that every city with a population over 2 million would have a metro.

In the automobile cities there has also been a big commitment to investment in transit, with most Australian, Canadian, and U.S. cities committing to new urban rail lines. In the United States, light rail grew by 190 percent between 1993 and 2011 on the basis of expansion or new building in eighteen cities, with dozens more under way. Heavy rail grew by 68 percent during this period, though bus patronage dropped by 3 percent, suggesting that transit speed has become critical in these automobile-dependent cities that are now stuck in traffic.[32]

Data from the Global Cities Database are summarized in table 2.4 to show how automobile speeds slowed in relation to transit during the period 1960–2005, especially where there was a rail option.

The ratio of overall public transport system speed to general road traffic speed increased from 0.55 to 0.70 between 1960 and 2005. The ratio of rail system speed to general road traffic speed went from rail being slower than cars in 1960 (0.88) to rail being on average faster in 2005 (1.13). And this trend has seen a steady increase.

Within the different global regions it can also be seen that even in 2005 in U.S. and Canadian cities, public transport overall was barely half as fast as general traffic speed, whereas these cities' rail systems were about 90–95 percent as fast, meaning that in many cases they were competitive with the car, especially into dense urban centers, where clogged highways lost out to fast rail systems time and again. Australian cities did a little better, with public transport overall only about 25 percent slower than cars, while the rail systems in 2005 were on average about 8 percent faster and had generally improved their competitive position since the 1960s and 1970s. When major corridors into city centers are considered, the rail systems are at a clear advantage in all cities, which is why cities everywhere are investing in them, even in the United States and Australia.

European cities generally had quite competitive rail systems in terms of speed, but they hit a high in this forty-five-year perspective by reaching an average of 28 percent faster than cars. Their overall public transport systems, as a result of their fast rail systems, were on average 90 percent as fast as the car. It is interesting to note, however, that European cities' rail speed relative to road speed dropped from 1.07 to 0.80 during the 1960s, when they opened up to cars and built a lot of roads. A similar trend was seen in

Table 2.4: Ratio of overall average transit system and rail speed to general road traffic speed, 1960–2005.

Comparative Transit and Automobile Speeds in Global Cities

Ratio of Overall Public Transport System Speed to General Road Traffic Speed						
Cities	1960	1970	1980	1990	1995	2005
American Cities	0.46	0.48	0.55	0.50	0.55	0.54
Canadian Cities	0.54	0.54	0.52	0.58	0.56	0.55
Australian Cities	0.56	0.56	0.63	0.64	0.75	0.75
European Cities	0.72	0.70	0.82	0.91	0.81	0.90
Asian Cities	N/A	0.77	0.84	0.79	0.86	0.86
Global average for all cities	0.55	0.58	0.66	0.66	0.71	0.70
Ratio of Metro/Suburban Rail Speed to Road Speed						
Cities	1960	1970	1980	1990	1995	2005
American Cities	N/A	0.93	0.99	0.89	0.96	0.95
Canadian Cities	N/A	N/A	0.73	0.92	0.85	0.89
Australian Cities	0.72	0.68	0.89	0.81	1.06	1.08
European Cities	1.07	0.80	1.22	1.25	1.15	1.28
Asian Cities	N/A	1.40	1.53	1.60	1.54	1.52
Global average for all cities	0.88	1.05	1.07	1.11	1.12	1.13

Source: Newman and Kenworthy, 2015

Australian cities, but after that rail speeds relative to car speeds rose quite consistently as investment in rail returned.

Asian cities in the sample had very fast rail systems compared with their crowded road systems, where in 2005 rail speeds were some 52 percent higher. This fluctuated somewhat over the decades, but rail speeds on average were never less than 40 percent better than road speeds, even in the 1970s. Such data give hope to the many emerging cities struggling with the car, indicating that rail systems can help them to develop a very different kind of overall urban transport system that is not so overwhelmed by the automobile. In the emerging cities traffic speeds were very slow (around the low 20s in kph), and bus speeds are always slower than this. Bangkok had a traffic speed of 14 kph and a bus speed of 9 kph in 1990. Thus as these emerging cities build rail (often above or below the traffic), the data will show dramatic improvement in transit speeds.

Corresponding to these data on speeds, it is becoming obvious that urban rail can compete with urban freeways in terms of cost. It is difficult to compare cost data between cities, but within cities the data can and should be compared on any project, though in the past road and rail projects were always planned and funded without analysis of comparative costs. In Perth a single lane of urban freeway cost $35 million per kilometer, whereas the railway down the middle of the same freeway cost $12 million per kilometer and carries the equivalent of eight lanes of traffic. This means that investing in traffic yields twenty-four times less value for money than investing in rail.[33]

Such numbers explain why twenty-two cities have removed urban freeways from their blighted urban landscapes and replaced them with transit and walkable urban spaces.[34] This trend is likely to continue and accelerate as the life span of many freeways is reached.

The Knowledge Economy and a More Urban Culture Are Driving Business and Community

If cities are shaped by transport infrastructure to enable reasonable travel times, what are the economic drivers that are locating work and housing? Two factors seem relevant: the rise of the knowledge economy and the rise of digital technology in changing culture.

The biggest change in the economy during the period leading up to and including the period of car use decline and rail growth has been the digital transformation and the consequent knowledge and service economy. Despite this being global and enabling long-distance communication, it has in fact been a concentrating force in terms of city structure and fabric. The data on global cities outlined earlier show a universal increase in density, and this is even more obvious when it is seen how knowledge economy jobs are focusing in city centers and subcenters.[35]

The knowledge economy and digital jobs are focused in city centers, as these are where the creative, face-to-face synergies occur between people.[36]

Old central business districts have been transformed back into functional walking cities, and those that have done this best have attracted the most capital and young talent to work there. The six most walkable cities in the United States have 38 percent higher gross domestic product (GDP). In Boston 70 percent of knowledge economy workers live in walkable locations.[37]

Transit systems and walking are the most spatially efficient forms of transport. As outlined in the earlier discussion of autonomous vehicles, if one kilometer of a lane of road is considered as a unit of travel, then car traffic can fit about 800 people per hour down that lane in a suburban street, a freeway up to 2,500, a busway around 5,000, light rail between 10,000 and 20,000, and heavy rail up to 50,000. These striking differences in spatial efficiency are translating into competitive advantage based on the need to bring people together in centers.

Transit city corridors are also regenerating because of these efficiencies, enabling linkages between city centers and subcenters, with their need to provide housing and work locations within the thirty-minute journey to work. The revival of the transit city is mostly related to the need to link universities, health campuses, and information technology job clusters, which have created their own centers for jobs, and the need to attract housing and transit to link them together efficiently. In all these places the waste of urban space to parking and large-capacity roads has become a major issue detracting from their competitive advantage. Only sustainable transport solutions can help resolve this.

Other parts of the economy, such as manufacturing, small and large industry, and freight transport and storage, have remained car based and are outside this new knowledge economy. They will remain as part of the consumption economy, but they are not where the growth in jobs or the growth in wealth is happening. Thus the automobile city economy and culture has become somewhat distinct from the new regenerated urban economy of knowledge and services, with their basis in walking and transit city locations.

As with many economic changes, there is also a cultural dimension to this change that perhaps explains the rapidity of the changes observed here as well as the demographic complexion of the change. Young people (especially those involved in knowledge economy jobs) are moving to reduce their car use and switching to alternative transport faster than any other group. This has been recognized by a few commentators and related to the use of social media devices.[38] While on transit or walking (and even to an extent while biking) young people are already connected by their smart technology phones and tablets. These are hardly usable while driving a car. A report by U.S. PIRG Education Fund authors Benjamin Davis, Tony Dutzik, and Phineas Baxandall shows that the mobile phone is a far more important device than a car for younger people.[39] This is a cultural revolution that partly underlies the rail revolution as well as the reurbanization of cities.

Baby boomers gained freedom and connection with a car; millennials are not needing one. They like to save time on a fast train, but they also like to use the time constructively, relating to their friends and work colleagues through smart technology devices. They are not put off by density, as they know it enables them to live closer to the city where all the action is and all the best jobs are. They are also more inclined to be part of the shared economy with innovations such as UberPool, which claims to have reduced London's vehicle miles traveled (VMT) by 700,000 in six months from its opening in November 2015.[40] This may, however, have taken people from transit; no survey was done to show what other mode they would have used. Such shared mobility is also much easier in London, where the urban fabric is mostly from the walking and transit eras.

The structural expression of this change is that younger people are moving to live in the walking city or transit city, as these locations more readily enable them to enjoy the urban experience and culture they aspire to, as well as save precious time. Thus they feed the market that enables peak car, the rail revival, and city center renewal to continue. They are the leaders in ending automobile dependence. This can explain why cities such as Washington, DC, and Portland, Oregon, are demonstrating the decoupling of GDP from car use per capita—see figure 2.8.[41]

So the trends to a sustainable mobility system are under way, but what can we expect into the future?

Can We Reduce Car Use 50 Percent and Oil Use 80 percent by 2050 and 100 percent by 2100?

A sustainable mobility system in a city would need to meet the goal of 80 percent less oil by 2050 and 100 percent less by 2100. This will require less car use as well as less oil use per vehicle. How much is it possible to change our cities? Is it possible to imagine an exponential decline in car use in our cities that could lead to 50 percent fewer passenger kilometers driven in cars to go with the technological changes in fuel and vehicles discussed earlier? The key mechanism is a quantitative leap in the quality of public transport accompanied by an associated change in land use patterns. Walking and transit city fabrics are relatively easy to regenerate and enable more

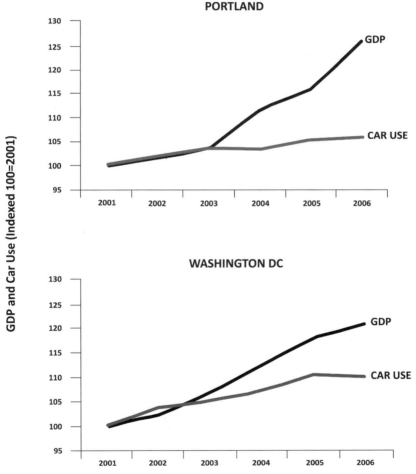

FIGURE 2.8: Growth in decoupling of car use from gross domestic product (GDP) in Portland, Oregon, and Washington, DC, 2001–2006. (Source: Kooshian and Winkelman, 2011)

people to walk and use transit. But how do we shape the automobile city fabric to enable a large percentage of people to overcome their automobile dependence?

Figure 2.9 shows the relationship between car passenger kilometers and public transport passenger kilometers from the Global Cities Database.

The most important thing about this relationship is that as the use of public transport increases linearly, the car passenger kilometers decrease exponentially. This is due to a phenomenon called "transit leverage" whereby one passenger kilometer of transit use replaces between three and seven passenger kilometers in a car as a result of more direct travel (especially in trains), trip chaining (doing various other things, like shopping or service visits, along with a commute), and giving up one car in a household (a common occurrence that reduces many solo trips), eventually resulting in changes in where people live as they prefer to live or work nearer transit.[42]

Using this relationship we can see that cities can project their continued transit growth and expect significant reductions in car use. Indeed it is feasible that each city could set a target of increases in passenger kilometers per capita for public transport in order to achieve 50 percent reductions in car use as part of their commitment to reaching the global goal of 80 percent reduction in greenhouse gases by 2050.

The biggest challenge in an age of radical resource efficiency requirements will be finding a way to build fast rail systems back into scattered automobile-dependent suburban areas. Rail reserves are not available, so many cities are choosing to tunnel or go aboveground on elevated structures—both are expensive. Many cities are building fast rail systems down freeways deep into car-dependent suburbs. Building fast electric rail down the middle of roads is easier than anywhere else, as the right-of-way is there and engineering in terms of gradients and bridges is compatible. If a median is not available, then a lane may need to be replaced by rail, but in an era of declining car use this should be possible. Freeways are not ideal in terms of ability to build TODs, but it can still be done using high-rise buildings as sound walls. Linkages from buses, electric bikes, and park and rides are all easily provided so that local travel to the system is short and convenient.

Speed of the transit system is key. In Perth the new Southern Railway runs down a freeway with a maximum speed of 130 kph (80 miles per hour) and an average speed of 90 kph (55 mph) that is at least 30 percent

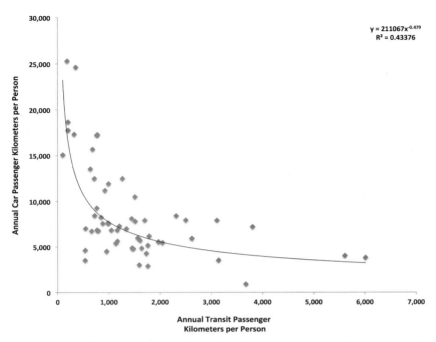

$$y = 211067x^{-0.479}$$
$$R^2 = 0.43376$$

FIGURE 2.9: The exponential relationship between car use and transit use in global cities. (Source: Newman and Kenworthy, 2015)

faster than traffic. The result is dramatic increases in patronage, far beyond the expectations of planners, who see such suburbs as too low in density to deserve a rail system. Perth's Mandurah line, serving the city's southern suburbs, opened in December 2007 and is now carrying 75,000 people a day, where the bus system carried just 14,000.[43] Little else can compete with this kind of option for creating a future in the car-dependent suburbs of many cities. Portland, Oregon; Denver, Colorado; and Washington, DC, have been moving fast rail out into their suburbs.

Light rail (and heavy rail) can be built back into automobile-dependent suburbs by using land value capture or land value creation.[44] Value capture is relatively well known, but value creation is new. We call this approach, which is based on urban regeneration, the "entrepreneur rail model." Urban regeneration is planned first so that the best sites are determined for new urban centers in the suburbs. The ability to fund a light rail system that can unlock the value in this land for redevelopment is then assessed. This is best done by seeking bids from consortia who can build, own, operate, and finance the light rail through their investment in the urban regeneration. This is how urban rail is built in Japan and Hong Kong and how it is beginning to be built in some Canadian cities and in Florida's Brightline system.[45] It is how urban rail was first built in the era of the transit city, from the late 1890s to the 1940s. It would seem that the new market for urban rail could unlock the development of a new type of polycentric twenty-first-century city, especially one that incorporates all the renewable innovations described in chapter 1.

Reducing Travel

There are many ways that technology can help us reduce the need to travel. Transport to meet people by long-distance or even short trips within cities may be considerably reduced once the use of broadband-based telepresence begins to make high-quality imaging feasible on a large scale. There will always be a need to meet face-to-face in creative meetings in cities, but for many routine meetings, computer-based meetings are taking a growing role, becoming more and more like face-to-face meetings. However, there does not seem to be a reduction in the attractions of city centers, and this is likely to continue. Cities that are attractive places to meet (walkable, safe, and lively) will thrive, whereas suburban areas with little more than scattered houses will find their economies being undermined.

The relationship between density and car use is exponential, as shown earlier. If a city slowly increases its density, especially in centers, then the impact can be more extensive on car use than expected. Density is a multiplier on the use of transit and walking or cycling, as well as reducing the length of travel. Increases in density can result in greater mixing of land uses to meet people's needs nearby. This is seen, for example, in the return of small supermarkets to the central business districts of cities as residential populations increase and demand local shopping opportunities within an easy walk. The same mix can be found in the repurposed suburban shopping center when people are attracted to live inside and over such areas. Overall, this reversal of urban sprawl will undermine the growth in car use.

The need to develop city centers is now shifting to the need to develop subcenters across the whole car-dependent city in order to help get people out of cars. This process aims to create transit-oriented developments

FIGURE 2.10: Toyko, a model walking city. (Source: Peter Newman)

(TODs). This will ultimately lead to the polycentric city, which is a series of subcenters or small cities in the suburbs all linked by quality transit but each providing the local facilities of an urban center. University of Utah professor Reid Ewing examined the "Newman-Kenworthy hypothesis" that more compact urbanity will reduce car use and concluded that we are correct.[46]

The need to facilitate TODs has been recognized by all Australian cities and most U.S. cities in their metropolitan strategies.[47] The major need for TODs is not in the inner areas, as these have many from previous eras of transit building, but in the newer car-dependent suburbs. There are real equity issues here, as the poor increasingly are trapped on the fringe, with high expenditures on transport. A 2004 study by the Center for Transit-Oriented Development shows that people in TODs drive 50 percent less than those in conventional suburbs. In the United States, according to a 2004 study, "shifting 60 percent of new growth to compact patterns would save 85 million metric tons of CO_2 annually by 2030."[48]

In both Australia and the United States, homes that are located in TODs are holding their value the best or appreciating the fastest under the pressure of changing real estate markets.[49] The report suggests that TODs would appreciate fastest in up markets and hold value better in down markets. This is the rationale for how TODs can be built as public-private partnerships (PPPs) in rail projects, as outlined earlier in the discussion of the entrepreneur rail model, due to the value benefits in TODs.[50]

Thus TODs are essential in responding to the need for low-carbon mobility, especially when they incorporate affordable housing.[51] The economics of this approach have been assessed by the Center for Transit-Oriented Development and the nongovernmental organization Reconnecting America. In a detailed survey across several states they assessed that the market for housing within a half mile of a TOD was 14.6 million households. This is more than double the number who currently live in TODs. The market is based on the fact that those living in TODs now (who were found to be smaller households, the same age and the same income on average as those not in a TOD) save some 20 percent of their household income by not having to own so many cars—those in TODs owned 0.9 car per household, compared with 1.6 outside. This frees up on average $4,000 to $5,000 per year. In Australia calculations have shown similar private savings.[52] Most important, this extra income is spent locally on urban services, which means the TOD approach is a local economic development mechanism.

TODs must also be PODs, that is, pedestrian-oriented developments, or they lose their key quality as a car-free environment, to which businesses and households are attracted. Urban designers need to ensure that public space is vibrant, safe, and inviting. Architect and urban designer Jan Gehl's transformations of central areas such as Copenhagen, New York, London, and Melbourne demonstrate how to improve TOD spaces so they are more walkable, economically viable, socially attractive, and environmentally significant.[53] Gehl's work in Melbourne and Perth has been evaluated after a decade of implementation and in both cases indicates substantial increases in walkability, numbers of pedestrians who use the city center for their work, shopping, education, and, especially, recreation. It will be important for those green developers wanting to establish credibility that scattered urban developments, no matter how green their buildings and renewable their infrastructure, will be seen as failures in a low-carbon mobility world unless they are building pedestrian-friendly TODs.

At the same time, TODs that have been well designed as PODs will also need to be GODs—green-oriented developments. TODs will need to ensure that they have full solar orientation, are renewably powered with smart grids, have water-sensitive design, use recycled and low-impact materials, and use innovations such as green roofs, as outlined in this book.

Reducing Demand for the Automobile

The real test of a 100 percent oil-free city will be how it can simultaneously reduce its oil consumption through new technologies and reduce the need to travel through urban design, while at the same time changing behavior to reduce the demand for car travel. The need for a parallel delivery of physical infrastructure and mental infrastructure will be essential for any city contemplating becoming oil free.

Every nation and city has its own way of making the adoption of more planetary lifestyles convenient and easy compared with more consumptive lifestyles. When it comes to cars, however, the more that a city is car dependent, the harder it is to use tax incentives to change people's lifestyles. European cities have much higher gasoline taxes than American and Australian cities, and accordingly they use cars less.[54]

In the car-dominated cities of North America and Australia, the major public policy to reduce the global and local impacts of the car has been through regulations on vehicles that have forced them to become cleaner. Vehicles are becoming much more energy efficient.[55] Following introduction of these, most urban atmospheres have become cleaner, although fuel use has continued to increase as vehicles have become bigger and their use has continued to grow. Regulations also are applied to safety and congestion management, but this will continue to worsen if more and more car use is facilitated. Regulations alone do not change behavior. The economic principle known as the rebound effect or the Jevons paradox—increasing efficiency means increasing consumption—has been found to apply to car use. If people buy cars that use less fuel, they just drive them more—undermining most gains made possible through the new technology.[56]

All of these necessary policy approaches will be wasted without education on a changed role for the car. Thus cultural change, to help people want to drive less, needs to be part of any city's policy arsenal if it is to face up to the challenge of growing a sustainable, low-carbon mobility city. TravelSmart is one such program that shows this is indeed possible.[57]

German sociologist Werner Brög developed TravelSmart based on the belief that behavior change toward less car dependence can work if it is community based and household oriented. After some trials in Europe, TravelSmart was adopted in large-scale projects in Perth. It has since spread across most Australian cities and to other European cities, especially in the United Kingdom, and has now been piloted in six American cities.

Good behavior change programs do not use media. So TravelSmart targets individual households directly, asking them if they would like to find ways to reduce their car use. Residents who show interest receive information and, for the few who need extra support, a visit from a TravelSmart officer or eco-coach, who encourages them to start with local trips. TravelSmart especially recommends starting with the school trip for children, which is now seen as an essential part of the healthy development of young people's sense of place and belonging in any community, as well as a way to reduce obesity.

TravelSmart has been found to reduce the kilometers traveled by vehicle by around 12–14 percent across whole communities—a result that seems to last for at least five years after the program ends. Where transit is not good and destinations are more spread out, the program may reduce car use by only 8 percent, but where these are good it can rise to 15 percent.[58]

Behavior change programs can develop social capital to support people as they try to get out of cars, and this can change local cultures. People show friends how much money they save, and they feel they are doing their bit for climate change and oil vulnerability. There is evidence in Brisbane, Queensland, Australia, that at least 50 percent more people than those involved in the initial household interviews were actually following the program when the surveys were done; in other words, people were spreading the message to their friends and colleagues.[59] When people start to change their lifestyle and can see the benefits, they become advocates of sustainable transport policies in general. The politics of change is easier to manage when communities have begun to change themselves.

In Perth the extension of the rail system to the far outer suburbs has been more positive and politically achievable than expected, with a massive 90 percent support for the last stage, the southern suburbs railway. In parallel to this political process, Perth had some 200,000 households undergoing the TravelSmart program; the suburbs where TravelSmart was conducted increased their public transport patronage by 83 percent, but in areas without TravelSmart it was 59 percent.[60]

TravelSmart has now been applied to more than 450,000 residents in Perth, at a cost to the state of under A\$36 per resident. Worldwide, TravelSmart's individualized approach to travel demand management has been delivered to approximately 5 million people. Taking into account the reductions in public and private costs of car use that it has achieved, the program saves \$30 for every dollar it costs.[61]

Behavior change programs can also work in the workplace. TravelSmart was found to work well when a TS Club was formed that enabled people to share experiences, bring in local speakers, and lobby for facilities such as showers for bike riders and transit passes instead of parking spaces. For example, the natural gas company Woodside in Perth involved its employees in planning their new building; a strong representation from the TS Club at Woodside led to good bicycle facilities being provided. The firm now has more employees biking to work than riding, and the subsequent saving in car parking spaces is considerable.[62]

TravelSmart has also used the "walking school bus" concept to enable children to safely walk to school. A variation is the "bicycle bus," in which adults supervise children riding their bikes to school. Walking or riding to and from school provides valuable exercise for children. It enables them to learn early that walking and cycling are very practical, pleasant, and healthy forms of local travel. At the same time, the adult supervision that walking school bus schemes provide ensures that children—especially very young ones—are safe, thus overcoming a barrier that causes parents to prevent their children from walking or cycling. The experience of walking or cycling teaches children about their neighborhood and environment, as well as teaching road safety skills and equipping them for independent mobility as they get older. Finally, these programs, if they are supervised by parents or volunteers, involve virtually no cost.

The changes in behavior being seen among young people in cities across the world, especially the United States, suggest that programs to assist this process may have considerable success in further reducing the demand for car use.[63] Much of this cultural shift appears to be because young people are connected substantially through social media devices rather than cars and to a growing use of Skype and other telepresence technologies to replace the need for travel by business. These cultural changes will help drive the transition to sustainable mobility.

There are many hopeful examples of cities moving in the right direction and of steps that can be taken to reduce our dependence on oil-consuming, greenhouse gas–emitting modes of transportation while retaining travel time budgets that are economically and socially realistic.

Conclusion

There are not many guidelines to the future of our cities and regions that take account of what could happen to mobility in response to the challenge of climate change. This chapter has examined what could happen, based on first, assessing the trends that are already leading to less oil and car dependence, and second, imagining this oil-free future given what we know about technology, urban planning, and behavior change possibilities available or emerging. The alternatives all require substantial commitment to change from government, business, and the community. As with renewables, we can now see that our cities will be better places to live with better economic opportunities. The transition will take time, but already it is clear that the early adopters in cities around the world are establishing economic competitiveness.

The first signs of change toward these emerging technologies can now be seen: the reurbanization of our cities with walkable centers; the dramatic growth in electric rapid transit; the 40 percent per year growth in electric vehicles and their ability to tap into solar energy, thus enabling renewable transport; the emerging use of natural gas and biofuels in transport; new telepresence technologies; and the obvious potential for lifestyle change indicated by behavior change programs.

Business will have more and more opportunities to help shape cities with entrepreneurial projects that build TODs with electric rail powered by the sun; industry will need to show the way on how to use non-oil alternatives for freight and aircraft.

Government has historically had the biggest role in transport and will continue to need to drive it for common good outcomes.

Community will need to support walkable urban regeneration, create lifestyles that are oil free, and buy into the new technologies and urban designs that are low carbon.

The potential for creating oil-free cities is here. The technologies and practices outlined here suggest that we can be oil free by 2050 and renewably based oil free by 2100.

CHAPTER 3

Foster Inclusive and Healthy Cities

The New Urban Agenda is an ambitious agenda which aims at paving the way towards making cities and human settlements more inclusive, [ensuring that] everyone can benefit from urbanization, paying particular attention to those in vulnerable situations. It is a vision of pluralistic, sustainable, and disaster resilient societies that foster green economic growth. Above all it is a commitment—a commitment that we will all together take the responsibility of one another and the direction of the development of our common urbanizing world.

—Joan Clos, secretary-general of the United Nations Habitat III Conference

A city is only as resilient as its most vulnerable residents. A resilient city provides access to healthy food, clean water and air, safe transportation infrastructure, healthy buildings, and health services *for all citizens*. But as the economic divide increases between the haves and have-nots, the health disparities increase, leaving the neediest with the fewest resources to face any type of disruption. "The gap between the rich and the poor in most countries is at its highest levels since 30 years," according to the report prepared by the United Nations' 2016 Habitat III Conference in Quito, Ecuador, which created the New Urban Agenda referred to in this chapter's opening quotation.[1] In cities in much of the developed world, air pollution levels have lowered as cars and industry have been regulated to reduce their emissions, while air pollution is rising in many of the worlds' poorest cities.[2] In the United States, as markets have responded to the demand for walkable, transit-oriented neighborhoods, those with access are increasingly upper-class residents, while lower-income residents retreat to the more affordable areas, where they are often left with limited access to jobs and few healthy transportation options. Todd Litman, executive director of the Victoria Transport Policy Institute, reports: "On average, the lowest income quintile (fifth of households) spends 40% of its budget on housing and 15% on transportation, leaving little money for other important goods. If lower-income households cannot afford healthy food or healthcare, the actual cause is usually high housing and transportation costs, since for each dollar spent on food and healthcare they typically spend three to five dollars on housing and transport."[3] While many reports of the resurgence of urban centers are largely stories of success, they reflect only part of the picture of these urban regions, where different zip codes may reflect very disparate health realities.[4] If the global knowledge economy is creating new jobs in dense urban centers, then how do we manage the growing loss of jobs and access to jobs on the fringes of our cities as they become fringes of the economy?

Most economic growth in developing countries over the past fifty years has been in big cities. Big cities, by virtue of their concentration of economic activities, usually attract capital investment for employment, education, and other opportunities. In most instances, however, they fail to absorb the ever-increasing demand for affordable housing and associated support infrastructure.

While there are disparities and growing inequities within each developed city, there are stark and startling disparities between the developed and developing worlds. Access to clean drinking water is something most residents of developed countries take for granted, yet worldwide, 783 million people do not have access to clean water and almost 2.5 billion do not have access to adequate sanitation.[5] In the United States in 2015, the inadequacy of our infrastructure, especially in lower-income communities, was highlighted by the disaster in Flint, Michigan, where residents' water was found to be contaminated by lead. "There is a widespread assumption that safe,

FIGURE 3.1: Currently, no place shows the danger of climate change and inequity more clearly than Haiti, the poorest country in the Western Hemisphere. The effects of natural disasters are exacerbated by deforestation and a lack of basic services and infrastructure. Hundreds of thousands of lives were lost in Haiti as a result of the earthquake of 2015 and the related cholera epidemic. (By EscombrosBelAir5.jpg: Marcello Casal Jr. via Wikimedia Commons)

affordable water for drinking and household use is available to all residents in the United States," notes Pacific Institute researcher Amy Vanderwerker. "The reality is that some low-income communities and communities of color lack access to water for the most basic human needs."[6]

As the world continues to urbanize, accommodating new urban citizens in a fair and humane way and offering access to basic human needs becomes more challenging. In "The Inclusive City," Franziska Schreiber and Alexander Carius write, "In addition to managing the integration of immigrants, cities and municipalities must provide sufficient infrastructure to accommodate their growing and diversifying populations and to avoid the emergence of new inequalities in urban areas while fostering social cohesion. For example, local governments must meet the increasing demand for housing and provide sufficient infrastructure and basic services, such as electricity, water, sanitation, health care, and education."[7]

This chapter will address the following questions:

1. What is an inclusive and healthy city?
2. What is inclusive and healthy housing?
3. Resilience for whom? How do we protect all citizens?
4. How can planners and policy makers work toward inclusive and healthy cities globally?

What Is an Inclusive and Healthy City?

The number of urban dwellers is not only increasing but also diversifying—by 2044, a majority of Americans will be people of color.[8] But economic benefits are not increasing equally, and the gap between the rich and poor continues to grow. In the United States, "full-time workers of color currently earn 23 percent less than their white counterparts—the gap is slightly more than in 1979, and is growing rather than shrinking."[9]

The most important attribute of an inclusive, healthy city is affordable, safe, and healthy housing within a supportive community, as addressed later in this chapter. But critical to this is workplace location, which impacts so heavily on inclusive job options and access to jobs through transportation options, as well as the community within which the housing is located.

Even in communities where basic human needs and services are provided, the physical environment may not offer healthy options, such as walkable infrastructure and access to open space. Dr. Richard Jackson, a physician who early on related health problems, such as obesity, to car dependence (to the chagrin of home builders, some members of Congress, and even some public health professionals), is now a sought-after expert on health and the built environment. Dr. Jackson believes that "we must rethink the ways in which our physical environments, homes, offices, neighborhoods, regions, and transit systems are designed and constructed, understand how they impact health, and ensure that they foster equity and sustainability."[10]

An inclusive, healthy city also offers accessible and affordable transportation alternatives to the car, such as walking, biking, and transit (sustainable mobility is covered more generally in chapter 2). In 2013, the Victoria Transport Policy Institute and the American Public Transportation Association (APTA) studied the health benefits of public transportation and came up with six primary benefits:[11]

1. Public transit users are more active (more than three times more active than individuals who don't use public transit).
2. Buses are safer than individual vehicles.
3. Public transportation reduces stress and encourages social interaction.
4. Public buses keep air cleaner (especially newer diesel and electric vehicles).
5. Riding public transportation saves money.
6. Public transportation provides access to essential needs later in life (a critical point, given that globally the population aged sixty or over is the fastest growing).[12]

Given the lack of federal investment in transit infrastructure and the cost to maintain existing systems, let alone improve them, fares in U.S. cities continue to rise as service is cut. "More than 70 percent of the nation's transit systems cut service, raised fares or both during the recession and its aftermath," according to APTA.[13] Programs to provide reduced fares for lower-income residents are once again being examined in many cities, most notably Seattle, Washington, which recently launched a program to provide reduced fares for residents "whose household income is no more than 200 percent of the federal poverty level—for instance, $47,700 or less for a family of four under the 2014 guidelines."[14] The cities of Charlotte, North Carolina, and Boston, Massachusetts, offer reduced fares through nonprofit groups. In New York City there is pressure from local advocacy groups for the Metropolitan Transportation Authority to offer reduced fares in light of a possible fare increase to $3.00 per ride for subway and bus.[15]

As transit fares rise and service becomes less predictable, urban biking has increased in popularity. Bicycling offers a healthy alternative for longer distances and has become an increasingly popular commuting option in many areas of the world, especially now that electric bikes can extend easy riding distances as well as helping people of all ages. In China there are now 150 million electric bikes. In more than 600 cities throughout the world, bike infrastructure has come to include bike-share systems, which provide access to bikes when owning one is not practical or affordable. Hangzhou, China, operates the largest bike-share system in the world, with 65,000 bikes.[16] As stated by the National Association of City Transportation Officials (NACTO), gains in safety and access to bikes are especially important to low-income residents. NACTO's research shows that in the United States, "49% of the people who bike to work earn less than $25,000 per year."[17] Tamika Butler, executive director of the Los Angeles County Bicycle Coalition, states that building better bike lanes and supporting riders with long-term community engagement is essential for safety and is also "an important step on the path to a more equitable bike infrastructure."[18]

Providing safe pedestrian and bicycle infrastructure increases these benefits, especially those related to physical activity. Walking has proven benefits of combating obesity, improving mental health, lowering stress, and reducing the risk of heart disease.

Australia has one of the highest obesity rates, ranking twenty-first in the world and third among all English-speaking countries, with much of Australia's adult population not getting enough physical activity to remain healthy. In a 2010 study, it was found that Australia's Physical Activity and Sedentary Behaviour Guidelines could be met easily by increasing active transportation. (The guidelines recommend that people should engage in thirty minutes of physical activity per day over five days of the week in order to be healthy and to be considered physically active.)[19]

It is estimated that in developed countries, 1.5–3 percent of total direct health-care costs are related to inactivity.[20] The cost of inactivity in Australia due to car dependence is estimated at $3.82 billion per year, and the total value of all Australian adults meeting recommended activity levels is estimated at $6.1 billion per year. Added to this, it was found that productivity increased by 6 percent when walking increased as a result of urban form improvements; this was from enhanced physical and mental well-being from walking.[21]

Streets that offer multimodal infrastructure have proven to be safer for people on all modes. Yet there is still resistance in most cities to adapting automobile infrastructure to accommodate other modes, even given the threats to life and limb. As a culture we have come to accept automobile-related deaths as an inevitable part of mobility. According to the World Health Organization, road traffic injuries caused an estimated 1.25 million deaths worldwide in the year 2010. That is, one person was killed every twenty-five seconds. This is much more than people killed in wars, but we accept it, as in most cities automobile-oriented planning and decision making still dominate. The only solution being offered on a large scale is autonomous vehicles, and, as outlined in chapter 2, there are still many questions about how well these can actually improve road safety.

In response, various efforts, such as a combined project by the Bloomberg Philanthropies Initiative for Global Road Safety, Cities Safer by Design at the World Resources Institute, the Global Designing Cities Initiative at NACTO, and the Vision Zero Network, have been working to raise awareness and provide tools, from policy to design solutions, to make streets safer in cities around the world. Vision Zero, a program that originated in Sweden in the late 1990s, has a goal of zero traffic deaths. Vision Zero has been adopted in cities around the world, and there is now a U.S.-based network of these cities, the Vision Zero Network.[22] There is also a federal program in the United States called the Road to Zero. Vision Zero promotes safer infrastructure, stronger enforcement, data collection related to traffic safety, education, and policy changes (such as lower speed limits) to make the streets safer. Advocates also work to change the language used in reporting deaths, with a "crash, not accident" campaign to emphasize that these tragedies are preventable.

Providing safe public spaces—from roads to plazas—is part of the movement to create "cities for people." Danish architect and urban designer Jan Gehl reacted to the modernist focus on design that prioritized automobile spaces over all else rather than considering spaces that might invite humans to stay. Working with his wife, Ingrid Gehl, a psychologist, he developed methods for observing people's use of public space in order to design the spaces to fit their needs, instead of designing with the expectation that users would fit their needs to an artfully designed place. Gehl has worked in cities around the globe to ensure that as these areas urbanize, there are safe, comfortable, inviting public spaces

Box 3.1 The Complicated Success of the Atlanta BeltLine

The Atlanta BeltLine is generally considered a shining example of how to rethink mobility options even in a car-committed city. It was the idea of Ryan Gravel, a graduate student at Georgia Tech, who proposed the idea in his master's thesis in 1999. The concept was straightforward enough—take advantage of the twenty-two miles of abandoned rail line that encircled downtown Atlanta and convert this corridor into a vibrant walking, bicycling, and transit corridor. Even more remarkable were the steps Gravel and others took to rally the community around the idea—a series of many presentations and discussions with a variety of community groups, leaders, and agencies. Soon the idea had traction.

Today the BeltLine is a reality. With around nine miles of the total walking and bicycling system completed (none of the transit elements has yet been built), it has already become one of the most popular places in Atlanta to visit and spend time. It has emerged as a vibrant, highly popular place to walk, stroll, jog, and bicycle and a major movement and commuting corridor through the city, connecting with important public spaces such as Piedmont Park. New housing is being built in close proximity to the BeltLine, and many properties—offices, residences, businesses—are benefiting from connecting to it.

Eventually the BeltLine will tie together some forty-five neighborhoods in the city. Funding for the BeltLine is coming from a number of sources, including a portion of a dedicated sales tax passed in the November 2016 election. This funding will permit the purchase of land and lighting for the

for all citizens. Such people-based cities are also low-carbon cities, but people, as well as the planet, are the real winners.

In New York Gehl worked with Janette Sadik-Khan on Times Square; after it was pedestrianized she said: "From the moment that we closed Broadway in Times and Herald Squares, the spaces were reborn and people immediately occupied every available square inch, while traffic moved on surrounding streets as well as or better than before. This also improved the economy. . . . The quality of the space was better, inviting people to stop and inspiring them to view streets differently."[23]

Gehl's work continues to influence cities directly and indirectly. Gehl Studio in New York collaborated with the J. Max Bond Center on De-

Box 3.1 *continued*

remaining sections of the twenty-two-mile corridor. One funding innovation is the tax increment financing zone created along the corridor, which essentially captures a tax increase resulting from the property value increase associated with this new amenity. A portion of these funds must be spent on affordable housing. But Gravel and a fellow board member of the Atlanta BeltLine Partnership have concerns that the benefits are not shared by lower-income residents in the areas surrounding the BeltLine, and they resigned from the board to bring light to the issue. In an interview published by *Metropolis* magazine,[a] Gravel addressed the challenges of creating large-scale urban reuse projects, such as the BeltLine, for all residents: "I talk and write a lot about these issues and similarly transformational infrastructure projects cropping up all over the country. They include the High Line (New York), 606 (Chicago), Lafitte Corridor (New Orleans), Bayou Greenways (Houston), Underline (Miami), and the grandmother of them all, the revitalization of the Los Angeles River. They are redefining the future of cities, leveraging existing assets to support interesting, diverse collections of communities. They're transforming historic barriers into public meeting grounds and they're working. They are changing our way of life. But they also share similar challenges and opportunities around equity, and if we want these places we love to remain lovable for everyone, we have to get ahead on these issues."

---

[a]Vanessa Quirk, "Citing Equity Issues, Founder of Atlanta Beltline Leaves Board," *Metropolis* (blog), September 27, 2016.

---

sign for the Just City and Transportation Alternatives to explore socially just public plazas in New York. They set out to answer the question "Can the design of public space have a positive impact on public life and urban justice?" The study found that "the addition of plazas improved equitable distribution of initial capital resources, increased neighborhood access to open space, and that users of the plaza seemed to equitably mirror the population of the local neighborhood. However, there was less than equitable funding for ongoing maintenance, management, and programming, which was directly related to the overall wealth of the plaza neighborhood."[24] Gentrification of neighborhoods is often about access to local government, with the wealthy having a loud voice; community groups that can act on behalf of neighborhoods to demand similar resourcing of such important public spaces is an important role for civil society.[25]

Parks are critical public spaces not only for recreation and community gathering places but also for access to nature. Leaders in many cities have recognized these benefits and invested in initiatives to increase access to parks, such as former New York mayor Michael Bloomberg's program to have every city resident within a ten-minute walk of a park. Urban parks have been proven to have a positive impact on physical activity, reduced obesity,[26] and mental health.[27] (Benefits of access to nature are discussed in more detail in chapter 5.) Urban trees can help provide some access to nature beyond parks. They also provide natural shading, reducing the urban heat island effect and the need for artificial cooling. According to the City Parks Alliance in Washington, DC, "urban trees in the U.S. remove 711,000 tons of air pollution annually, at a value of $3.8 billion, not only saving money but also improving public health."[28]

What Is Inclusive and Healthy Housing?

Matthew Desmond states in his book *Evicted*, "Decent, affordable housing should be a basic right for everybody in this country. The reason is simple: without stable shelter, everything else falls apart."[29] As income disparities increase, housing that is healthy, safe, transit accessible, and within financial reach for lower- and middle-income residents is increasingly difficult to find in many global cities. Skyrocketing housing prices in major cities are sending residents to outlying areas in search of less expensive housing. This phenomenon of "drive until you qualify" may result in residents paying lower direct costs for rent or mortgage, but when transportation costs are added to housing costs, a much higher percentage is paying above the "30 percent of income" rule of thumb for housing affordability. "Today," Desmond notes, "over 1 in 5 of *all* renting families in the country spends half of its income on housing."[30]

The details of affordable housing finance are beyond the scope of this book, but there are many tools available for the provision of affordable housing. The challenges are (1) ensuring that people of all races, ethnicities, religions, and sexual orientations have equal opportunities for safe, affordable housing and (2) providing housing in healthy, walkable, transit-oriented communities that offer adequate services and educational opportunities.

Housing that is affordable is often sited in the most vulnerable locations, such as in contaminated areas and in low-lying areas near coastlines. The late geographer and anthropologist Neil Smith observed: "Put bluntly, in many climates rich people tend to take the higher land leaving to the poor and working class land more vulnerable to flooding and environmental pestilence."[31] Lower-income residents would also benefit most from energy- and water-efficient housing that results in lower utility expenses and increased health.

The Enterprise Green Communities program at Enterprise Community Partners recommends three primary ways that healthy housing can help: (1) health: green, healthy housing offers better indoor air quality and promotes healthy and active living; (2) energy savings: nationally, energy efficiency upgrades can produce cost savings of as much as $9.2 billion for property owners and tenants; and (3) climate change resilience: people in low-income households, who tend to be renters, are disproportionately affected by extreme weather events. Almost half of households in New York, New Jersey, and Connecticut that requested federal aid following Hurricane Sandy had annual incomes of less than $30,000. Every dollar spent on resilience measures reduces the cost of damage from extreme weather events by four dollars.[32]

Inequity is an ugly problem that demands new solutions. "A problem as big as the affordable-housing crisis calls for a big solution," Matthew Desmond writes. "It should be at the top of America's domestic-policy agenda—because it is driving poor families to financial ruin and even starting to engulf families with moderate incomes."[33]

Resilience for Whom? How Do We Protect All Citizens?

Parul Sehgal, a writer for the *New York Times*, commented, "I think that resilience is key to happiness. But how people are resilient and what resilience entails has become somewhat misunderstood. What seems to me to get people through these kinds of trauma are other people. It is an ability and an opportunity to talk about one's pain. It is an opportunity to be vulnerable and to change and dictate the course of one's life."[34]

After Hurricane Katrina in New Orleans, which largely impacted lower-income communities of color, there was a reaction to the term "resilience." Tracie Washington, president of the Louisiana Justice Institute, explained that the term "represents an unnatural state" because it is basically conditioning people to expect more hardships and learn to bounce back from them.[35]

For the people of New Orleans, there were few resources for recovery, and many parts of the city continue to struggle to "bounce back" more than ten years after the storm. "The only reason New Orleans came back," said former deputy mayor Andy Kopplin, "was that the people scrapped and clawed and figured out a way when there was none."[36] As Barack Obama, then an Illinois senator, said, "the people of New Orleans weren't just abandoned during the hurricane" but were "abandoned long ago."[37]

Neil Smith, in the blog *Understanding Katrina*, writes that "it is generally accepted among environmental geographers that there is no such thing as a natural disaster. In every phase and aspect of a disaster—causes, vulnerability, preparedness, results and response, and reconstruction—the contours of disaster and the difference between who lives and who dies is to a greater or lesser extent a social calculus."[38]

The larger systemic issues of discrimination in housing and economic disparities to a large part determine who will be resilient to a disaster, but there are some lessons from disasters.

The United Nations has looked at Cuba as a model. Hurricane Ivan hit the Caribbean in September 2004, resulting in deaths in Florida and Granada but none in Cuba, which was also hit directly. As Neil Smith explained, the United Nations and Oxfam attributed this to several factors:

First, Cubans learn from an early age about the danger of hurricanes and how to prepare and respond. Second, before the hurricane hits, local communities organize cleanup to secure potentially dangerous debris. Third, preparation and evacuation are organized and coordinated between the central government and local communities, and transportation away from danger is organized as a social community project rather than left to the private market, as happened in New Orleans and Houston. To prevent fires, gas and electricity supplies are cut off before the hurricane hits. During a hurricane, pre-organized state-sponsored emergency teams guarantee water, food and medical treatment—2,000 such teams in the case of Ivan. The government also organizes resources for communities to reconstruct.[39]

How Can Planners and Policy Makers Work Toward Inclusive and Healthy Cities Globally?

If we do not plan inclusively, then we lose our legitimacy for any kind of urban outcomes. In the words of Garrett Jacobs, executive director of the Open Architecture Collaborative:

> Now more than ever, designers need to confront the actual economic and social systems we work within. We need to confront our privileged ability to capture leaders' attentions, and acknowledge that most people don't have that power. We need to use our comprehension of intentionally exclusive codes, policies, and economic models for inclusion, translating the complex language for those marginalized from the very systems we help coordinate. We need to ask, quite literally, whom do we work for, because social justice no longer has an advocate at the top.[40]

In 2010 and 2014 the International City/County Management Association (ICMA) conducted surveys of city and county governments to determine how they were addressing issues of social equity and whether they were coordinating these issues with sustainability goals. ICMA found that although the number of government entities addressing issues of social equity increased between 2010 and 2014, surprisingly few considered coordinated sustainability and equity goals: "The social equity dimension of sustainability refers to how burdens and benefits of different policy actions are distributed in a community. The more evenly they are distributed, the more equitable the community is, and this even distribution is reflected in economic, ecologic, and social outcomes."[41]

Todd Litman of the Victoria Transport Policy Institute addressed this issue by considering how better to frame discussions about making cities more compact and walkable; for many people this would appear socially irresponsible (high density) and expensive, shutting out many people. In his summary, he suggests that planners need to work harder to bridge the divide evident from the 2016 U.S. election: "Planners generally try to be responsive and inclusive, but the recent presidential election is a reminder that we must do even better to address some citizens' alienation."[42]

Some cities are taking steps to ensure that in their resilience planning

FIGURE 3.2: A slum in Addis Ababa. (Source: Zafu Teferi)

they address equity issues directly, thus serving as models for others. Boston hosted a meeting, attended by 600 residents, to discuss racism and resilience, the first of a series of discussions on the topic. Mayor Martin Walsh said of the initiative, "At this moment in history, Boston will take a stand. We'll answer the call to put the safety, the rights and the equity of everyone in our city at the top of our agenda, every day. If we want to be a strong city, we have to be able to depend on each other, trust each other and understand each other."[43]

Inclusive Cities in the Developing World

The challenges facing planners in countries with a high proportion of slums are overwhelming in terms of health (sanitation, clean water, clean air, access to health care) and access to economic opportunity. The 2013 report on the state of global cities by the United Nations Human Settlements Programme (UN-Habitat) suggests that sub-Saharan Africa has the highest level of urban population in slums, at around 72 percent.

Around 32 percent of global urban populations and 43 percent of urban populations in the developing world live in slums. South Central Asia has a slum population of 262 million, representing 58 percent of the total urban slum population of the world. By far the greatest share of health problems in rapidly urbanizing contexts is attributable to living and working conditions in slums.[44]

Slums are generally characterized by four main conditions:

1. They are illegal and hence often do not have formalized tenure. This leads to social and economic exclusion due to lack of formal recognition of their address, and hence slum dwellers regularly encounter different forms of deprivation.[45]
2. They are vulnerable, as they are often built on steep slopes or riverbanks, the only land available. Mudslides and floods often mean they are very dangerous places to live, so authorities are often looking to have them moved.[46]
3. They are usually not old, as informal settlements put up in former times are incorporated generally into the formal city and upgraded to make them seamlessly part of the city.[47]
4. They are poorly serviced with basic infrastructure, leading to inadequate and overcrowded housing, unhealthy and unsafe working conditions, and lack of access to clean water and decent sanitation.[48]

So what can be done to make slums more inclusive and healthy as well as ensuring they are not making a bigger environmental footprint?

This agenda is being addressed by the United Nations Environment Programme as a way of applying metabolism to informal settlements; its publication is called "City-Level Decoupling: Urban Resource Flows and the Governance of Infrastructure Transitions."[49] A similar approach that we call the "extended metabolism model," outlined in more detail in chapter 6, suggests we should try to measure how settlements can reduce their environmental footprint while increasing their livability.[50] This approach has been applied to two sets of urban slums—one in Jakarta, Indonesia, and one in Addis Ababa, Ethiopia. In both places the settlements were surveyed to analyze their environmental footprint from energy consumption, water consumption, and waste production and their livability in terms of health, housing, employment, income, education, and community. In both places the old informal slums were compared with the footprint and livability in a new government apartment complex built for slum residents. The differences between the building typologies are very stark, with glass, concrete, and steel going up twenty stories compared with organic houses made from any bits of building materials and, like ancient cities, with only small alleyways linking the buildings together. The slums have no infrastructure for water, energy, or waste because they are illegal constructions, but the householders generally find ways of accessing such facilities. The results are provided in appendix tables A.1–A.4 for Jakarta and Addis Ababa.[51]

The results show the following:

1. The physical environment in the new apartment blocks was significantly improved. The apartment dwellers used a little less energy and water than the slum dwellers and their waste management was considerably better, particularly since the slum dwellers in Jakarta put most of their waste directly into the river.
2. In human terms, the apartment dwellers had improved incomes and employment (they were better able to enter the formal economy) and had similar levels of accessibility and health compared with those who lived in the slum.
3. In terms of community parameters, the slum development was far superior because the layout of the housing encouraged people to know and trust their neighbors. More than 80 percent of people were able to trust their neighbors and lend them things, while this was less than 20 percent in the high-rise development. The lack of community orientation in the high-rise design questions the fundamentals of its development ethos.

The solution to this would appear to be a less modernist approach; rather than using standard high-rise buildings, it would be better to shift to a more organic renewal of the slums themselves, bringing in infrastructure for power and water and improving houses but maintaining the basic community structure. Zafu Teferi, one of the researchers from Addis Ababa, stated that "much greater attention needs to be given to rehabilitating houses in situ or to developing household designs that reflect the organic interactions of community life." This approach has characterized informal urban developments for thousands of years as they have shaped our cities through renewal and rebuilding. The new technologies for energy, water, and waste that are distributed and small in scale lend themselves to such urban structures. Obviously, dense high-rise housing will be needed as well, given the sheer numbers of migrants coming to the city, but even in these, community-based approaches to cooking, washing, and recreation can be explored so that people are not isolated in their individual units.[52]

Solutions and policies must aim toward transforming slums by taking into consideration not just the physical environment but also residents' quality of life, health, access to water and sanitation, and opportunities for income generation. However, the physical environment can be improved without expanding fossil fuel use. The data showed not only that the new apartments used less resources than those in slum accommodations but also that new technology for solar photovoltaics and small-scale water and waste systems can be fitted into slum neighborhoods, given their size and ease of management. This kind of leapfrog approach to infrastructure needs to be the new agenda for informal settlements in the developing world, as they create more resilient cities. This is the New Urban Agenda.

Conclusion

The need for inclusive and healthy cities is a powerful driver in both global and local politics. We have shown that these goals can be achieved while overcoming fossil fuel dependence. In other words, it is not necessary to consume increasing amounts of coal, oil, and gas to overcome poverty in developed or developing cities. Nor does the sustainable transport or sustainable housing agenda need to discriminate based on socioeconomic status.

Within urban design, planning, and policy we need to confront bias and discrimination, subtle or overt, wherever we see it, particularly in the structures that exclude rather than include.

To foster inclusive and healthy cities will require the following actions.

Business

Planning consultants and developers need to provide housing designs that are more affordable and inclusive of green features in a fully integrated way. New businesses that can enable distributed infrastructure in slums need to be developed into a mass market.

Government

Affordable housing options need to be increased in areas with access to services, including transit. In slum communities, housing and infrastructure must be regenerated without damaging the community. We also need more government officials in power who better represent our communities. Justin Garrett Moore, executive director of New York City's Public Design Commission, observes that while there has been increased discourse on social equity among people who design, plan, and manage our cities, a disconnect remains between the people who run our cities and the demographics of those who live in them.[53]

Community

Public spaces and community facilities need to be resourced no matter what the income of the area, and community groups need to constantly emphasize the need for affordable and accessible housing, as well as better accessibility. The need for community engagement tools that can highlight exclusion and enable inclusion need to be constantly addressed and embraced by communities.

CHAPTER 4
Shape Disaster Recovery for the Future

I've always said that if we just rebuild the city we've achieved nothing. If you just put back what you had before then you have all the same problems: aging population, centers of the city no longer functioning as they once did, the suburban centers sucking life out of the city. We have a chance to do something different. —Bob Parker, mayor of Christchurch, New Zealand, on recovery after the 2011 earthquake

Every city has a disaster at some time in its history. A few may have been mild, as in Perth, which has experienced only mild earthquakes and flooding, but urban history is dotted with disasters. The ancient city of Megiddo in the Middle East—after which the word "armageddon" was derived to mean "a dramatic and catastrophic conflict, especially one seen as likely to destroy the world or the human race"—is now just a large archaeological mound. Those working on the site have found twenty-two cities buried beneath the surface that were built and destroyed at some point in history. Megiddo's problem was that it lay in the path of invading armies from the east and west.

If disaster is part of urban life, and it is likely to increase substantially as global warming leads to more extremes in weather, then we need to prepare for it. Every city needs a disaster preparedness plan, and every family needs to think about what they would do.[1] Most large cities, especially in the global North, have well-developed disaster preparedness or emergency management plans. The names vary, but it has become a common local government function and planning activity, often coordinated by a city's office of emergency management. Such plans seek to lay out a framework for actions to be taken before and after a disaster by various agencies and actors, from police and fire departments to specialized search and rescue teams. Increasingly these plans take an all-hazards approach, ideally considering the full range of potential natural and technological hazards faced by a city. Urban resilience must be measured in part by how a city is able to respond and cope with, for instance, an oil spill or hazardous substance spill or even a terrorist attack. Though most of what we discuss in this chapter relates to natural disasters, it is important to recognize the need to plan for and respond to this fuller set of crises and disasters that cities will face.

For those who think a lot about hazards and disasters, there are clear steps toward strengthening resilience that can and should be aimed at all four of the oft-cited *stages* of disaster planning: preparedness, response, recovery, and mitigation. Preparedness entails all those things a city can do in advance of a disaster event to minimize damage and loss of life. In the face of an oncoming hurricane, for instance, cities can and must evacuate populations in low-lying and especially hazardous parts of the city. After the event occurs, whether a hurricane, fire, or earthquake, a resilient city must be able to swiftly respond to the crises at hand—for instance, to find and rescue, treat, and care for affected residents. Following these more immediate response concerns and demands is the longer-term recovery process a city faces. During this process, as the examples from Christchurch and elsewhere show, cities can rebound and recover in ways that enhance long-term sustainability, safety, and quality of life. For instance, rebuilding can impose new and stronger construction standards or relocate buildings and people out of a floodplain or other high-risk location. Such a recovery strategy not only minimizes the likelihood of damage and loss of life in future events but also has a range of co-benefits, including an agenda to overcome fossil fuel dependence.

Such a disaster recovery strategy is commonly referred to as hazard mitigation—actions, policies, and decisions that a city can take today to minimize exposure and loss in the future—and is the fourth stage in the disaster planning model. Much of what cities can and must do to be resilient is to take sometimes courageous steps to reduce long-term risk and exposure—before the disaster strikes. Examples of hazard mitigation include the following:

- Identifying especially risky locations where growth and density should be reduced
- Strengthening building codes and construction standards
- Disaster-proofing vital urban infrastructures and lifelines to enhance their resilience
- Replanning coastal cities by setting developments back from areas that will be subject to sea level rise and repurposing them as biodiverse natural parks and buffers

These four stages can be understood as circular or spiral, with post-disaster recovery leading into and contributing to long-term pre-disaster mitigation.

The big question underlying this book is whether we just bounce back from a disaster or whether we can bounce forward to use the rebuilding as a way of claiming a future without fossil fuels and then use this experience to help us all in disaster preparedness. There are also cities that have slowly emerging disasters, especially as a result of climate change, that need to be addressed and used to create a better future for the city.

This chapter will address the following questions:

1. How can a city recover from a disaster in a way that creates a better future for the city?
2. How can a city respond to a slow-moving disaster in a way that creates a better future for the city?
3. How can smart technologies and systems help in disaster preparedness while reducing fossil fuel use?

How Can a City Recover from a Disaster in a Way That Creates a Better Future for the City?

When Hurricane Sandy crossed the coast in Connecticut, it left a trail of destruction. In the cleanup after the event a decision was made to create a more distributed electricity microgrid for cities in Connecticut to enable a better response to future emergencies as well as to use the rebuild to create a better city for the future. The city therefore invested $30 million in solar power and battery storage. Other cities have similar motivations in setting up smart microgrids, such as Lancaster, Texas; San Diego; and a number of remote Native American settlements.

Doug Peeples, editor of a Smart Cities Council blog, wrote: "Microgrids do more than simply provide stand-alone emergency backup power. They can help communities integrate renewable energy resources and energy storage, decentralize their sources of power while maximizing those assets and help ensure that power quality remains reliable, even in the immediate aftermath of climate-related disasters. . . . It's something to consider when your city is working on its resiliency plans."[2]

Similar approaches can be taken to transport, which is one of the first types of infrastructure, along with power, to be challenged by disasters such as floods, storms, earthquakes, and fires. The Hurricane Katrina disaster in New Orleans left one-third of the residents stranded, as they did not have cars to take them out of the city when it was being threatened, and there was no viable rail option. Yet school buses were left to rot when the flood-waters swept in.

A more coherent approach has now been built into the city's disaster preparedness plans, with many areas being set aside as no longer suitable for urban development, a much greater commitment to managing the natural wetland defense system, and strengthening of the front-line engineering protection systems. And in the process of replanning after Katrina, signifi-cant improvements in rail and bus transit have been made.

John Renne, who was a professor at the University of New Orleans during Katrina, has taken a leading role in post-disaster transport planning.[3] He was sensitized by Katrina to issues of how transport systems should respond to disasters, and when the *Deepwater Horizon* oil rig disaster happened in April 2010 in the Gulf of Mexico, John brought together a team to focus on why cities should become less oil dependent.[4]

Cities can take the opportunities created by disasters to prepare for a different future, not just rebuild the way they were.

In the story that follows we look at Christchurch, New Zealand, which was destroyed by a series of earthquakes in 2011. Tim Beatley, Peter New-man, and Linda Blagg made a film about the city's rebuilding process called

Christchurch: Resilient City,[5] from which much of the story and many of the quotes that follow have been taken.

This chapter's opening quotation, from the mayor at the time of the earthquake, Bob Parker, suggests that the city is not just bouncing back but bouncing forward. Critical to this was a highly engaged community process that was instigated early in the rebuilding, which showed that community members were keen to demonstrate how they could build a city with much less dependence on fossil fuels and with a range of other environmental and social benefits similar to the multiple co-benefits outlined in the six principles in this book. The case study also shows some powerful examples of how government, the business community, and civil society can play extremely important roles in both recovery and preparedness.[6]

The earthquake, in February 2011, killed 185 people and injured 164. One-third of all housing was damaged, and the central business district was basically leveled, as that was where most of the old masonry buildings were located. Christchurch was not expecting earthquakes; experts had suggested that the fault line was in the mountains fifty kilometers away, but this one threw the city up one meter into the air and then turned it slightly before

FIGURE 4.1: A memorial to those lost in the 2011 earthquake in Christchurch, New Zealand. (Source: Peter Newman)

FIGURE 4.2: Shigeru Ban's Cardboard Cathedral, a sustainable approach to rebuilding a church destroyed in the Christchurch, New Zealand, earthquake. (Source: Peter Newman)

it fell. Thousands of smaller earthquakes followed over the next few years. Devastation was everywhere, with many deaths caused by new high-rise buildings later found to be structurally faulty. The pressure forced a mud-clay mixture (caused by a process called liquefaction) to bubble up into houses and streets, sometimes a meter deep. The Avon River corridor was the most affected, shifting its banks and flowing into buildings.

Within hours the local community and its emergency response teams began working with the most affected people. Volunteers, farmers and students especially, were galvanized into action by leaders who used social media to communicate. People poured in to help dig out the dead and injured and remove the liquefied soil. Water supplies were shared wherever they still worked, emergency power and cooking facilities were provided, and temporary shelters were set up for people to sleep in. For several weeks people lived closely together, helping each other to get through.

Anglican bishop Victoria Matthews said that Christchurch went through a deeply spiritual experience, "learning what it is to be human all over again. We rediscovered that life is an extraordinary gift; by reaching out to each other we rediscovered who we are." The nineteenth-century Anglican cathedral was something of a symbol, as Christchurch was an Anglican colony first established on the banks of a river they called the Avon. Ruined beyond repair, the Christchurch Cathedral became the focus of much bitter commentary because, instead of restoring the building at great cost, the bishop said she would build a modern low-cost, low-carbon Cardboard Cathedral (designed by the Japanese disaster architect Shigeru Ban) in the middle of the worst affected area. The building was an immediate success when it opened. The bishop explained that she realized she had been the target of much of the deep anger in the city because "it's totally unsatisfactory getting angry with God; a bishop is much better."

Evan Smith and Professor Bryan Jenkins from the Avon-Otakaro Network had been reestablishing a river park that went from the origin of the spring-fed Avon River through the city and to the coast some twenty kilometers away. The earthquake exposed the fact that much of the housing on the banks of the river should never have been built. As these houses had to be destroyed, a whole new vision for the river corridor could be developed. Within six months the network had developed the concept with the community and submitted to the government a petition signed by 18,000 people proposing to create a river park from the city to the coast. The proposal included restoration of the original vegetation in the corridor where the most devastation happened, including the whole suburb of Bexley, built on a former wetland but now abandoned. The project met with widespread support because for many it represented a healing of the whole city, reestablishing the city with a more harmonious relationship to its river. Restoring the river was therefore a "source of healing" on a personal and public level.

Sam Crofskey, the owner of C1 Espresso, was able to quickly restart his restaurant in one of the few buildings in the central business district that were not damaged. He decided to rebuild C1 as a model of sustainability, using waste heat from the kitchen to heat the building, growing vegetables and herbs in gardens around the restaurant, using recycled furniture and fittings from buildings that were being demolished, and even using the roof to produce organic wine and honey alongside solar panels. By using solar power, a backup generator, and water tanks the restaurant was able to function without utility supplies. Sam said, "We don't want to be closed for another day, another hour, another minute." Then, pursuing the idea of local self-sufficiency, C1 began growing coffee in nearby Samoa as an aid project. The restaurant was a huge success, becoming the main place for businesspeople, government workers, and creatives to meet in the old central business district while redevelopment continued.

Bailey Peryman was a young food activist who had started Garden City 2.0 to promote food resilience. Food and its origins became an issue in the earthquake's aftermath. Bailey extended his food resilience network by linking peri-urban farmers and local community gardens across the city; he set up distribution outlets through farmers' markets and community-supported agriculture. Garden City 2.0 continues to grow, delivering food to more than one hundred households, and with many more permaculture farmers signing up to join their new venture, Ooooby (Out Of Our Own Back Yards).

Matt Morris, the University of Canterbury's sustainability advocate, became a major player in determining how the university could rebuild its many damaged buildings and face a less certain future in terms of students wanting to come to the earthquake-ravaged city. He was able to ensure that buildings had green roofs and green walls as well as much better energy efficiency and strength; he lobbied for more cycling infrastructure, added fruit trees to the campus landscaping, and restored creeks running through the campus. All of this had been on the agenda but now became essential to do. He created a new course on sustainability and resilience that would enable students to study the university's and city's responses to the earthquake. A new, and growing, set of students interested in issues of urban resilience were attracted to study in Christchurch.

Ryan Reynolds, an American filmmaker who had been drawn to live and work in Christchurch, was in the badly damaged city center when the earthquake hit. He immediately saw that the city's social infrastructure had been destroyed and a new kind of organization was needed to provide activities that could replace the city center's social function. With others he set up a group called Gap Filler to find creative projects to entice people into the city and reactivate not just spaces but also the life of the community. Projects were workshopped and then built with artists and students from many backgrounds, including some very clever engineers. The projects included the following:

1. *Cycle-Powered Cinema.* In the early weeks it was clear that there was no functioning cinema. A bicycle-powered cinema was built outdoors so that people could come and share the social activity of not just watching a movie but also powering it by riding one of three bikes linked to the projector.
2. *The Dance-O-Mat.* A proper sprung dance floor was built, and a jukebox that plays iPhone music was provided. The first reaction was "Cantabrians don't dance in public," but almost immediately it was used for seven hours a day, and visitors including Prince Charles joined in.
3. *The Arcades Project.* A set of wooden arches was designed and put up without council permission on an abandoned site, ensuring that a demolished building would not be rebuilt, as it had prevented pedestrian and bicycle access.
4. *The Pallet Pavilion.* A temporary function area and restaurant were built as a meeting place using $80,000 raised by crowdfunding, volunteer labor, and recycled pallets from freight containers.
5. *Grassroots bottom-up initiatives.* These included a book exchange in old fridges on sites of mourning where houses had been removed, a mini golf course across the city, and many outside workshops for children. Similar projects were generated by Greening the Rubble, which created gardens and landscaping on empty sites, often in concert with Gap Filler.[7]

The Gap Filler motto was to experiment with prototypes of the future, something that planners and technical people rebuilding the city cannot do. A new role for civil society was created with significance for any city seeking to be more resilient. A similar exercise was started by the central business district business community when they created a container-based pop-up shopping area called Re:START Container Mall. The pop-up area had a highly activated front that replaced the modernist internal-facing shopping mall. The pop-up mall was very successful and helped the city to reimagine how to make a more attractive and successful shopping area in the future.

Roger Sutton was the head of the energy utility when he was approached to be the inaugural chief executive officer of the Canterbury Earthquake

Redevelopment Authority. Reflecting on the scale of the damage, he said it was around NZ$40 billion, roughly twice the city's annual gross domestic product. The biggest issue would be ensuring that the public came along for the long term. "It will take time, and keeping people patient is the biggest issue in disaster recovery. The blueprint is generally accepted to make the city more interesting, more compact, more green, with a river park vision that replaces hundreds of houses. This will work, and people will be able to fish again in the river in the CBD [central business district]." But how do you make people continue to believe in the long-term vision? One failure of government was that despite a high-priority request during the community engagement process, the idea of light rail for Christchurch was not agreed to, though some plans left it as a possibility.[8]

Lianne Dalziel, then New Zealand Parliament member for Christchurch and now the city's mayor, was amazed at how people committed to helping each other, how so many students and farmers poured into the city and dug out the liquefaction in Bexley, where she lived. "Now," she said, "the suburb is returning to nature, so it is an eco-recovery to go with the economic and social recovery."

The port area of Lyttelton suffered significant loss of housing and businesses, as the old town had many masonry buildings and was directly over the epicenter. However, the community's response was dramatically helped by a group called Project Lyttelton, whose membership included most of the town's population because of a sustainability commitment to create a food-based cooperative and a social capital project. Margaret Jefferies, the founder of Project Lyttelton, explained how 170 members of the community bought the Harbour Co-Op building to act as a conduit for food resilience, linking local growers into a distribution center and providing a base for schoolchildren. Their social capital project was the Lyttelton Harbour TimeBank, where people share skills and work based simply on the time it takes. A review of the Christchurch earthquake points to the Lyttelton TimeBank as a key reason why so many people received help so quickly. Members knew one another, the emergency authorities knew how to get local tools and skills to help with the emergency recovery and rebuilding, so the TimeBank provided a model for resilience. Developing social capital through groups such as this is a deep way to prepare for any disaster.[9]

In the conclusion to the film on Christchurch, Tim and Peter say that so often the community and its leaders could describe their experiences only in spiritual terms, using words such as "hope," "spirit," "soul," and "love." It was the only way to convey the depth of experience, the preciousness of life, the strength of people telling their stories, the emerging vision of what the city could be, and how most people have become stronger as a result of the disaster. A student in Christchurch, Kristina Carrick, has the last word in the film as she reflects on the many opportunities now provided in the city: "I always loved the city, and I love the city even more now."

Bob Parker, who as mayor led the city through its darkest times, summarized the approach he adopted by saying: "The government agenda will always be the economic agenda—get things up and running, rebuild—whereas my agenda, and I think [that of] most people in the community, is reimagining what we can be, recreating who we are in the city, rediscovering the strengths of what came out of the trauma."

How Can a City Respond to a Slow-Moving Disaster in a Way That Creates a Better Future for the City?

Most disasters happen quickly, especially earthquakes, floods, fires, cyclones, hurricanes, and typhoons. We know that climate change will cause an increase in many of these, and we certainly need to prepare for them. But some disasters creep up on us, and we need to be just as resilient in our response. Climate change induced by use of fossil fuels and other human activities can be the cause of these creeping, slow-moving disasters, as well as the rapid ones.

Many water systems around the world are running dry or changing their flow patterns drastically as a result of climate change.[10] David Brown, a long-time development worker in Vietnam, now focuses on how the Mekong River faces multiple pressures that begin in the mountains and are multiplied at its confluence. He says, "The Mekong is an example of a slow-moving disaster we can all learn from."[11] There are many complexities of a major river passing through many countries, with its source changing as a result of climate change pressures and its usage increasing as it flows through cities and regions with growing populations and changing economies. The key lesson from Brown's work is that most of the big issues were not addressed as they slowly accumulated. In the next section, we discuss an example in which the slow-moving disaster suddenly accelerated and demanded critical action.

The Perth Water Supply

The story of Perth's water supply is an example of how a thirty-year decline set in motion a process for dealing with a creeping disaster.

Perth has a Mediterranean climate with most of its rainfall occurring in a six-month period from May to October, a result of low-pressure systems moving around the southern part of the globe that were known in the past to mariners as the "roaring forties." These would just tip the south-west corner of Western Australia and created the forests, agricultural areas, and cities of that region. Perth has grown from its start in 1829 with the assumption that this corner of a very dry, but mineral-rich, state would always have water. Economic development enabled the water to be shared hundreds of kilometers out into the agricultural and mining region.

However, in the 1970s, water planners began to worry. It was just not raining as it had for the past hundred years. Climate change modelers informed the city that it was probably because the low-pressure systems were being pushed farther south as a result of increased global warming and were thus missing the southwest corner. It was not a drought; it was climate change. Figure 4.3 shows these trends in rainfall runoff and the subsequent reduction in water supply capacity through traditional rain-fed dams.

The Water Corporation of Western Australia moved to alternative water sources and began by extracting groundwater from shallow aquifers in the Perth region. This filled the immediate gap but began to deplete the aquifers. What to do next?

Tim Flannery, author of *The Weather Makers*, predicted in the 1990s that Perth would be abandoned because its water supplies were not sustainable. All of the climate change models continued to predict a drying climate in this corner of the world, and this has been observable, with forty years of reduced rainfall. The sudden drops in rainfall coincide with what Flannery calls "magic gates," periods when there is a major shift in the climate system. In 1976 the first magic gate meant that instead of 340 gigaliters (GL) of rainfall runoff in its catchments, Perth averaged only 160 GL. Then again in 1998 another magic gate reduced the rainfall runoff to 111 GL, a reduction of about one-third from what it had been receiving.[12]

Don McFarlane, a scientist with Perth's Water Resources Division of the Commonwealth Scientific and Industrial Research Organisation, said: "Climatologists tell us that [Perth] is the most profoundly affected

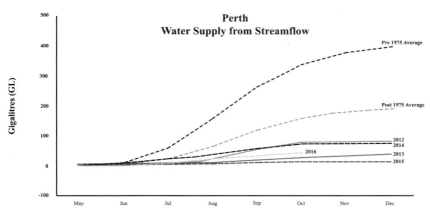

FIGURE 4.3: Water supply from streamflow has continued to decline in Perth's region for forty years. (Source: Water Corporation of Western Australia, 2009)

city in the world. People have accepted that it is climate change. In other parts of the world people are thinking it's something that's going to happen to them in the next 10 or 30 years and that they've got time to adjust. We've found we've been living with it for 30 years now and we're having to adjust very quickly."[13]

Dams and groundwater would never be enough if rainfall kept declining. As a result, the planners in the Water Corporation decided, well before climate change became a political football, that it was real. Perth was a miner's canary for how cities must face a slowly arriving disaster.

In 2001 a political crisis emerged when the rain did not come at all. Apart from immediate conservation measures, the long-term solution was seen to be a large, deep aquifer in the southwest called the Yarragadee. A detailed sustainability assessment was conducted, which showed it was a possible source, but civil society could not accept that stressing a natural system in a drying climate would do. No other options were available, but recent work on desalination had suggested that this process may have become significantly cheaper. Thus a rapid investigation was conducted, which suggested desalination might be possible. Because of the enormous energy inputs required, only a few cities in the Middle East had used desalination for their water supplies, but new German membrane technology could reduce the energy required significantly. The politicians made a decision: go for wind-powered desalination.

The first plant built was small and provided 10 percent of the city's water supply without a significant increase in cost. The impact from the saline wastewater was minimal, and no distribution issues were found, as the water could be pumped up to the dams, enabling the system to continue as it had before. Then a decision was made to build a much bigger plant, and within a few years more than 50 percent of Perth's water supply was coming from the Indian Ocean. The city breathed a sigh of relief as the rain continued to bypass it.

So what can be done next? If rain levels continue to decline, then even more radical solutions are needed. The long-term plan was to be much cleverer with local distributed systems and to recycle wastewater, as treated sewage was historically pumped out to sea. Research was conducted on whether the local sand would manage to process gray water and whether recycling the sewage through deep sands would enable it to be recycled back into the groundwater and reused for water supply. The science showed that both would work, but the public needed to be sure, so a series of demonstrations were started. The resulting water was declared clean not only by health and environmental agencies but also by interested members of the public who were willing to try it out.

The result is that there has been a significant uptake of gray water systems at the household level, and recycled sewage has begun to be pumped into groundwater sites. The treated sewage will filter for decades through sand before being available for water supply again and recharging the depleted aquifers. Perth is now largely climate proofed, having become one of the first cities to successfully introduce wind-powered desalination along with recycled gray water and sewage. It is a remarkable turnaround from the dire predictions of Tim Flannery, but the journey is not over and considerable work is still needed to reduce demand.

This journey began with the insights of the scientists who confirmed the likelihood that reduced rainfall could be a permanent reality. The public in the whole of Perth and in the southwest region was highly sensitive to the issue and pushed the politics of resilience planning to the limit, basically saying no to using the Yarragadee Aquifer as the next major source. Desalination and recycling of gray water and sewage were therefore the only real options remaining. Despite being the first developed city to attempt it, the politicians moved quickly to affirm desalination and get it into the water supply system. They have been proved right.

In a strategic planning document called "Water Forever: Towards Climate Resilience," the Water Corporation set out its vision for a continuous reduction in demand and a shift away from rainfall-based water supply. The projections (see figure 4.4), almost unimaginable a few decades ago, are now well accepted by government, business, and the community.[14]

A further phase of water-sensitive urban design is now being tried out to enable Perth to better reduce its need for water. The White Gum Valley project, discussed in chapter 1, is not only demonstrating zero-carbon urban development but also trying out zero-mains water, or at least a movement toward it. Houses will be provided with tanks to collect rainwater for use as the major source during the wet season and a few months into the dry season. Highly efficient water appliances will be required. Then community-scale gray water will be used as the basis of garden irrigation through a well-developed piece of technology that has been tested in individual houses across Perth. As more than half of Perth's water is used to irrigate home gardens, it is imperative that this process is

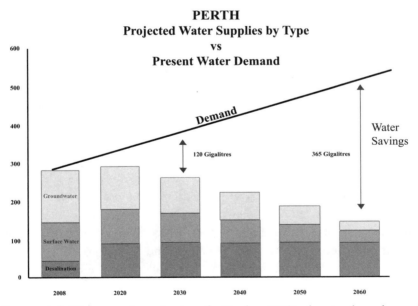

FIGURE 4.4: Water supply projections for Perth to 2060, showing how demand declines and new forms of water supply are phased in. (Source: Water Corporation of Western Australia, 2009)

managed well and monitored to ensure it has no side effects. This gray water and a rainwater sump converted into public open space will be monitored and managed by a citizen utility working with the local authority. A similar project in a large new suburb will be using an even more dramatic recycling process by mining the sewer line to obtain water for irrigation of gardens and open space.

All of this work is based on detailed research by Josh Byrne, the television personality and researcher mentioned in chapter 1. Josh built two simple homes in a normal Perth suburb and fully monitored them to show not just how well the solar-battery system worked but also how well the water could be managed while having a flourishing garden. His work has been filmed and his results provided on a Web site (http://joshshouse.com.au) that has had millions of hits, as it shows practical solutions for any family wanting to contribute to making a more resilient city. His work is now being tried out in the larger precincts and suburbs of Perth with the potential of demonstrating regenerative outcomes.[15]

As climate change continues to destabilize water supplies for cities across the globe, we will need to find similar solutions that utilize new technologies and involve citizens in determining how their water is to be provided. Resilient water systems can become regenerative projects that create whole new urban systems with positive effects on their bioregional environments, despite continued impacts of climate change.

There are of course a host of other ways that cities will be vulnerable in the future, and climate change will lead to many long-term stresses, crises, and disaster events that resilient cities must anticipate and work toward addressing. In addition to water shortages, these include droughts and heat waves, flooding and coastal storms, and long-term sea level rise, the latter especially serious given the significant (and growing) populations at risk in coastal cities. Few resilience challenges are as serious and difficult to solve as the combination of sea level rise and the increase in storms and other extreme weather events (and, often, potent combinations of these). Cities such as New York, following the devastation of Hurricane Sandy, have taken a number of steps to address these problems, including some retreat where sensible and, in other places, testing of new ideas such as dynamic, multipurposed shorelines that will serve at once as barriers to flooding and as places that can occasionally flood with little or no damage or lasting impacts. The so-called Dryline, a portion of which is now under development along the lower Manhattan shoreline, is one example of this new creative and flexible approach that many coastal cities must take.[16]

How Can Smart Technologies Help in Disaster Preparedness and at the Same Time Reduce Fossil Fuel Dependence?

Technology that is now part of the "big data" revolution in our cities can be used in a variety of ways, some not very attractive, such as the continuous surveillance of citizens as they go about everyday life, the astonishing collection of data on our consumption habits fed back to us to encourage more consumption, and the invasion of privacy by people who somehow get to know our phone numbers. However, very clever things can now be done with smartphones, drones, surveillance cameras, and sensors to alert us to disasters, assist us during them, and prepare us for a better future that is more inclusive, more healthy, and without fossil fuels.

The unpredictability of weather is one of the biggest fears of the climate change era we are living through. Storms, fires, and floods are all dependent on extreme weather. The increased ability to track weather is thus a big advantage in how we receive proper warning of a severe event and, afterward, in tracking exactly where disaster has struck. When roads are cut, a drone can get in well before people in vehicles. If centralized power is down, the distributed power of solar and batteries can keep some places going with their smartphones and other communications largely intact.

Thus, after a disaster, we can now more effectively rebuild with renewables and distributed power, all linked with smart control systems, sensors, and emergency links to core services without the need for fossil fuels. The best way to approach this is to bring everyone together: emergency services, government agencies, business leaders, and most of all community leaders, who can see very clearly that the longer-term future of the city must be on the agenda while facing up to the trials of the short term.[17]

To facilitate evacuation, before a disaster, of people of all incomes, ages, and levels of ability or disability, it is now possible to have all this information available to emergency agencies, just as the big advertising agencies have it. Thus as services to evacuate are implemented, people can be coordinated far better than in the pre-Katrina panic, when one-third of the residents were left behind because they had no private vehicles. Smart systems can be used to make our cities more sustainable, more resilient, and eventually more regenerative.

Conclusion

The case studies presented here show how disaster recovery, from a sudden disaster or a slow-moving disaster, can enable cities not only to bounce back stronger but to bounce forward with their agenda for change. These lessons can be the basis for disaster preparedness and for continuing the journey toward a resilient city. For a start, if a city is able to leapfrog into a future with low-carbon, low-water infrastructure, buildings, and industries, then its economy will be well prepared.

The leadership needed to enable recovery and preparedness includes the following actions.

Business

Business leaders can prototype new ideas for business that emerge out of opportunities in the new city. Business associations can challenge businesses to take stock of the ways they are likely vulnerable to future disasters and to make the necessary investments to ensure continuity in the face of a future event.

Businesses can also recognize new commercial opportunities that are emerging much earlier than elsewhere because of slow-moving disasters associated with climate change.

Government

Governments need to prepare strategies for greater local self-sufficiency in energy, water, food, and other material needs. They also need to rebuild natural features that can help with the healing process and restore important natural features around new urban ecologies—from urban wetland systems to dynamic shorelines to eco-roofs—that at once restore urban nature and reduce future impacts and disaster vulnerability. They can assist disaster preparation and recovery by demonstrating new technologies and new urban governance techniques, such as distributed infrastructure.

Governments also need to anticipate and plan for future disaster events and be ready to capitalize on windows of opportunity to further enhance physical, social, and economic resilience. To help with this, they can use smart technologies that not only help with disasters but also help the city move away from fossil fuels.

Community

Engaging deeply with the community before, during, and after a disaster can help the community see what is needed for the long term, not just for rebuilding. New digital tools for this need to be used regulary.

Civil society groups can prototype place-making ideas, as Gap Filler did in Christchurch. They can generate social capital through cooperative and collaborative community businesses. Overall, the community needs to accept and act on the fact that disasters are a deeply spiritual experience that will draw on all the city's strengths, experience, and institutions. They are also an opportunity to create hope for the future, including reduced fossil fuel dependence.

CHAPTER 5

Build Biophilic Urbanism in the City and Its Bioregion

By assigning value to a variety of indicators influenced by biophilic design, the business case for biophilia proves that disregarding humans' inclination towards nature is simultaneously denying potential for positive financial growth. —Bill Browning et al., in "The Economics of Biophilia"

Biophilic urbanism is based on the knowledge that humans have an innate connection with nature that should be expressed in our daily lives, especially in cities. This has not been a strong feature of architectural principles (even though there is a long tradition of landscape architecture), yet potentially it offers great rewards if it is implemented in the structure of the built environment. This chapter looks at the multiple co-benefits of biophilic urbanism within the city and how it can help in overcoming fossil fuel dependence and making a more resilient city.

A bioregion is defined by natural borders rather than by political borders, as in the Yellowstone to Yukon bioregion, which traverses state and national borders. Bioregional natural systems are critical for cities to function, but they are usually assumed to be separate from the built environment. These natural systems that surround the city include the water supply, local food and timber supplies, local materials for building, local waste-absorbing processes in air, water, and soils, local biodiversity that provides the fundamental life forces of the regional ecosystem, and bioregional recreation spaces for the city.[1]

As cities grow and consume or erode the natural environment, they must ensure that there is some conservation, management, and rejuvenation of natural systems. If the natural systems are impacted too heavily, they can collapse. The science of how cities interact with natural systems is only just beginning to be studied in ecological circles, and new ideas of resilient or regenerative design are being applied. Many ideas for managing the increasing effects of climate change rely on multi-use infrastructure, which uses natural systems to provide functions that traditionally were achieved by gray infrastructure systems (e.g., green space to absorb flooding, oyster beds to revive rivers).[2] Many of these projects go beyond resilience to actually regenerate the centuries of damage to their surrounding bioregion. The idea of regeneration is discussed further in the following chapter.

Biophilic urbanism in cities and their bioregions can make a better city, a place that can more easily overcome its fossil fuel dependence, and at the same time can help the healing of a city's natural systems.

The chapter will address the following questions:

1. What is biophilic urbanism, and how does it fit into the urban fabric?
2. Why is biophilic urbanism a necessary part of overcoming fossil fuel dependence in cities?
3. What are other benefits of biophilic urbanism and building?
4. What is the role of biophilic urbanism in helping city management repair bioregional systems?

What Is Biophilic Urbanism, and How Does It Fit into the Urban Fabric?

"Biophilia" was a term first brought to life in the 1960s by the psychoanalyst Erich Fromm in his exploration of the "essence of man." He saw that humans' awareness of their mortality separates them from nature, causing deep anxiety and conflict. Humans try to overcome this anxiety by either a regressive path of narcissism, incestuous symbiosis, violence, and necrophilia or a progressive path of altruism, freedom, and biophilia. "Biophilia" was defined as a love of life and living processes.[3]

The concept of the biophilic human being was then examined and popularized in 1984 by the sociobiologist E. O. Wilson in his book

Biophilia. Wilson defined biophilia as "the innate tendency to focus on life and lifelike processes." He utilized the term "biophilia" to describe his deep feelings of connection to nature during a period of exploration and immersion in the natural world. Wilson's special insight was that this biophilic propensity developed as part of evolutionary survival, so it encompasses certain characteristics that remain with humans even in modern cities.[4]

Today biophilic urbanism has become a major social movement within city policy and practice. The movement from ecology to the built environment can be seen, for example, in the collected work edited by Stephen Kellert and colleagues, *Biophilic Design* (2008), largely focused on the building

---

Box 5.1: My Wild City

One premise of biophilic urbanism is that urban environments can and do harbor a great deal of wildness. Elements of natural wildness are all around us in cities. They are a source of awe and wonder and are important elements in creating meaningful lives and resilient communities. Examples of celebrating wildness are everywhere—from catching a glimpse of an orca in the Georgia Strait near Vancouver Island to assembling in Arlington, Virginia, to watch migratory swifts swoop en masse down narrow chimneys to listening to the night sounds of katydids and tree frogs in many cities, there is wildness all around us.

Partly this is about shifting our point of view and imagining cities in new ways. Instead of just visiting a park or forest within a city, might we aspire to living in the forest or in the garden? This is the goal in Singapore, a "city in a garden." In the United Kingdom, similar thinking has been taking place in the city of Bristol, with the help of the Avon Wildlife Trust, a nonprofit working to protect nature and educate people about it. Several years ago Bristol started a campaign called My Wild City, with the tagline "Help make Bristol a nature reserve." Among the key activities undertaken has been the preparation of a series of beautiful maps, making visible the nature in different neighborhoods and in the city as a whole. These maps are helping to shift the "mental maps" of residents and their ability to see and be curious about the nature around them. And the Trust has been helping residents take many important steps to expand and enhance wildness.

continued on page 130

Box 5.1 *continued*

The Avon Wildlife Trust also has projects called My Wild Neighborhood, My Wild School, and My Wild Church, among others, showing how wildness can be introduced into many different urban spaces. Many steps can be taken to enhance wildness in each of these places. My Wild Street has seen, for instance, the creation of a "wildlife-friendly urban street" through sponsorship by the local law firm Burges and Salmon and volunteer help from its staff. The aim of the improvements was to bolster biodiversity and also the quality of the street. The team of volunteers made the improvements over a ten-day period, installing a series of box planters, front yard ponds and gardens, and even bug hotels. The result is at once beautiful and biophilic, enhancing habitats for many species and bringing together the street's residents and tenants to effect positive changes, with impressive results. The full story can be seen in a short film at www.avonwildlifetrust.org.uk/mywildstreet.

Wildness in cities can be strengthened and experienced in many different ways, of course, from urban hiking and wildlife watching to participating in local nature clubs and encouraging residents to convert their balconies and backyards into wildlife habitats.

Challenging urbanites to understand their very urban lives through the lens of wildness is another step. Here, a recent U.K. national campaign called 30 Days Wild is instructive. Residents were asked to commit to undertaking one "random act of wildness" each day for the month of June. Social media were a big part of the campaign, and participants were asked to tweet and blog about their wild acts. The campaign was a huge success, and it was estimated that more than a million acts of random wildness were undertaken during the month. Participants planted, hiked, watched and listened to nature, went on picnics and spent time outside, wrote poetry, and generally actively sought out wild nature.

level, and in Timothy Beatley's book *Biophilic Cities* (2011).[5] There is now a Biophilic Cities Network with membership across the globe. With twelve cities in the network, biophilic urbanism is becoming mainstreamed into the policies and practices of these cities.[6]

In chapter 2, on sustainable mobility systems, we set out three types of urban fabric that were formed around different transport systems. It is possible to delineate two other types of urban fabric that are of much

Table 5.1: Two additional urban fabrics important to resilient and regenerative cities.

Urban Fabric	Function	Transport Priority	Speed (Kilometers per Hour)	City Radius (Kilometers)	Land Use Pattern
Peri-urban	Urban and village support functions	Some long-distance rail and road connections for occasional urban trips; local transport for daily activity	50–80	40–80	Intensive agriculture, recycling, industry, water servicing, open space, and villages (new and old)
Bio-regional	Natural system support functions: water, energy, materials, waste management, biophilics	Mostly car and truck	50–80	80–several hundred	Rural land uses for production of food, water, materials, and energy, as well as waste disposal and ecological functions

relevance to this issue of bioregional regeneration: the peri-urban fabric and the bioregional fabric. These are set out in table 5.1.

Peri-urban and bioregional areas are not generally part of the daily commute and are therefore not considered part of the core city. However, these areas are still related to the city, as they are fundamental to its functioning in terms of its natural resources and materials as well as its waste management and ecological functions. Peri-urban areas are much more intensively used than the areas farther out. Many small villages in older areas of Europe are being drawn into cities; new kinds of settlements are emerging in such areas, offering new possibilities for resilient and regenerative outcomes.

Peri-urban areas are likely to be able to have rail access but are likely to need electric vehicle car-share or cooperative bus services to link them to it and hence to the city. Local transport can use such vehicles and also electric bikes. Peri-urban areas will grow in their usefulness to the rest of the city, as all settlements move away from fossil fuels, for the following types of functions:

- Local food production based on intensive permaculture that has short food miles and local types of food, including native food species, which are increasingly being found to have nutritional value
- Waste-recycling centers that cannot fit into the more built-up part of the city, for example, the recycling of treated wastewater to recharge groundwater systems
- Utility-scale solar farms
- Lifestyle villages for retirees and others wanting a life near the city but not on a daily basis, where experiments in regenerative design can be conducted[7]
- Biodiversity experiments that are based on restoring native species and habitat but that need intensive manpower to manage the areas and prevent exotic and feral animals and plants from invading[8]

Bioregional fabric is essentially rural, but of course it still has small settlements that service the city area and thus should be seen as part of the city. Transport can still become zero carbon but is likely to involve biofuels from locally grown cellulose-based systems. The functions of bioregional areas will include all of those described for peri-urban areas but on a bigger scale.

The key to understanding a biophilic urbanism approach to peri-urban and bioregional areas is to see that the same underlying philosophy applies about human settlements and nature: human beings cannot live properly without a daily dose of living nature. Thus these areas need to build that into all that drives the human activities in the two fabrics. They do provide more easy opportunities to be exposed to nature, but every building and activity can be used to separate human activity from nature or integrate it. The integration process will ensure that the activities are more respectful of the area's underlying ecosystems and also enable the removal of fossil fuels from the area's structure and activities.

The city uses the peri-urban and bioregional areas for various productive land uses, and these all need to be part of the agenda for phasing out fossil fuels and creating regenerative urbanism, in which the city is in fact restoring and renewing the various productive and ecological functions. These peri-urban and bioregional parts of the resilient city need to be just as creative and experimental in being inclusive, safe, resilient, and sustainable as the more built-up areas.

The special niche of biophilic urbanism has been its focus on getting greenery into and onto the buildings that make up our cities, predominantly through green roofs and vertical greenery, or green walls. These have changed buildings from being concrete and steel, designed to separate urban life from nature, to having living walls and roofs, now seen as habitat sites with a new kind of design aesthetic. As a result, a wide range of designs and methods for integrating nature into the built environment have emerged and continue to evolve.[9] The broad elements of biophilic urbanism that overlap with landscape architecture and environmental planning are covered later in this chapter; first we address the two areas in which most new science and engineering for bringing nature into cities have grown: green roofs and green walls.

Green Roofs

Green roofs are being developed across the world using a range of new materials and new technologies as well as new science regarding what kinds of plants will work in different areas. They are also being built for different reasons. North America is discovering that they are a very effective and popular option for managing storm water and reducing the urban heat island effect—the warming of cities as a result of their own energy usage turning into waste heat. The urban heat island effect is increased by concrete and bitumen surfaces that absorb heat. Chicago was one of the first cities to recognize that heat stress in certain months was killing people and that much of the heat was created by excessive human energy use. The city began to create opportunities for green roofs to help cool the city. Chicago first conducted a green roof trial on its city hall, and its success led to incentives and regulations to encourage further green roofs in the city. By 2010, Chicago had 359 green roofs totaling 51 hectares (126 acres). The city hall's green roof has become an icon for Chicago's sustainability movement.[10]

In Switzerland, the city of Basel has been installing green roofs for the past sixteen years with a focus on increasing biodiversity. Where there may be a sole initial driver for a green roof installation, multiple benefits are discovered, leading to a ripple effect of further green roofs being installed in the surrounding area.[11]

Green roofs can be extensive, such as the roof of the California Academy of Sciences in San Francisco, or they can be intensive gardens that fit into recreational spaces with roof gardens or are part of landscaping to ensure all parts of a building can have easy access to nature. Millennium Park in Chicago is an extensive green roof covering 10 hectares (about 25 acres) built over parking lots and an end-of-line train station. The park has increased tourism and spurred further development, bringing $3–$5 billion in economic benefit to the area.[12]

Green roofs can become part of a city's building policy with strong incentives, such as extra density, if provided or with just the encouragement of a city policy. Germany began offering incentives in 1983, followed by Switzerland in 2000, particularly in Basel. Both countries currently have a high number of green roofs, which are now an accepted form of practice there. Washington, DC, initiated a green roof rebate program in 2005 and, as part of its Sustainable DC strategy, aims to have 20 million square feet of green roofs by 2020. Many other cities have initiated some form of incentive encouraging green roof construction. Globally, there is a growing tool kit of options for biophilic urbanism policy. Few cities have gone as far as Singapore, with its "green floor plate ratio" requiring buildings to replace the floor plate of a building with at least the same and sometimes twice as much greenery.[13] This requires not just green roofs but green walls as well.

Green Walls

French botanist Patric Blanc was the first to demonstrate extensive green walls; he created large, artistic, and prominent green walls with plant species selected from waterfall rock-face plants. Blanc's walls are hydroponic panel systems that are quite thin, thus enabling them to be wide and tall. Since the creation of these spectacular examples, green walls of all kinds have sprouted across the world.

Green walls are suitable for both indoor and outdoor locations. The

FIGURE 5.1: Green wall of the One Central Park building, Sydney, New South Wales, Australia. (Source: Peter Newman)

resulting benefits vary with the site; in some climates indoor placement brings greater benefits. Toronto, Ontario, has discovered this with indoor biofilter green walls developed from space technology research by the U.S. National Aeronautics and Space Administration (NASA). These biofilter green walls significantly improve indoor air quality through a filtering system primarily involving the plant roots and soil microbes. Toronto's indoor biofilters have been a popular addition in developments, with recognition of their social, environmental, and economic benefits.[14]

Biofilter walls are also being recognized scientifically: in Australia, a two-year study of an installation in Sydney, New South Wales, suggested significant reductions of indoor particulates and carbon dioxide.[15]

Why Is Biophilic Urbanism a Necessary Part of Overcoming Fossil Fuel Dependence in Cities?

Biophilic urbanism can help cities overcome fossil fuel dependence in three obvious ways: making density more appealing, sequestering carbon, and reducing the urban heat island effect.

Making Density More Appealing

Perhaps the most significant way biophilic architecture helps reduce the use of fossil fuels is by enabling higher density to be attractive. Denser cities have much lower fossil fuel footprints, as well as enhanced economic productivity resulting from reduced costs of sprawl, improved agglomeration economies, and greater opportunities for attracting knowledge economy capital (as discussed in chapter 2). However, cultural and political barriers to density can prevent these benefits from being achieved. By introducing biophilic architectural features into dense buildings, the chances of delivering these benefits are greatly increased.[16]

Carbon Sequestration

Plant photosynthesis in cities can help reduce airborne carbon as long as carbon sequestration in the wood created for long-term carbon storage is able to last long enough. Many cities, such as Singapore, have revegetated by planting trees in open spaces and roadways. These large-canopy trees, such as rain trees (*Samanea saman*), can last hundreds of years and store a lot of carbon. One estimate suggests that carbon sequestration by urban trees can reduce a city's carbon dioxide (CO_2) level, with each 50 square meters (59.8 square yards) of tree crown sequestering 4.5–11 kilograms (9.9–24.2 pounds) of carbon. Carbon in plants can also make its way into the soil when the plant dies or goes dormant and can stay there for hundreds of years.[17]

How this can be measured and used as part of urban development standards, and even carbon markets, is not yet clear. Thus the Intergovernmental Panel on Climate Change has not yet been able to advise cities other than to say that revegetation has multiple advantages. It is possible that biophilic design initiatives, especially incorporating green rooftops and green walls, will be able to demonstrate carbon sequestration on a scientific basis, although large-scale demonstrations are still required.

Reduced Urban Heat Island Effect and Reduced Energy Consumption

With increasing urbanization, urban vegetation is being replaced by low-albedo surfaces, such as concrete and asphalt, which along with less evapotranspiration lead to the urban heat island (UHI) effect. Appropriate use of

Box 5.2: Planting Healthy Air

October 2016 saw the release of the first global study of the potential of urban trees and tree planting in addressing particulate air pollutants and urban heat. The study, "Planting Healthy Air," undertaken by The Nature Conservancy, examined data from 245 cities around the world.[a] The study specifically explored whether and to what extent tree planting was a cost-effective strategy. The report concludes that trees and tree planting do indeed represent an important and very cost-effective strategy in tackling particulates and heat. Another key conclusion of the study is that there is significant variation among neighborhoods within cities, and variation among cities around the world, in the return on investment they realize from planting trees. As a result, the authors argue for the importance of "targeting" tree planting in those neighborhoods with the highest rate of return, which tend to have the highest levels of particulate pollutants and heat and the highest population densities. Similarly, certain cities—notably dense cities of the global South, with high population densities and high levels of air pollution—will benefit most and realize the highest rates of return, so targeting at a global scale makes sense as well. (Tree planting in dense cities has been pioneered by Singapore, as addressed in this chapter.) The report concludes that cities that will see the highest return on investment will include Dhaka (Bangladesh), Karachi (Pakistan), Mumbai and Delhi (India), and Ho Chi Minh City (Vietnam), among others. A relatively modest global investment in urban tree planting will deliver substantial benefits. The report estimates that an annual global expenditure of $100 million will result in 77 million urban residents experiencing reductions in particulates and some 68 million experiencing reductions in urban heat.

[a]The Nature Conservancy, "Planting Healthy Air: A Global Analysis of the Role of Urban Trees in Addressing Particulate Matter Pollution and Extreme Heat," October 2016, https://global.nature.org/content/planting-healthy-air.

vegetation in the built environment can help adjust the urban microclimate and improve thermal behavior of building envelopes.

Studies have estimated that around a 25 percent reduction in net heating and cooling energy use could be achieved in urban areas by planting street trees; for example, sixteen shade trees were found to save 30 percent in energy cooling in an area of one city.[18] Vegetated building facades have the same effect on exterior temperatures, as well as reducing interior temperatures by delaying solar heat transfer, leading to reductions in energy consumption used in air-conditioning. Green roofs and green walls can reduce the UHI effect by around 2°C, improving air quality, thermal comfort, and human health, with a 5–10 percent savings in electricity consumption. Research in Hong Kong revealed a maximum temperature decrease of 8.4°C when both green walls and green roofs were used to create a green urban canyon, or street canyon, which is vegetation planted on streets between high-rises.[19]

What Are Other Benefits of Biophilic Urbanism?

Many pioneers in the biophilic design movement recognized the potential environmental benefits of restoring and enhancing nature in architectural design. These emergent biophilic design advocates primarily focused on the human-nature connection, with obvious human health and psychological benefits, though they acknowledged the possible benefits for the environment as well. Once the biophilic design movement, especially Tim Beatley and his research group, saw the broader urban issues, biophilic urbanism researchers and professionals began to see the feasibility of environmental restoration and regeneration of urban areas. These multiple benefits suggest that biophilic urbanism can be a major tool in decreasing fossil fuel dependence and increasing economic performance. The detailed evidence is set out in the following sections.

Water Management

The ability of vegetation to take up and absorb storm water provides a successful strategy to manage runoff and associated waterway pollution. Soil and vegetation together are much better at slowing water flows than are concrete and bitumen. Significant reductions in storm water runoff can be achieved, especially through the use of green roofs, as they provide a larger potential area of absorption. The amount of retention varies according to climate, seasons, plant type, slope of roof, and substrate depth, but the appropriate combination can achieve average retention rates of 70 percent or more. Biophilic design in the form of green roofs and rain gardens along roads significantly aids storm water reduction. Green roofs are particularly appealing, as they potentially utilize unused or underused areas and do not compete with public space. Vertical green walls, in addition to reducing storm water runoff, have the potential to reuse reclaimed gray water and recirculate excess drainage water.[20]

Water Quality

"Phytoremediation" is the term for using plants and associated soil microbes to reduce the concentrations or toxic effects of contaminants in the environment; the plants clean, or remediate, the surrounding air, soil, or water. Gravity encourages water to flow down a living wall and through the plant's growing medium, which, depending on the living wall system, can act as a biofilter for the water. The large vertical root zone typical of a living wall can also efficiently purify water through phytoremediation. In many U.S. cities, storm water management is a significant issue because of heavy rainfall along with urban hard surfaces that collect impurities. Substantial contributors to water pollution in the United States are the combined sewer systems commonplace in the Northeast, Great Lakes, and Pacific Northwest areas, and as urban storm water runoff increases, so does the problem. Heavy rain events result in more frequent combined sewage overflows, carrying both household pollutants and surface pollutants into waterways. The U.S. government has introduced regulations and policies to mitigate waterway pollution through control of storm water runoff. The Clean River Act in Washington, DC, is an example of the outcome of one of these policies, an initiative that has catalyzed the introduction of green roofs throughout the city.[21]

Air Quality

Airborne pollutants, such as ozone (O_3), nitrogen oxides (NO_x), sulfur dioxide (SO_2), ammonia (NH_3), nitric acid (HNO_3), carbon monoxide (CO), and particulates, can be remediated by urban vegetation. Street canyons can reduce particulate matter by as much as 60 percent and nitrogen dioxide (NO_2) by 40 percent. Particulate matter adhering to leaf surfaces is absorbed into the plant, or at least diluted, when it is released. In the root area, contaminants are broken down by interactions between plants and the soil. In the plant tissue, compounds are chemically transformed. Phytoremediation involves different mechanisms and different processes, so particular plants are better suited than others for particular pollutants. Although few studies have yet appeared, this well-known science would suggest that mechanical filtration and phytoremediation could enable gray water to be used to irrigate green roofs and living walls in hot areas with minimal use of water and substantial reduction of pollutants.

Ongoing research conducted by NASA on the potential of plants to assist air purification in closed systems has evolved from a focus on air quality in space stations and closed-system buildings, with particular attention to the removal of formaldehyde and other volatile compounds. Studies conducted in a primary school that monitored temperature, CO_2, CO, volatile organic compounds (VOCs), carbonyls, and particulate matter with and without plants corroborated NASA's findings. NASA's research also revealed that the soil, particularly if it contained activated carbon, played an important part in the absorption of pollutants, storing them until the plants were able to utilize the pollutants for food. The U.S. Environmental Protection Agency's chief of indoor air quality critiqued NASA's research, however, arguing that it would take 680 plants in a typical house to achieve the same results as in the tests. Further research showed that it was mostly the soil microbes that removed indoor air pollution.[22]

Thus indoor green walls that support a large number and variety of plants, along with a variety of soil microbes, can be effective indoor biofilters. The University of Guelph's Controlled Environment Systems Research Facility designed its first indoor biofilter living wall in 2001, installing it at the university in 2004. Toronto now has a growing number of indoor biofilter living walls. With successful outcomes and responses, architects are discovering that developers are cutting costs in other areas to pay for the installation of indoor green wall biofilters. These complement the green roofs now required to be installed on applicable developments since the passing of a 2009 bylaw.[23]

Biodiversity Conservation

With declining global biodiversity, increasing habitat in cities through increased urban vegetation is an obvious focus for progressive cities. The United Nations' 2012 conference on biodiversity pledged to increase commitment and spending to halt the rate of species loss, but it is mostly cities that will be able to do this. Green roofs and green walls have multiple benefits, but if carefully integrated into urban landscaping and bioregional ecosystems they can also help with biodiversity.

Cities in Switzerland, particularly Basel, have been studying the progression of biodiversity associated with their green roofs with encouraging results, resulting in mandatory green roofs on new flat-roofed buildings, similar to what is being done in Toronto. Some bird species are beginning to colonize Swiss green roofs. In a study of 115 "wild colonized" green roofs in cities in northern France, 86 percent of the colonies were found to be composed of native plants. This suggests that once established, biophilic architectural features could act as important sites for biodiversity colonization from the surrounding bioregion.[24]

Singapore's Khoo Teck Puat (KTP) Hospital incorporated greenery and biophilic design throughout its campus in the hope of encouraging butterflies to return. A goal of 100 butterfly species was set. After three years, 102 species were sighted on the hospital grounds, indicating that the goal had been reached. Peter Newman, in the journal *Australian Planner*, made an assessment of Singapore's biophilic urbanism and showed that the value of high-density cities for biodiversity is the access to intensive labor for careful attention and maintenance, and much greater variety in the structure of habitats, especially at vertical sites. The assessment shows that habitats in high-rise areas can create biological habitats similar to forests. There is much more scientific work to be done in designing and evaluating biophilic architecture for its biodiversity, but the early signs are encouraging, and a whole new set of ecological techniques could be emerging.[25]

Sociopsychological Benefits

Although the value of biophilic urbanism in reducing use of fossil fuels has been established, if this process of removing fossil fuels is to go mainstream, there must be obvious sociopsychological benefits. The established benefits of biophilic urbanism include improved mental health and reduced stress; attention restoration; increased well-being and productivity; faster healing; and decreased violence and crime with greater altruistic behavior.

Improved Mental Health and Reduced Stress

Roger S. Ulrich, who cofounded Texas A&M University's Center for Health Systems and Design, developed a theory about stress reduction through significant exposure to nature. He employed electrocardiograms; measurements of pulse rates, frontal muscle tension, and skin conductance; and self-ratings of emotional states to investigate subjects' physiological relationships with nature. Both physiological and verbal results indicated that recovery from stress was faster in a natural setting than in an urban

FIGURE 5.2: Along the daylit Cheonggyecheon River in Seoul, South Korea. (Source: Jeffrey Kenworthy)

one. The physiological results also suggested an involvement of the parasympathetic nervous system. Ulrich proposed a psycho-evolutionary theory that nature has a restorative influence by increasing positive feelings, positive physiological responses, and sustained involuntary attention.[26]

Attention Restoration and Increased Well-being and Productivity

Rachel Kaplan and Stephen Kaplan, in their 1989 book *The Experience of Nature: A Psychological Perspective*, suggested that people exposed to nature can concentrate better as a result of restored vitality, mood, and creativity. In more recent studies the physiological response was measured using salivary cortisol as an indicator of stress. Results suggested that even short-term exposure to nature had positive effects on stress reduction, which could be expressed in a renewed ability to focus on work or other activities. This is now called the attention restoration theory.[27]

In his best-selling book *Last Child in the Woods: Saving Our Children from Nature-Deficit Disorder*, journalist Richard Louv brings together research showing that direct contact with nature—whether an urban park, a backyard, or a mountaintop—is essential for healthy childhood development.[28] This has spurred a major global movement, with, for example, all cities in Australia establishing Nature Play areas for children to experience nature directly instead of with plastic, cement, and rubber play area constructions.[29]

Studies in workplaces have confirmed that this approach works in offices as well. In a study of office workers, Tom DeMarco and Tim Lister studied the ability to focus. They compared "lean" and "green" office spaces and concluded that lean offices were worse than green offices not only because they were less pleasing to the workers but also because organizational output and productivity was significantly less in the lean offices.[30]

Research on the physiological and psychological responses of office workers to a vase of roses has demonstrated reduced heart rate variability, slower pulse rate, and strong subjective responses, evaluated through a profile of mood states (POMS) questionnaire. The study showed that by simply viewing roses, office workers experienced increased parasympathetic nervous system activity, indicating lower stress and a greater sense of well-being.[31]

Faster Healing Rates in Hospitals

Hospitals are an ultimate expression of modernism with all their amazing functionality, but they sometimes lack a human dimension, and some hospital administrators are now realizing that more access to nature should be provided for staff and patients. Psychological testing of responses to images revealed that stressed individuals feel considerably better when exposed to views of nature. Recovery times were found to be faster for patients who have a view of nature, along with less need for pain relief.

The obvious conclusion was that plants should be used in hospitals as a supplementary healing mode. One study found that indoor plants "enhance patients' physiological responses, with lower ratings of pain, anxiety and fatigue, and more positive feelings and higher satisfaction with their hospital rooms." A study in Michigan revealed a 24 percent decrease in frequency of health-care visits among prison residents who had views of nature. Measurements of hospitalized elderly women who were exposed to a green rooftop forest showed that they were more physiologically relaxed and restored.

Similar studies have emerged from Japan on the effects of the traditional practice of *shinrin-yoku*, or "forest bathing." Physiological research has demonstrated that exposure to nature reduces heart rate variability and pulse rate, decreases blood pressure, lowers cortisol, and increases parasympathetic nervous system activity while decreasing sympathetic nervous system activity, all of which are helpful in healing.[32]

Decreased Violence and Crime with Greater Altruistic Behavior

Nikos Salingaros has developed a unified architectural theory that relates design to human behavior. He suggests that "environments devoid of neurologically nourishing information mimic signs of human pathology. For example, colorless, drab, minimalist surfaces and spaces reproduce clinical symptoms of macular degeneration, stroke, cerebral achromatopsia, and visual agnosia." Environments devoid of any representation of nature not only can make people psychologically unwell and regressive in their behavior but also can cause them to display physical symptoms and responses. The primal fight-or-flight response is increased when individuals are exposed to hard-edged architecture rather than curving contours, and this effect is heightened when a person is already in a stressful environment. Increasing greenery in housing developments has resulted in less violence and aggression, less crime, and better interpersonal relationships. Others have suggested that greener environments in lower-income public housing reduce mental fatigue and assist "residents' psychological resources for coping with poverty" and that short immersions in nature elicited a more positive mood and a greater desire to help others.[33]

Economic Benefits

Sociopsychological and environmental benefits are likely to combine to contribute to significant economic benefits, such as better workplace productivity, improved health and healing, increased retail potential, decreased crime and violence, increased property values and employee attraction, and increased livability in dense areas. These are set out in table 5.2 along with estimates of economic benefits.

Table 5.2: Sociopsychological, environmental, and economic benefits of biophilic urbanism.

Area of Benefit	Estimated Economic Benefit
Better workplace productivity	$2,000 per employee per year from daylighting $2,990 per employee over 4 months when desks angled to view nature[a]
Improved health and healing	$93 million per year in reduced hospital costs if natural features provided in U.S. hospitals[b]
Increased retail potential	Skylighting in a chain store would result in a 40% sales increase, ±7% 25% higher sales in a vegetated street frontage[c]
Decreased crime and violence	Public housing with greenery had a 52% reduction in felonies Biophilic landscapes introduced across New York City would save $1.7 billion through crime reduction[d]
Increased property values	Biophilic buildings attract higher rental prices, 3% per square foot or 7% in effective rents, selling at prices 16% higher[e]
Employee attraction	Biophilics attract and retain high-quality workers[f]
Increased livability in dense areas	Green features increase salability of dense apartments[g]

[a]Browning et al., 2012
[b]Browning et al., 2012
[c]Erwine and Heschong, 2000
[d]Kuo and Sullivan, 2001; Browning et al., 2012
[e]Wolf, 2005
[f]Heerwagen, 2000
[g]Green and Newman, "Demand Drivers," 2017

Source: Summary of literature, with particular acknowledgment to Söderlund, 2015

What Is the Role of Biophilic Urbanism in Helping City Management Repair Bioregional Systems?

Biophilic urbanism has all the marks of a social movement. Social movements begin with a few concerned individuals bringing others together and move from "emergence to coalescence to mainstreaming." Jana Söderlund outlined how biophilic urbanism moved through these stages as it began to emerge as a collaborative idea in the United States in the 2000s as a range of people saw a need for a better understanding and a better delivery of natural experience and natural values in urban life.[34] It began to coalesce as a number of books were written and Tim Beatley's Biophilic Cities Network was formed. Today it is mainstreaming.

Cities around the world are recognizing the power of nature and the need to integrate nature into urban design and planning. Cities such as Melbourne, in Victoria, Australia, have set new ambitious goals for urban tree planting; Melbourne aspires to double its tree canopy coverage by 2030 (from its current 22 percent to 40 percent).[35] As with Singapore, Melbourne's vision of the future is of an immersive urban nature—not just more trees in the city but a "city in a forest." Other cities, from Oslo to Los Angeles, are recognizing the power of water and are restoring and renaturalizing rivers that touch many neighborhoods. In the United States, shrinking Rust Belt cities are seeing the opportunity to convert vacant lots into parks and orchards, as in the HOME GR/OWN initiative in Milwaukee, Wisconsin. Many cities, from Rio de Janeiro in Brazil to Vitoria-Gasteiz in the Basque Country of Spain, are further developing networks of urban trails that connect residents with parks and green spaces and provide opportunities to spend more time outside and in closer contact with the natural world. And in many coastal cities, from Wellington, New Zealand, to Boston and New York and Seattle, there are impressive new efforts to provide physical connections and access (as well as visual access) to nature in aquatic and marine environments.[36]

Biophilic goals and targets are commonly included in city comprehensive and sustainability plans. Vancouver, British Columbia, for instance, in its "Greenest City 2020 Action Plan," established the goal of every resident living within a five-minute walk of a "park, greenway or other green space."[37] The sustainability plan for Washington, DC, sets a similar goal (ten-minute walk) as well as other biophilic targets, for instance, that 75 percent of residents live within a quarter mile of a "community garden, farmers' market, or healthy corner store."[38]

Moreover, many cities are establishing biophilic ordinances and codes. Like Singapore, cities such as Chicago and Toronto have adopted a mix of requirements and incentives to promote biophilic urbanism. Toronto was the first North American city to mandate installation of green rooftops for new buildings over a certain size (with a sliding scale mandating that larger buildings must cover a higher percentage of roof area). Seattle, Washington, and Washington, DC, have adopted minimum green area ratio standards, and many cities require or incentivize biophilic measures and projects through storm water management ordinances. Philadelphia, Pennsylvania, has adopted an ambitious twenty-five-year plan and vision called Green City, Clean Waters.[39] Implemented largely through the Philadelphia Water Department, the program has implemented a variety of green infrastructure projects, including rain gardens and bioswales, schoolyard greening, green rooftops, and many others aimed at decreasing impervious surfaces and increasing storm water retention. These green projects result from a mix of direct grants, incentives (e.g., reduced storm water fees), and requirements under the city's storm water management standards. The city's first public rooftop park, Cira Green, resulted from compliance with the city's storm water management requirements.

Although only five years into the implementation of this visionary plan, as of June 2016 Philadelphia had made green infrastructure improvements at more than 440 sites, resulting in an estimated reduction in discharge of nearly 2 billion gallons of polluted water.[40]

Many city officials understand the numerous different yet complementary benefits provided by biophilic urbanism—trees shade and cool cities, sequester carbon, retain storm water, and provide important habitat for birds and wildlife. These same trees also significantly reduce long-term chronic stress and serve to soften the urban setting (a recent study showed that the perceived wait time for buses decreased when bus stops had trees around them.[41] Many North American cities, including Philadelphia and Washington, DC, are struggling with the problem of combined sewer overflow, and urban trees, green rooftops, and gardens help in important ways to reduce this problem. The green infrastructure projects undertaken through Philadelphia's Green City, Clean Waters program do much to enhance the natural qualities of their neighbor-hoods. Tim Beatley visited several of the city's "green streets," where new rain gardens and bioswales have been installed—they will enhance the permeability of the urban streetscape and add much to the greenery and nature residents experience there.

Few cities do as much as San Francisco to return built-up areas to nature in small parks and greenspaces. This city, where International PARK(ing) Day started, has been a global leader in innovative ways to create small urban parks, especially through its Pavement to Parks program. An important part of this initiative is the option of creating "parklets"—converting two to three on-street parking spaces into small parks and gathering spaces. This project has been a great success, and since its inception, in 2010, more than fifty parklets have been created throughout the city. Like many cities, San Francisco is looking for other ways to integrate nature, including a living alleys initiative, extension of its network of urban trails, and a new urban forest plan, among others. And it is also, like many cities, beginning to plan for the many other species that occupy space in the city, for instance, adopting bird-safe building standards that mandate window and building facade treatments that minimize fatal bird strikes.

In San Francisco, as in many emerging biophilic cities, the agenda of integrating new nature has been advanced and supported by a robust net-work of nonprofits. These have included the good work of advocates such as local architect Jane Martin, who founded Plant*SF.[42] Martin pushed the city to create a special sidewalk landscaping permit allowing residents to take up some of the hard surface spaces in their neighborhoods and plant beautiful, lush gardens. Since 2006, when this permit was created, some two thousand of them have been issued by the city, allowing residents to plan and organize their own sidewalk greening projects. The results are especially evident in the Mission District, where Martin lives, with new flowers, plants, and trees strategically planted along sidewalks, on curb extensions, and along the edges of buildings.

Lessons Learned from Singapore

Biophilic urbanism is not just an American phenomenon. Without calling it by this name, Singapore has shown, perhaps more than any other city, how a dense city can bring in nature in new and exciting ways. Perhaps the most important outcome of Singapore's biophilic urbanism is that it has proved not only that density does not preclude a city from bringing nature more intensively into its daily life but that density may in fact assist this. Three key conclusions about the future of resilient cities can be drawn from the biophilic urbanism demonstrated in Singapore: (1) density can be an advantage, not an obstacle, in creating green cities; (2) biophilic cities can make important contributions to local biodiversity; and (3) biophilic urban design can encourage new types of urban biodiversity.

Density as an Advantage in Biophilic Urban Design

Singapore's biophilic urbanism has shown the world how a dense city can regenerate natural systems and create far more natural urban systems. It is doing this between buildings and all over buildings using their structures to create new urban ecosystems never considered possible before. Singapore has demonstrated that density probably helps this process in two ways. First, it enables the development of such concepts as Singapore's Park Connector Network and Gardens by the Bay, which involve intensive land uses in small areas. Second, it enables the height of buildings to be used to help create a third dimension in an urban ecosystem. This means that a structure for biological activity can be created around buildings similar to the structure of a tall forest.

Singapore was built as a "garden city" but now wants to be seen as a "city in a garden" or even a "city in a forest." Thus another positive element of biophilic urbanism is that dense cities with high-rise buildings may offer more opportunities to build biophilic urban ecosystems than is possible in low-density suburbia, given the extra habitat opportunities provided by high walls and flat roofs in dense cities. This is a big issue, as the findings shown in this book point to a powerful need for increased densities to prevent car-dependent urban sprawl with all its oil, climate, health, and economic implications. However, the need for natural systems to be part of this policy has always been a question that threatens to undermine the value in more compact cities. Might biophilic urbanism be a way to facilitate green and attractive cities that are also far more efficient in resources? To take away the stigma of density would be a significant planning contribution from biophilic urbanism, now clearly demonstrated in Singapore.

Biophilic Cities' Contributions to Local Biodiversity

Singapore's National Parks Board (NParks) started measuring biodiversity when the city began its biophilic experiments. NParks pioneered the City Biodiversity Index (CBI), also known as the Singapore Index on Cities' Biodiversity (SI), which has been adopted by many cities worldwide. These data show that new and rare species are being found in Singapore long after they were thought to have disappeared from the urban area. The many local examples set out in a series of beautiful publications from the city show rapid increases in bird life and other biodiversity as soon as habitat is provided, whether involving local species or not. Indeed, many of the tree species used to provide structure for Singapore's urban ecosystems are not native, such as the rain trees used for canopy cover over roads and parks because their root systems fit into urban areas. Singapore's KTP Hospital measures biodiversity in birds, fish, and butterflies, and all are increasing as the hospital's biophilic features mature.

Biophilic urbanism such as that demonstrated in Singapore is unlikely to recreate the pre-urban ecosystem, nor is that ever claimed. But it can do far more to recreate the ecosystem structure in any area, as it can use the diversity of a city's built forms and microclimates to create urban ecosystems far more biodiverse and structurally complete than in the unidimensional urban parks and gardens we are used to. In this it is more like the regenerative design paradigm discussed in chapter 6.

Emergence of New Types of Urban Biodiversity

As Singapore's biophilic urbanism spreads and matures into a more complete coverage of the urban environment, it can be expected that it will not only increase local biodiversity but also provide a better understanding of urban ecosystems that can help bioregions regenerate. Although Singapore's mature biodiversity will not be the same as the pre-city rain forest, it will have many features of a rain forest and will also contain a city full of people.

In two new projects, Singapore is redeveloping areas for extra housing and in the process regenerating the area's natural features. One project, restoration of a former river delta that had been drained and channelized into concrete drains, will recreate some of the former river

FIGURE 5.3: Biophilic Singapore. (Credit: Skye Duncan)

mouth ecosystem. It will then bring some of this ecosystem's features into landscaping around and on buildings in the new housing area. It will thus join the area's natural features to the built form and regenerate the former ecosystem. The other project, involving a reclaimed area and concrete wall on the coast, will use coastal ecosystem features to regenerate a thriving natural area; it will then bring these features into the green roofs and green walls of the new housing area.

The rapidity with which Singapore has made the transition from being a modernist city, where nature was kept at a distance from urban development, to embracing nature at every point of the city's development and buildings, suggests that any city wanting to contribute to biodiversity and to create a healthier and more complete urban ecosystem can now do so. The technology of green walls and green roofs is available and needs to be tried out in many different urban environments. The results can be a city where a new kind of urban nature develops that fulfills the functions of the ecosystem displaced by the city and that contributes to local biodiversity improvements.[43]

Other Bioregional Benefits

The examples given here, especially those in Singapore, show cities repairing their urban ecosystems. Most cities have a much larger bioregional ecosystem that they draw from for energy, water, food, materials, waste processing, and other urban activities, such as recreation. These areas around the built-up city also need regeneration if a city is to be truly resilient.

Biophilic urbanism has been applied not just to roofs and walls but also to the hard concrete and bitumen surfaces that have been part of the modernist approach to cities. From 1986 to 2007, Singapore increased its natural plant coverage by 40 percent by putting a canopy cover over most roads, installing biophilic features on buildings, increasing plantings in its famous gardens, and building a series of park connectors that provide a biological and recreational link across the city to its major open space regions such as water catchments. Wherever possible, the city has replaced concrete drains and bitumen roads with natural features.

Many cities are using such processes, which in the past have been called "water-sensitive urban design"; for example, gardens are often created alongside roadways and paved areas to alleviate storm water runoff. Portland, Oregon, has a program called Depave in which city roadsides are planted with "rain gardens" and unnecessary roads are removed and replanted.[44]

In Australia, Melbourne also has reduced and replaced road space to create more green areas, and many local governments are replacing drains with natural features, as at Sydney's Clear Paddock Creek.

In Boulder, Colorado, this process of making creeks and drains more natural has been associated with another great feature of that city, extensive off-road cycle paths that follow the creeks and go under crossroads wherever the engineering can be done. These creeks go right out into the surrounding bioregion and generally have days of flooding; clever engineering has enabled the floods to spill out onto the cycle path in order to be contained.

Such clever and creative use of infrastructure has enabled Boulder to fit naturally into its bioregional system and yet enable people to use the green corridor to commute to their workplaces. Cities need to find more and more of these creative solutions linking their built environment to the bioregions upon which they depend.

FIGURE 5.4: Biophilic cycle paths down regenerated creeks in Boulder, Colorado, with flood control opportunities down the paths. (Source: Peter Newman)

Conclusion

Biophilic urbanism is a great tool for helping cities overcome their fossil fuel dependence. It has multiple co-benefits, with a strong psychological and physiological rationale for an innate human-nature connection, solid local environmental evidence of the value in environmental planning, and, finally, a good economic case for bringing natural systems more into the core of architecture and urban development. Developers, designers, planners, and urban politicians can no longer neglect the value of biophilic urbanism and bioregional planning. The Biophilic Cities Network demonstrates that many cities now include the following:

Business that can see the economic opportunities in biophilic urbanism;

Government that wants to regulate to require as many biophilic features as possible, especially in dense urban areas and in bioregional natural systems; and

Community that wants to include biophilic urbanism in all its visions of the resilient city of the future.

CHAPTER 6

Produce a More Cyclical and Regenerative Metabolism

The metabolic requirements of a city can be defined as all the materials and commodities needed to sustain the city's inhabitants. . . . The metabolic cycle is not completed until the wastes and residues of daily life have been removed and disposed of. . . . As man has come to appreciate that the earth is a closed ecological system, casual methods that once appeared satisfactory for the disposal of wastes no longer seem acceptable.

—Abel Wolman, in "The Metabolism of Cities"

As we approach the end of this book, we look toward some more visionary unfinished agendas for resilient cities that are also related to overcoming fossil fuel dependence. In recent years there has been a focus on the nine "planetary boundaries" that show how human activities, mostly in cities, are setting up limits to our growth.[1] The constraints are dominated by climate change and biophysical integrity, which we have addressed so far, but the main agenda is that more focus is needed on the metabolism of our cities. How can we reduce the flow of nutrients and materials that end up in wastewater and landfill and also reduce the flow of fossil fuels into greenhouse gases and waste heat? Can cities take up the urban metabolism agenda in new and creative ways, maybe even creating a regenerative metabolism?

The idea that cities have a metabolism, with resource inputs and waste outputs, as does any living plant or animal, was popularized in 1965 by Abel Wolman (see the chapter opening quotation). In most cities energy, water, and materials flow through the urban metabolism in a linear system. However, in all of life this metabolism is optimized to enable the ecosystem within which the living parts are located to be more cyclical as a system. Resource inputs of energy, water, and materials are shared and the wastes minimized as they flow into a circular system that converts them mostly to useful resources. We believe that a city can also create a more circular urban metabolism, as exists in natural ecosystems (see figure 6.1).

Why do our cities not follow this model? For the most part, we are highly exploitive of the energy, water, and materials that we bring into our cities, and we treat our wastes as something to simply get rid of, without seeing their beneficial uses within the urban system. This cannot continue, as cities are driving us toward planetary boundaries, not just climate change, and all cities are involved.

Cities need to become much more aware of their metabolism and do something about reducing their footprint. The size of the impacts has caused scientists to suggest we are in a new geologic epoch called the Anthropocene.[2] Experts have sometimes panicked—suggesting that we need massive intervention called geoengineering to steer away from these

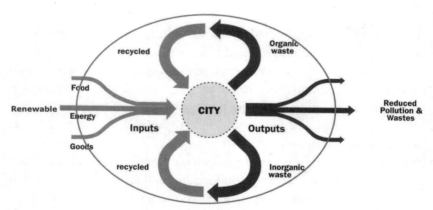

FIGURE 6.1: Circular urban metabolism in theory. (Source: Newman and Jennings, 2008)

impacts. Proposed large-scale global engineering experiments such as pouring iron filings into the ocean and firing sulfur into the atmosphere have generally been rejected as far too risky, with the potential of causing more damage than they would fix.[3] In this chapter we suggest that small-scale geoengineering in cities is a viable alternative to large-scale geoengineering.

The road to resilient cities requires finding ways of relating urban metabolism to practical, daily urban planning. We suggest that it can be done by examining urban metabolism in each of the urban fabrics. How can the materials and resources they use be regenerated and foster a mutually beneficial relationship between urban areas and the planet?

This chapter will address the following questions:

1. What are planetary boundaries and the Anthropocene, and how do they prevent our continuing with the extractive city?
2. Can urban geoengineering prevent the Anthropocene?
3. How can urban metabolism help cities move beyond resilience to regeneration?
4. How do the different urban fabrics vary in their metabolism?
5. How can each urban fabric develop a more regenerative metabolism?

What Are Planetary Boundaries and the Anthropocene, and How Do They Prevent Our Continuing with the Extractive City?

Planetary boundaries suggest a set of limits, which have been controversial since the time of Thomas Robert Malthus in 1798 and, in modern times, the Club of Rome's *Limits to Growth* in 1972. Debates over these limits helped to frame sustainability as they tried to bring together open-ended economics, which saw growth as limitless, and closed-system ecology, which saw growth as always limited. The resolution has tended to be that growth in pollution and other negative environmental impacts needs to be curtailed and reversed, but growth in practices that enable this curtailment and reversal can be the basis of a new economics.[4]

Over the past two decades there have been attempts to define global environmental sustainability empirically, including concepts such as "tolerable windows," wherein minimum societal needs form the lower boundary and maximum environmental limits form the upper boundary; "critical natural capital," defined as environmental systems that perform irreplaceable functions; and "environmental guardrails."[5]

Another common approach, as set out by The Natural Step, has been a general set of rules for use in decision making, typically prohibiting the following:

1. Increasing concentrations of substances from Earth's crust,
2. Increasing concentrations of substances produced by society, and
3. Increasing degradation by physical manipulation or overharvesting.

A fourth rule pertains to societal well-being.[6]

Perhaps the most popular definition of environmental limits is contained in the concept of environmental footprints, which is based on the capacity of a given area to produce renewable resources and absorb waste from human impacts.[7] The environmental footprint is most commonly used to compare national impacts in relation to the area available on the planet, but it is also used to measure the impacts of individuals, products, organizations, cities, and regions.[8] However, there is no scientific consensus as to the amount of biocapacity that should be set aside for ecological purposes, with estimates ranging from 12 percent to 75 percent.[9]

One criticism of many environmental limits is the need for a value judgment in their definition. There are no biophysical laws that can be used to determine the limits—just human ones.[10] The planet can be expected to survive extreme climate change, as there have been periods in history far hotter and far colder than today, and the Earth has continued. Human civilization, however, is at risk, and thus we need to set limits that will enable our grandchildren and successive generations to survive. Humanity has survived through many different geologic eras, including several ice ages and a brief period much warmer than the current climate; however, for 150,000 years during harsh and changing climates we subsisted only as hunter-gatherers, until approximately 10,000 years ago, when we entered the Holocene, the current geologic epoch. Within this constant and nurturing climate humans thrived and developed into the advanced civilization we know today.[11] Today our limits are all about how cities can be enabled to survive and thrive in a way that overcomes the threats outlined in the planetary boundaries.

The new debate about limits centers on the premise that we have left the Holocene and entered into the next epoch, the Anthropocene, which is defined by human activity. Thus future geologic formations will show levels of human activity laid down in rocks and soils similar to global geologic processes. As the Holocene is the only planetary state we know of that provides favorable conditions for humanity, it seems reasonable to suggest that humans should be aiming for the Anthropocene to resemble the Holocene by dealing with the planetary boundaries.

The planetary boundaries framework, first introduced in 2009 and updated in 2015, is the first attempt to define boundaries that, if respected, would allow us to maintain the planet's Holocene-like state within an era driven by the activities of people in cities.[12] The developers of this framework reviewed Earth system processes and identified nine that have critical tipping points that are influenced by human activity; see figure 6.2A–I.

Despite inevitable criticisms about limits, the planetary boundaries concept has been widely taken up.[13] Although not specifically referred to in the United Nations' final Sustainable Development Goals (SDGs), the concept was included in many of the original SDG proposals and is likely to stay on the global agenda.[14] The SDGs, however, show that in meeting such planetary boundaries we must meet the other economic and social goals at the same time.

The planetary boundaries framework is set out in table 6.1, which shows the response of two of the first countries (Switzerland and South Africa) to estimate the limits they saw driving their nations.

The limits outlined obviously are not just the greenhouse gas (GHG) limits set out by the Intergovernmental Panel on Climate Change (IPCC), but they raise the same kinds of issues: how best do you go about reducing the causes of these impacts so that the limits are not breached? We believe that the same approach is needed as we have suggested for GHGs. Indeed, this approach completely aligns with the climate change agenda of removing fossil fuels—it requires cities to create a more regenerative future.

Can Urban Geoengineering Prevent the Anthropocene?

The need for rapid large-scale decarbonization has driven investigations into a simple "silver bullet" for climate change mitigation. This has led experts to look toward geoengineering, defined as "deliberate, large-scale

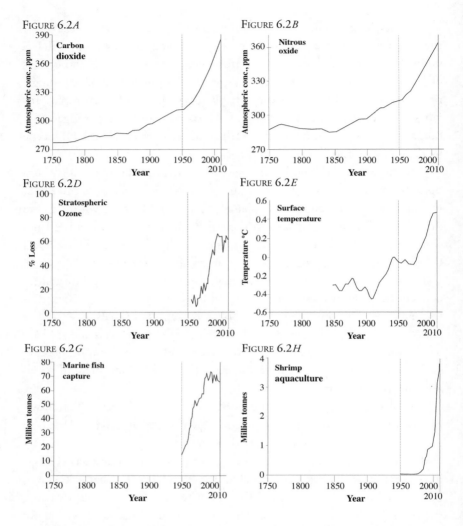

modification of the Earth's climate systems for the purposes of counteracting climate change."[15] Geoengineering approaches can be divided into two major classes, carbon dioxide (CO_2) removal and solar radiation management; the latter involves reflection of the sun's rays and is more a temporary management tool for extreme events.

The IPCC's Working Group III, concerned with mitigation of climate change, accepted that in the face of extreme climate events there may be the need to quickly offset warming. However, the report warns that terrestrial

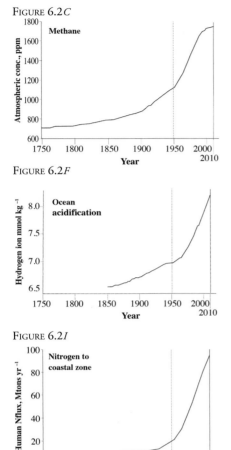

FIGURE 6.2C

FIGURE 6.2F

FIGURE 6.2I

FIGURE 6.2: The takeoff, from 1950, in critical human activity levels impacting the planet, leading to the idea of the Anthropocene epoch. *A*, carbon dioxide; *B*, nitrous oxide; *C*, methane; *D*, stratospheric ozone; *E*, surface temperature; *F*, ocean acidification; *G*, marine fish capture; *H*, shrimp aquaculture; *I*, nitrogen flow to coastal zones. Units of measure in *A–C* are parts per million (ppm); in *F*, millimoles per kilogram of water (mmol/kg^{-1}); in *I*, millions of metric tons per year (Mtons/yr^{-1}). (Source: Steffen et al., 2015)

geoengineering techniques would require large-scale changes in land use involving substantial local and regional risks, while ocean-based techniques (such as iron fertilization) would involve "significant transboundary risks for ocean ecosystems." Similar risks exist for solar radiation management, which involves introducing reflective particles or aerosols such as sulfur into the upper atmosphere. The IPCC's report addresses cost, risk, governance, and ethical implications of such interventions. These ethical issues were the focus of the Oxford Principles, developed in 2009 to provide a

Table 6.1: Planetary boundaries and how they have been interpreted in Switzerland and South Africa.

Earth System Process[a]	Planetary Boundary Threshold	Adapted Boundary for Switzerland (Global Limits)[b]	Adapted Boundary for South Africa (National Limits)[c]
Climate change	Atmospheric CO_2 Change in radiative forcing	CO_2 emissions 12.3 Gt CO_2eq	CO_2 emissions 451 Mt CO_2
Biodiversity loss	10 species/million species extinct per year	Biodiversity damage potential 0.16	Endangered and critically endangered ecosystems 0%
Nitrogen and phosphorus cycle	Nitrogen removed from the atmosphere Phosphorus flowing into oceans	Nitrogen emissions 47.6 Tg Phosphorus fertilizer consumption 38.5 Tg (global limit)	Nitrogen application rate for maize production 144 kg N/ha Total phosphorus concentration in dams 0.1 mg/L
Stratospheric ozone depletion	Concentration of ozone	Not considered, as currently phased out	Annual HCFC consumption 369.7 ODP
Ocean acidification	Mean saturation state of aragonite 2.75	CO_2 emissions 7.6 Gt CO_2	Replaced by marine harvesting
Freshwater use	Freshwater consumption 4,000 km³/year	Not included, as considered a regional issue	Consumption of available freshwater resources 14,196 mm³/year
Change in land use	Land cover converted to cropland 15%	Surface of anthropized land 19,362,000 km²	Rain-fed arable land converted to cropland 12.1%
Chemical pollution	N/A	Rationales lacking in setting limit	Not given due to lack of detailed and accurate data
Atmospheric aerosol loading	Aerosol optical depth	Rationales lacking in setting limit	Replaced by air pollution

[a]Rockström et al., "Safe Operating Space," 2009
[b]Dao et al., 2015
[c]Cole, Bailey, and New, 2014
Note: CO_2 = carbon dioxide; CO_2eq = carbon dioxide equivalent; Gt = gigatons; ha = hectare; HCFC = hydrochlorofluorocarbons; kg = kilograms; km² = square kilometers; km³ = cubic kilometers; mg/L = milligrams per liter; mm³ = cubic millimeters; Mt = megatons; N = nitrogen; ODP = ozone depletion potential; Tg = teragrams.

code of conduct for geoengineering research. They suggest that the risks are likely to be high. The U.S. National Academy of Sciences in 2015 stated that geoengineering "is no substitute for reductions in carbon dioxide emissions and adaptation efforts aimed at reducing the negative consequences of climate change." Nevertheless, this agenda continues to be seen as a potential backup for emergency intervention.[16]

The practical, ethical, and governance problems of large-scale geoengineering are too great to be easily dismissed. In light of this uncertainty about global-scale top-down geoengineering, we suggest city-centric urban geoengineering with a local urban planning and urban development approach.

Jonathan Fink of Portland State University suggests that "urbanisation could constitute a successful form of distributed, bottom-up geoengineering" and that "urban redesign carries a lower risk and offers more ancillary benefits than most other geoengineering schemes." Tim Flannery, author of *The Weather Makers* and, more recently, *Atmosphere of Hope*, suggests that large-scale geoengineering should be abandoned in favor of "third way" technologies. First way technologies involve adaptation, and second way technologies involve mitigation; third way technologies can actually extract CO_2 from the atmosphere—they regenerate the atmosphere. Third way technologies "recreate, enhance or restore the processes that created the balance of GHG, which existed prior to human interference, with the aim of drawing carbon, at scale, out of the Earth's atmosphere and/or oceans." Some examples of third way technologies are given in box 6.1.[17]

Urban development that reduces resource use through efficiency and recycling, renewable fuels, and third way sequestration technology has the potential to fulfill a major geoengineering function. The decarbonizing potential of cities is only beginning to be understood, and there is the potential for far greater capacity. This approach has been called the "carbon positive" approach by architect William McDonough.[18] He says that if we "design with the natural cycle in mind to ensure that carbon ends up in the right places," we can create carbon positive outcomes. By this he means that we need to curb "fugitive carbon," which is released when we try to make energy or we leak methane or put plastic in the oceans; preserve the "durable carbon" in durable wood products, geologic formations such as limestone, and new products used in third way sequestration; and cultivate

Box 6.1: Techniques for Urban Geoengineering

Urban geoengineering, in combination with renewable energy in a low-demand and highly efficient urban environment, can turn cities into sequestration machines while reducing emissions at their source. Techniques for urban geoengineering include the following.

1. Carbon negative construction using technologies such as these:
   a. Carbon-absorbing cement, produced by removing CO_2 from industrial waste and incorporating it into cement (e.g., Solidia Cement™)
   b. Carbon negative plastics, which capture CO_2 from the air (e.g., Newlight Technologies' AirCarbon™)
   c. EnergyPlus buildings, which generate more electricity than they consume, thus offsetting high-carbon energy sources
   d. Prefabricated low-carbon housing made from biogenic materials (e.g., cross-laminated timber, straw composite), which effectively sequester carbon if the biogenic materials are harvested from plantation sources
2. Carbon negative landscaping using serpentine rock, which when crushed absorbs CO_2 from the air
3. Carbon negative waste streams, such as biochar from combustible timber waste (e.g., from sources such as biogenic building material offcuts and forestry and agricultural waste)
4. Carbon negative industrial products, such as carbon nanofibers manufactured for many functions and carbon fiber replacing steel
5. Urban and bioregional forestry and biophilic urbanism to absorb carbon biomass

"living carbon," produced by living materials that provide food and fiber and soil organisms that continue the cycles of nature. McDonough points to a special issue of the journal *Nature*, "The Circular Economy," as the kind of approach he is advocating.[19]

How Can Urban Metabolism Help Cities Move Beyond Resilience to Regeneration?

The best way to see if cities are bringing about sufficient change to enable the kind of planetary healing envisaged is to measure the flows of sustainability performance through a material and substance flow analysis mapping the flow of resources through the city. This is a well-established tool and is usually described as urban metabolism modeling.

Urban metabolism modeling provides a tool for understanding and monitoring the performance of urban systems, not just in terms of GHG emissions but also as they relate to the other planetary boundaries. All of these broader sustainability elements are linked to how we use energy, water, waste, transport, building materials, and food, as well as the economic and social outcomes that are part of livable cities, as outlined in chapter 3. We have called the model for understanding these factors the "extended metabolism model," as it shows how important it is to simultaneously reduce metabolism of cities while improving livability in all of its dimensions.[20]

Good governance will drive more sustainable urban infrastructure that can simultaneously create circular metabolism in cities, with lower emissions, reduced water demand, cleaner energy, local food, and more efficient waste recovery, as well as better livability. This is the goal of a more circular and regenerative metabolism.

The ideal regenerative city (resulting from regenerative urbanism) would allow a settlement to do the following:

- Create more energy than it needs.
- Use water sparingly, with full recycling, to eliminate the need for external supply and to enable regeneration of groundwater systems and rivers.
- Regenerate natural systems in degraded areas to support biodiversity of a complexity similar to the pre-settlement bioregion's natural capacity.
- Reduce the scale and extent of centralized energy, water, and storm water infrastructure and the embodied and operational energy required for this infrastructure.
- And regenerate the economy and community at the same time!

Regenerative design aims to eliminate waste, finding new uses for residual products by treating them as resources; for example, waste food becomes compost, thereby reducing the waste going into the environment (such as a landfill) and in turn reducing the need to import fertilizers. Urban material flows are optimized from their design through to their disposal with the intent to create a circular urban metabolism. Applying a regenerative design approach to urbanism allows cities to begin to perform a restorative role in the biosphere. The process requires local management of resources and will help build a local green economy.[21]

The regenerative potential of a location will vary, and specific needs will be highly dependent upon the climate. In this respect regenerative design represents a very different approach from the universally applied modernist International Style, which has dominated city planning for most of the past century. A growing body of literature on the theory of regenerative design and regenerative cities documents the feasibility of this approach as early innovators deliver demonstration projects that are beginning to show the possibilities. Such changes can rapidly mainstream and set off exponential growth in regenerative urbanism. There are numerous emerging examples with a variety of governance systems, such as the following:

- West Village, University of California, Davis—the largest net zero carbon development in the United States—was created by UC Davis with the local government.
- White Gum Valley (WGV), Perth—a net positive energy precinct based on solar power and battery storage, with zero waste and high water goals—was created by the government of Western Australia, the Fremantle City Council, and Curtin University.
- Vista Carbon Challenge, Peterborough—in 2012 the largest zero-carbon development in the United Kingdom—was led by the U.K. government as a Carbon Challenge demonstration site and delivered through a public-private partnership.
- Hammarby Sjöstad and the Stockholm Royal Seaport—created by the Swedish and Stockholm governments—are regenerative in energy and water and exhibit extremely high recycling waste rates (enabled by automated vacuum waste collection streams).
- Vauban, Freiburg, Germany—with its net positive renewable energy system, dubbed the "greenest city in Europe"—was led by a nonprofit civic group with facilitation from the local government.[22]

Delivering the regenerative city requires a paradigm shift from current conventional practice. Cities have generally been designed as extractive engines drawing resources from natural systems, processing these resources to generate value, and producing wastes, the impacts of which are externalized. Urban systems must be planned to more closely resemble the cyclical resource flows observed in balanced natural systems; urban metabolism must then be constantly monitored to ensure that the city is moving in a regenerative trajectory.

How then can we bring urban metabolism into town planning and urban development practice so that the concepts can be mainstreamed? We suggest that using the approach of urban fabrics can enable this to happen.

How Do the Different Urban Fabrics Vary in Their Metabolism?

The three kinds of urban fabric outlined in chapter 2—the walking city, transit city, and automobile city fabrics—have significant differences in their areas, elements, and qualities that can form the basis of statutory and strategic town planning. Each fabric can also be shown to have different metabolism qualities. The variations are discussed here with a focus on energy and the materials used in a city, mostly for construction, but as discussed in chapters 2 and 3, there are human and livability components as well.

Energy

Cities' consumption of transport fuel has been shown to vary exponentially with density.[23] The data make sense in terms of the theory of urban fabrics:

- The *walking city* requires little transport fuel, as it was designed and built around walking. Today it will have some cycling and transit use. These help maintain the intensive land use of a walking city, especially rail systems, the most spatially intensive transport modes next to walking. The walking city will also have cars, as the automobile city fabric has been laid over all parts of the city. However, there is very little space for cars, and hence it is primarily a walking-based area. In Melbourne and Sydney the central areas have 80 percent and 92 percent walking, respectively, as the daily activity of the area. Thus the transport fuel use is likely to be little more than 5 to 10 gigajoules (GJ) per capita in walking city urban fabric.
- The *transit city* is shaped primarily by a corridor of electric rail supplemented by buses. Cars are more likely to be part of this area, as there is more space than in the walking city in the medium-density housing, but there are options for using transit and walking that the automo-

bile city just does not have. Transport fuel use is therefore likely to be around 15 to 25 GJ per capita in the transit city urban fabric.

• The *automobile city* is built around cars, with few alternatives other than for short trips to local shops, schools, and recreation areas, but most journeys are long and scattered without a fast transit option. In this case, the automobile city urban fabric is likely to use anywhere from 30 to 80 GJ per capita. Cities such as Atlanta stretch this further, with more than 100 GJ per capita.

Just as transport energy varies across the city, so too does building energy, as this also varies with density.[24] Thus if urban fabrics vary so much in energy use, the obvious conclusion is that we need to use the character of low-energy urban fabric when we build more urban fabric. But the planetary boundaries are about more than just energy, so we will also look at how some of the material inputs and outputs to a city vary with the different urban fabrics.

Basic Raw Materials

Basic raw materials (BRM) are the sand, clay, wood, and stone that form the foundation for building construction. They literally are built into the fabric of a city.

BRM studies are rare, but here we summarize a study conducted in Perth to outline the significant variations that can be observed in urban metabolism across different fabrics of the city.[25] The study examined the normal quantities of material that went into construction in three parts of the city: central or inner city, which is very similar to the old walking city; middle suburbs, which are similar to the transit city; and outer or fringe suburbs, similar to the automobile city.

The variations across the city are demonstrated graphically in figure 6.3, and the data are shown in tables A.5 and A.6. The variations are huge (resulting from the amount of material required in construction) and are even greater when technologically innovative construction techniques are applied. In figure 6.3, the area of the circles represents the proportional volume of BRM required for new building types per person for both business as usual (BAU) and technology and construction innovation (TCI). TCI includes more efficient building practices such as prefabricated construction.

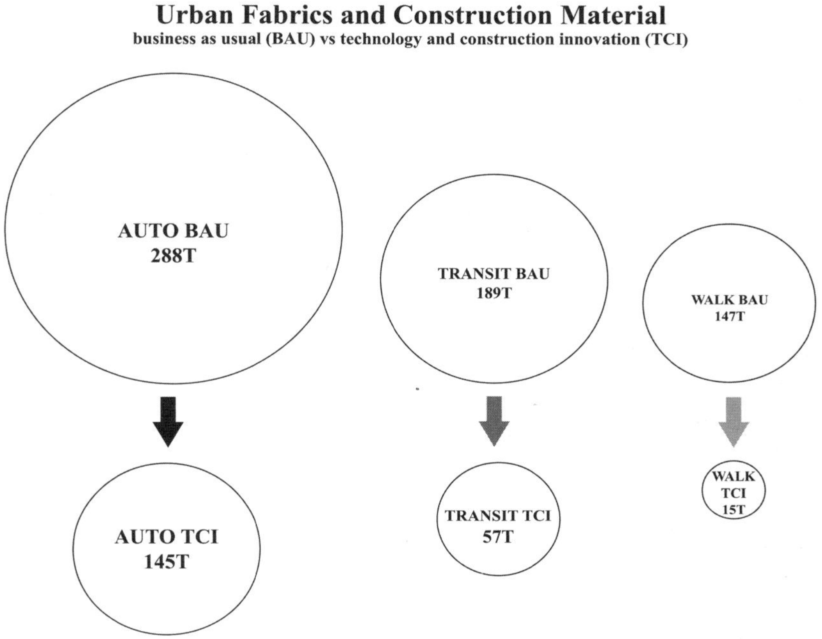

Urban Fabrics and Construction Material
business as usual (BAU) vs technology and construction innovation (TCI)

FIGURE 6.3: Perth's demand for basic raw materials (BRM) in terms of three urban fabrics. The circles' relative areas indicate proportions of BRM, measured in metric tons (T) per person, under the business as usual (BAU) and technology and construction innovation (TCI) scenarios. (Source: Gardner and Newman, 2013)

Metabolism of the Three Urban Fabrics

The full urban metabolism of Perth is set out in terms of its three urban fabrics in figure 6.4 and appendix tables A.5 and A.6. These data show the variations in energy, water, land, food, and BRM in the three areas of the city as well as the wastes produced in the three urban fabrics. The metabolism flows in the three fabrics are significantly different. As figure 6.4 shows, these differences can be reduced by technologies for construction innovation. In terms of urban planning's role in helping to create a more regenerative city that can live within planetary boundaries, it would seem obvious that we need more walking and transit urban fabrics, as well as technological innovation in the construction and management of our city's metabolism.

Urban Fabrics and Urban Metabolism
(per person per year)

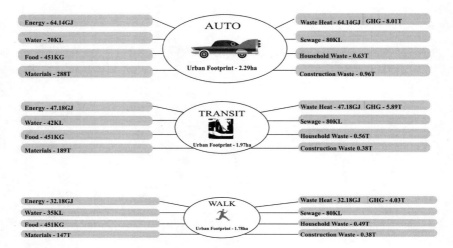

FIGURE 6.4: Perth's different urban metabolisms in terms of three urban fabrics. Figures shown are per person per year. GHG = greenhouse gas emissions; GJ = gigajoules; ha = hectares; kg = kilograms; kL = kiloliters; T = metric tons. (Source: Gardner and Newman, 2013)

The fundamental structural difference in the three urban fabrics dominates the differences between the three kinds of urban systems in all aspects of urban metabolism.

The following guidelines show how urban metabolism can be reduced by transitioning to a higher proportion of walking and transit urban fabrics, with all of their planning implications. If a city is to regenerate its urban metabolism, it will need to introduce a series of key technological systems in the areas of energy, water, biodiversity, and material waste along these lines:

1. Energy can become regenerative if the fuel used to build and operate buildings and to build and run transport is renewable and if more is produced than is consumed by the city. The excess can help power and fuel the surrounding bioregion. This is likely to be renewably powered electric systems in buildings and transport as well as renewably produced natural gas (see chapters 1 and 2).

2. Water can become regenerative if it is fully collected at its source within a city, as well as being recycled from gray water and black water (wastewater) and used to help regenerate aquifers and water bodies in the bioregion. This can be done with technologies such as desalination and wastewater recycling (see the story of Perth's water supply in chapter 4).

3. Biodiversity can become regenerative if it is built into every part of the urban fabric, including green roofs and green walls. Bioregional biodiversity can be assisted by the city with its different structural habitats and intensive human power (gardening and urban conservation projects).

4. Waste of materials can be reduced to very small amounts, but materials cannot be regenerated unless very large amounts of energy are used, given thermodynamic limitations. However, carbon, phosphorus, nitrogen, and other trace elements can be returned to soils in the surrounding bioregion through recycling.[26]

How Can Each Urban Fabric Develop a More Regenerative Metabolism?

Table 6.2 sets out the characteristics of each urban fabric in general terms, showing how the three fabrics are structured, their associated resource consumption and waste outputs, and some of the livability parameters for each fabric.

The perspective shown in table 6.2 is that the walking and transit fabrics have many strong livability functions as well as having lower metabolism than the automobile fabric.

Town Planning Implications

The new era of cities appears to be shifting away from the automobile urban fabric, and this transition needs to be facilitated for many more reasons than simple transport functionality. It is an opportunity to help make cities a force in geoengineering, a mechanism for regenerating local and global ecosystems. This demands that we have a more coherent set of planning norms that can more easily accommodate a reduction in metabolism and improved livability associated with less automobile urban fabric. The town planning system will, however, need to change, moving away from its statutory regulations on densities, car parking, mixed use, and other key

Table 6.2: Urban fabrics: fundamental structural differences and differences in metabolism and livability.

Fabric Area	Walking City	Transit City	Automobile City
Dimensional radius	0–2 km	0–8 km	0–20 km
Outer dimensional circle	1–2 km (less intensive)	8–20 km (less intensive)	20–40 km (less intensive)
Fabric Elements			
Street width	Narrow	Wide enough for transit	Wide enough for cars, trucks
Squares and public spaces	Frequent, as very little private open space	Less frequent, as more private open space	Infrequent, as much greater private open space
Street network	Permeable for easy access; enables good level of service for pedestrians	Permeable for pedestrians, networks to reach transit stops; corridors enable good levels of transit service	Permeability less important, enables high levels of service for cars on freeways, arterials, and local roads; bus circulation often restricted by cul-de-sac road structure
Block scale	Short blocks	Medium blocks	Large blocks
Building typologies	High density, usually minimum 100 people/ha	Medium density, usually minimum 35 people/ha	Low density, < 35 people/ha, often much less than 20 people/ha
Building setbacks	Zero setbacks	Setbacks minimal for transit noise protection and more space	Setbacks large for car noise protection
Building parking	Minimal for cars, seats for pedestrians, bike racks	Minimal for cars, seats for pedestrians, often good bicycle parking	Full parking in each building type
Level of service for transport mode	Pedestrian services allow large flows of pedestrians	Transit services allow large flows of transit users	Car capacity allows large flows of cars

Table 6.2 *continued*

Fabric Functions and Lifestyles	Walking City	Transit City	Automobile City
Movement/ accessibility functions			
	High by walking	High by transit	High by car
	Medium by transit	Medium by walking	Low by transit
	Low by car	Medium by car	Low by walking
Consumer services			
Shopping, personal services	High locally, especially niche services	High in corridors, especially subcenters	High, especially in shopping centers, but dispersed
Large-scale consumer services			
Hypermarkets Warehouse sales Car yards	Low	Medium	High
Industry functions			
	Small—more white-collar	Medium—more labor-intensive, e.g., hospitals, education	Large—more blue-collar
Face-to-face functions			
Financial and administrative Creative decision making Knowledge exchange The arts	High	Medium	Low–Medium
Car-less functions			
	High	Medium	Low
Lifestyles			
Walking city lifestyles	Major	Possible	Not possible
Transit city lifestyles	Possible	Major	Difficult
Automobile city lifestyles	Possible	Possible, common	Major

continued on page 174

Table 6.2 *continued*

Fabric Qualities	Walking City	Transit City	Automobile City
Urban form qualities			
Density	High	Medium	Low
Mix	High	Medium	Low
Transport qualities			
Car ownership	Low	Medium	High
Level of service	High level of service for pedestrians	High level of service for transit users	High level of service for car users
Transport activity	High pedestrian activity	High transit activity	High car activity
Economic qualities			
Development infrastructure cost per capita	Low–Medium	Medium–Low	High
GDP per capita	High	Medium	Low
Labor intensity	High	Medium	Low
Social qualities			
Difference between rich and poor	Low	Medium	High
Ability to help car-less	High	Medium	Low
Health due to walking	High	Medium	Low
Social capital	High	Medium	Low
Personal security	Variable	Variable	Variable
Traffic fatalities	Low	Low	Medium–High
Environmental qualities			
GHG per capita and oil use per capita	Low	Medium	High
Waste generated per capita in buildings and households	Low	Medium	High
Footprint per capita	Low	Medium	High

Note: GDP = gross domestic product; GHG = greenhouse gas; ha = hectares; km = kilometers.

Sources: Newman and Kenworthy, 2015; Newman, Kosonen, and Kenworthy, 2016

regulations that end up producing automobile urban fabric even when a city is trying to do something different.

Wherever possible when planning for greenfield and brownfield urban areas, automobile fabric should be minimized in favor of higher-density transit and walking fabrics so as to maximize resource efficiency for the more difficult urban components, such as transport fuel, solid waste, and building materials. But particular strategies will still be needed for each component of the urban footprint to collectively work toward the delivery of a regenerative city, as follows:

- Renewable energy will be more regenerative than the energy consumed only if the buildings are highly energy efficient and all available sites are used to create renewable energy from sun, wind, and geothermal sources.
- Water will be more regenerative than the water consumed only if there is a big emphasis on water efficiency and on collecting rainwater and groundwater and recycling wastewater.
- Biodiversity will be more regenerative only if biophilic urbanism strategies are in use that enable green roofs, green walls, and water-sensitive design to create more habitat opportunities than previously existed on the site.
- Waste of materials can be significantly reduced if new technologies in building materials and construction techniques (such as modular) are used and recycling is optimized.

In addition, new developments should seek infrastructure synergies at the energy, water, and waste nexus; such integration of utilities can optimize efficiency of each through an industrial ecology that makes the most of distributed and local technologies and governance.

But even with all these characteristics, the regenerative city will need to have all the livability features of an inclusive and economically productive city. Such integration points us to minimizing automobile city fabric and creating more walking and transit fabrics using all the best practice technologies and planning systems. Ending fossil fuel dependence will be a significant part of this transition to meeting the nine planetary boundaries, but the world's cities will need to take on this bigger journey as well.

Conclusion

The planetary boundaries that have been demonstrated by the world's scientists demand a response. The initial top-down global-scale geoengineering solutions are clearly not safe enough to be considered further. Local-scale urban engineering shows much more promise, and this chapter shows how detailed audits using urban metabolism studies can set up urban geoengineering strategies. These will need to have elements of demand reduction, operational efficiency, new technologies, and sequestration systems such as the third way technologies discussed earlier in the chapter. They will also need to bring along the economic and social goals of cities in an integrated way to achieve a more resilient and, eventually, regenerative city.

Urban geoengineering will require regenerative design perspectives and integrated urban planning at all scales, from regional to household, as well as considerable modification of existing legislation, policies, and codes driven by all levels of government. The first case studies are beginning to emerge that demonstrate this should be feasible and cost-effective and should also build community.

Fundamental to achieving more circular and regenerative urban metabolism will be the recognition of how large are the differences in urban fabric types in all aspects of their metabolism. Building more walking and transit urban fabric out into automobile urban fabric will be an essential part of how cities need to face their future. This will become even more important when the regenerative city and the need for urban geoengineering are firmly on the global agenda.

The articulation of a regenerative city vision provides a clear and positive direction for the application of urban metabolism models; however, as with all visions, its implementation will depend upon strong leadership in business, government, and community.

Business should seek new opportunities in the innovative technologies in energy, water, waste recycling, and construction, especially the third way technologies, which create more circular metabolism.

Government should create strategies to address planetary boundaries, especially with regard to climate change, and apply these strategies to each urban fabric in the city in a way that is integrated with economic and social goals. Planning strategies and regulations will need to favor walking and transit fabrics for their full urban metabolism benefits.

Community should be constantly drawing cities forward with visionary and creative expressions of why cities must become regenerative in order to address planetary boundaries.

CONCLUSION

Growing Regeneratively

The driving force for global resilience will continue to be cities. This book has suggested six principles to create resilient cities and, perhaps, even regenerative cities. We need to create cities that rapidly accelerate the process of decoupling economic growth from fossil fuels. We need to use the knowledge and creative force of cities to build rooftop solar systems and utility-scale solar and wind farms instead of continuing with coal and gas power stations. We need to use the innovative skills of urban design to create walkable, transit-oriented cities with new and exciting ways of using solar-based electric transport instead of using oil. We need to use integrated co-design and partnerships with business, government, and civil society to make cities more inclusive, healthy, disaster ready, biophilic, waste-free with more circular metabolism, and regenerative.

Underneath the six principles of resilient cities are some fundamental ideas that support the whole foundation of city building. We need to create cities of hope, not fear, and this means grasping the opportunities that cities create, opportunities for change in how we live and work and how we manage the planet. We need to create more opportunities for overcoming poverty, and we need to do it without fossil fuels. We need to accept that this means our cities will grow economically, but at the same time we need to be prepared for managing this growth in an inclusive and sustainable manner.

How do we approach growth in cities? There are two approaches to the science or analysis of urban growth, which can be labeled "agglomeration" and "anxiety."

Agglomeration is how economists and engineers look at the benefits of cities. The economies of scale and density are analyzed in terms of how clusters of different skills and jobs can create positive agglomeration elasticities. Engineers and planners seek how to make more opportunities through simple analysis of density and scale efficiencies: better public transport, better recycling, better shops and services, better markets, and better universities all depend to some degree on increasing the size and density—the agglomeration.[1]

Anxiety is the basis of urban impact analysis. Planners, engineers, environmental scientists, and economists worry about certain trends, certain possibilities that may follow from the new development, the new road, the new technology, the increased size and density. So they seek to outline how the impacts could happen and how to avoid them.[2]

The approach we suggest is to use the growth of cities to create new opportunities (productive sciences based on agglomeration analysis) but to do it with minimal impacts (impact sciences based on anxiety analysis). This integrated duality is how we need to approach growth in cities.

It is possible to picture these approaches as either optimistic or pessimistic, but together they provide a balance—both approaches need to be integrated to create good urban futures. Agglomeration and anxiety each contain truths that we can use. The hope for our cities is that we can take the benefits of urban agglomeration and learn from the issues of urban impact analysis. Despair is created when we blindly accept growth and learn nothing from the anxiety associated with it. But despair is also created when we accept anxiety as a state of permanent fear about the future for any growth in our cities. It is not hard to see how imbalances in this integrated approach can powerfully influence politics and lead to a rethinking of how to make a more resilient outcome in our cities and their regions.

Productive sciences are usually the ones to which politicians listen, but if they keep saying that bigger is better, no matter what, then they will become victims of their own rhetoric. Most cities have mega-projects being proposed, usually by road agencies, that are rationalized by saying the projects will create shovel-ready jobs followed by more new jobs in the community. In Australia the conservative prime minister Tony Abbott talked up $40 billion worth of big roads without doing any serious analysis of their cost-benefit ratio or detailed impacts, just to get infrastructure spending into the economy. Most of these projects are dying. "Just do it"—without careful consideration of the benefits and impacts—does not work in our cities.

Anxiety about growth can lead to positive changes that ensure growth really does lead to a better city. But there are a few areas that are anxiety cul-de-sacs and don't lead anywhere helpful. Fear of population growth, migration, and increased density are a few of these cul-de-sacs. And there is little benefit to detailed thinking about an apocalypse, which leads only to paralysis instead of forward progress. Hiding out in the hills is not likely to work for many. The apocalypse is best left to Hollywood and scary novels. Climate change is not included in this category. We have been well warned about how our cities and regions are causing this and what can be done about it. We don't need to be scared into action; we need to embrace it as part of the next phase of urban growth. Indeed, it needs to be seen as a major force in achieving the transformation to resilient and, eventually, regenerative cities. It needs to be the new basis of economic growth.[3]

So how can the ideas of agglomeration and anxiety be balanced to manage growth for increased resilience? The most significant response to anxiety about population and density is to emphasize the importance of design. The great cities of the world, such as Paris, London, Barcelona, and New York, have design traditions that have shaped their urban growth into urban legacies that we would all like to emulate. Density is not feared when we look at those cities, as there has been a history of urban design sensitive to the human qualities of community, creativity, and aesthetics.[4] This applies to any city, no matter what its size or density.

Resilient design facilitates growth with positive outcomes for everyone and for the planet, through better urban land use and infrastructure, with creative integration of all the best technologies and processes for solar, walkable, healthy, inclusive, disaster-ready, biophilic cities.

Most cities have a strategic plan to help achieve their long-term goals, including how they cope with growth. However, there are only eleven cities in the Organization for Economic Cooperation and Development's wealthy cities category that are "big," which means they have a population of more than 5 million. But preparing for a "big" future needs to be on the agenda for many cities.[5] For example, in Australia, Perth and Brisbane are projected to reach populations of 5 million, and Sydney and Melbourne to reach 8 million, by 2050—just as we are meant to be removing 80 percent of fossil fuel dependence across the planet. Cities must embrace this growth and put it to use in developing the housing, commerce, industry, and infrastructure that will achieve 80 percent less fossil fuel use.

City design scenarios need to be considered with different models that can reduce traffic (and related emissions), reduce energy and water use, reduce waste, and reduce damage to water systems and biodiversity while increasing opportunities for jobs, education, recreation, health, and well-being. Regenerative demonstrations should abound.

Urban designers need to understand and consider how to use the design elements that can lead to improved resilience, and they must do this by thinking beyond disciplines and in response to residents' needs. The six principles outlined in this book overlap significantly when design is the focus. For example, use of solar photovoltaics and batteries, which can enable any development to be zero carbon at lower cost than if using coal-fired power (as set out in chapter 1), would eliminate the health threat from coal and give citizens greater control over their power source while increasing resilience to a disaster that may affect a centralized energy source. Biophilic urbanism, discussed in chapter 5, encourages the integration of green walls and green roofs into designs, especially in dense developments. Green walls and green roofs cool buildings and neighborhoods, reduce storm water pollution, increase biodiversity, and improve human health and well-being.

Digital planning tools are available that can enable an informed, multidisciplinary approach to achieving such integrated outcomes. Planning is one of the last professions to go digital, as it has been dominated by paper reports and architectural drawings. This is rapidly changing, so it will not be long before every development being considered will be submitted online, put out to the public for consideration online, and assessed online. Digital planning tools will be essential requirements for planners in all cities in preparation for developments and will be used by developers, communities, and authorities to help resolve the issues of agglomeration and anxiety.[6]

This process will considerably reduce preparation time and, it is hoped, will enable communities to recognize how best to integrate their concerns with the need for development and change. Having the ability to try out multiple scenarios for development that show the impacts on financial viability, community facilities, carbon, water, traffic, human health, biodiversity, waste, disaster preparedness—the full resilience agenda—should enable us to create better outcomes in design. Peter Calthorpe, an urban designer and cofounder of the Congress for the New Urbanism, developed software that has been used to calculate urban footprints of developments in California.[7] Similar work has been developed in Australia.[8]

The digital tools of twenty-first-century planning can be used to assist with local planning and can be used to demonstrate compliance with overall strategic planning goals. However, to do so we will need a local deliberative system that locks in genuine community-based feedback.[9] Such approaches can include the participatory budgeting that now is finding such positive integrated and visionary outcomes as government, business, and community outcomes are seen to coalesce and integrate as they should—agglomeration and anxiety are always resolvable.[10] These approaches have been used in wealthy cities and in emerging cities.[11] And, as always, a metropolitan-scale plan is needed that sets some guidelines and goals as well as the local processes so that broader citywide goals can be seen by those at local levels.

While design processes and technology are important, in the end much depends on our imagination. How do we imagine our future? Can we begin to see not just a city that manages the integration of productive and impact sciences, not just a city that eases the anxiety as it grows, but a city that absolutely inspires us?

The need for hopeful, global, inspirational solutions drives us into new ways of building cities, which is why the idea of the regenerative city is emerging. This is a city that not only says no to the extractive city of the past, with its constant consumption of more and more resources in exchange for urban growth. It acknowledges that a sustainable city is not enough even if it begins to reduce the resource inputs and waste outputs, but the truly resilient city of the future, as set out in figure I.4 in this book's introduction, will be regenerative as it phases out fossil fuels and begins addressing other planetary boundaries. The regenerative city will create more and more human opportunities in jobs and services while also regenerating what has been destroyed by its environmental footprint. This can mean creating more water resources than it consumes and creating more renewable energy than it consumes so it can support its regional resource needs and even begin extracting carbon from the atmosphere. It means recycling wastes and water in a way that helps its region to create more food than it consumes. All of this while creating more opportunities in a fairer city.

The regenerative city concept is gaining considerable global support. In 2013 the UN-Habitat publication *The Future We Want, The City We Need* stated, "The city we need is a regenerative city." Also in 2013 regenerative design in relation to urban environments was the topic of a special volume of the *Journal of Cleaner Production,* and around the same time leaders in the field at the University of British Columbia established the university's Regenerative Neighbourhoods Program. Since then academic publications on this topic have flourished, and the subject is beginning to infiltrate the mainstream. For example, the American Planning Association's 2016 conference hosted a session titled "Regenerative Urbanism Rising: Next-Generation Practice." In 2016 the University of Melbourne established its Thrive Research Hub, focused on regenerative urbanism, and Curtin University began planning its new campus as a city of innovation, with the goal of being an innovator in regenerative precincts and cities.

But such an inspirational concept must begin with some practical steps. So, for example, what would be a regenerative design approach to the automobile city? What can be done for the middle suburbs now fifty to sixty years old and looking their age, as well as the newer outer suburbs on the edge? Most planners want to bring more transport options and more centers with substantial density of jobs, services, and houses into such car-based suburbs that either are beginning to decay as they lose their younger demographic or are just too far from everything. But how can we do this in a way that not only reduces fossil fuel use but even begins to regenerate the local and global environment?

As outlined in chapter 2, we need to push new electric rail lines through into the middle and outer suburbs, to the edge of the city.[12] We need to make a series of smaller centers along such lines, all providing solar power for recharging the train at every station and for recharging local electric bikes and electric vehicles. But somewhere in the outer areas, perhaps at the end of the line, we need to imagine a big new walking-oriented city to be built with no car dependence at all. Such a city should be a major attractant for jobs, services, and dense new residential development. It should be a model regenerative city with complete independence from fossil fuels; it should have sufficient rooftop solar to export back into the rest of the city; it should be dripping with biophilic features so it is much cooler and more walkable in its streets than any other part of the city; it should have a completely circular metabolism in terms of its water and waste and materials. Its materials and construction fabric will be literally sucking carbon dioxide out of the atmosphere.

Such a city will be a twenty-first-century model for how to live without fossil fuels and will have the dense urbanism that attracts young people and investment. It will feature affordable housing and all the best of solar passive design and water-sensitive design. It will be the embodiment of a city completely decoupled from fossil fuels and a model of how economic growth can be regenerative of the local and global environment.

To do this will require new planning approaches that will enable the urban development system to put aside its old tools based on automobile dependence and fossil fuels. The new city will require an understanding of how narrow streets and dense urbanism of the old walking city can be combined with the new technologies of solar, biophilics, electric mobility, circular metabolism, third way carbon sequestration technologies, and the best of new materials and building design. It will immediately set up a corridor that is two-way in terms of flows of people and ideas between the old walking city and the new walking city. So it will require a different and more decentralized, distributed governance from the utilities—not just for renewable power systems post-coal and post-gas but also for the transport systems post-oil. This will be expressed through the local governments, business, and the community, who will need to recognize the need for an urban fabric different from what we have been generating for the past fifty years. It will require new partnerships between the global world of scientists and the local world of urban professionals to create the tools to achieve this regenerative city.

As we approach the next phase of urban growth in cities across the world, we need to embrace their agglomeration benefits and ensure that we deal with their impact anxieties—at the same time. Businesses need to create new markets for resilience and regenerative urbanism; government needs to provide the regulations and processes that enable, and not prevent, the changes; and communities need to keep providing the vision that we can do much better in our cities. Such markets, regulations, and visions can create new partnerships that form the basis of the next phase of economic growth. It will be a phase driven by cities growing regeneratively.

Appendix: Metabolism Tables

1. Metabolism and Livability in Slum Settlements

Table A.1: Resource inputs to Ciliwung River slum settlement and high-rise apartments, Jakarta, Indonesia.

Input	Slum Settlement	High-Rise Apartments
Water (L/household/day)	248	188
Energy (MJ/household/day)		
Electricity	2.30	1.20
Kerosene	60.80	57.00
Charcoal	0.90	0.15
Gasoline	3.99	7.05
Diesel	3.27	2.35
Total	71.26	67.75
Land (m²/person)	4.57	0.91
Building materials	Bricks, wood, bamboo frame; tile or tin roofs (very poor quality)	Bricks, ceramic floors, tile roofs (good quality)
Food	Inadequate intake	More balanced but minimal intake

Note: L = liters; MJ = megajoules; m² = square meters.

Source: Teferi, Newman, and Matan, 2016

Table A.2: Waste outputs from Ciliwung River slum settlement and high-rise apartments, Jakarta, Indonesia.

Output	Slum Settlement	High-Rise Apartments
Solid waste (kg/household/day)	216 *(82% into river)*	1.66 *(100% collected)*
Liquid waste (L/household/day)	248 *(directly into river)*	188
Air waste (g CO_2)		
Electricity	626	326
Kerosene	4,487	4,206
Charcoal	85	14
Gasoline	284	502
Diesel	241	173
Total	5,723	5,221

Note: g CO_2 = grams of carbon dioxide; kg = kilograms; L = liters.

Source: Teferi, Newman, and Matan, 2016

Table A.3: Livability of Ciliwung River slum settlement and high-rise apartments, Jakarta, Indonesia.

Parameter	Slum Settlement	High-Rise Apartments
Health	Environmental health very poor 42 ill in 3-month period	Environmental health relatively good 34 ill in 3-month period
Employment	55% street traders 19% employed in private business 0% home industries Most participate in informal economy	6% street traders 40% employed in private business 2% freelance workers Most participate in formal economy
Income (average)	Rp151,000	Rp252,000
Housing	Poor 82% want to move	Relatively good Do not want to move

continued on page 189

Table A.3 *continued*

Parameter	Slum Settlement	High-Rise Apartments
Education	94% primary school and below	44% primary school and below
Community	High level of community 92% know > 20% by first name 90% happy to live there 100% trust neighbors 100% feel secure 100% borrow tools from neighbors 100% borrow money from neighbors	Not high level of community 44% know > 20% by first name 76% happy to live there 52% trust neighbors 4% feel secure 70% borrow tools from neighbors 22% borrow money from neighbors

Note: Rp = rupiah, Indonesia's basic monetary unit.

Source: Teferi, Newman, and Matan, 2016

Table A.4: Sustainability of Arat Kilo slum settlement and Ginfle high-rise condominiums, Addis Ababa, Ethiopia.

Parameter	Slum Settlement	High-Rise Condominiums
Resource consumption and environmental footprint	60% solid waste collected 210 L liquid waste/household/day (65% release wastewater directly into river) 22% use fuelwood 30% use kerosene 37% use electricity Environmental health very poor	90% solid waste collected 175 L liquid waste/household/day 3% use fuelwood 10% use kerosene 80% use electricity Environmental health relatively good

continued on page 190

Table A.4 *continued*

Parameter	Slum Settlement	High-Rise Condominiums
Livability: economic	30% employed in private business, government, and NGOs 30% self-employed (informal activities) 29% unemployed 3% pensioners Average income Br10,560	45% employed in private business, government, and NGOs 43% self-employed (informal activities) 7% unemployed 5% pensioners Average income Br17,600
Livability: housing	Constructed from wood and mud Cooking and sleeping take place in same room 70% government owned No bathrooms; pit latrines and communal electric meters 43% wish to live there with minor improvement 30% need everything unchanged	Constructed from concrete blocks Separate bed and kitchen rooms available 100% privately owned Privately owned bathrooms and electric meters
Livability: education	67% primary school and below	30% primary school and below
Livability: community	High level of community 80% happy to live there 95% feel secure 93% enjoy access to at least one informal borrowing or lending network 97% trust neighbors	Low level of community 50% happy to live there 7% feel secure 42% enjoy access to at least one informal borrowing or lending network 34% trust neighbors 60% have social tie with previous communities

Note: Br = birr, Ethiopia's basic monetary unit; L = liters.

Source: Teferi, Newman, and Matan, 2016

2. Metabolism of Resource and Waste Flows in Perth with Urban Fabric Types

Table A.5: Resource input variations between urban fabric types in Perth.

INPUT (Per Person per Year)	Automobile City	Transit City	Walking City
Resources			
Fuel (MJ)	50,000	35,000	20,000
Power (MJ)	9,240	9,240	9,240
Gas (MJ)	4,900	2,940	2,940
Total energy (GJ)	**64.14**	**47.18**	**32.18**
Water (kL)	70	42	35
Food (kg)	451	451	451
Land (m²)	547	214	133
Urban footprint (ha)	2.29	1.97	1.78
Basic Raw Materials (BRM) for New Building Types per Person			
Sand (T)	111	73	57
Limestone (T)	67	44	34
Clay (T)	44	29	23
Rock (T)	66	43	33
Total BRM (T)	**288**	**189**	**147**

Note: GJ = gigajoules; ha = hectares; kg = kilograms; kL = kiloliters; m² = square meters; MJ = megajoules; T = metric tons.

Source: Thomson and Newman, 2017

Table A.6: Waste output variations between urban fabric types in Perth.

OUTPUT (Per Person per Year)	Automobile City	Transit City	Walking City
Greenhouse gases (fuel, power, gas) (T)	8.01	5.89	4.03
Waste heat (GJ)	64.14	47.18	32.18
Sewage, including storm water (kL)	80	80	80
Construction and demolition (C&D) waste (T)	0.96	0.57	0.38
Household waste (T)	0.63	0.56	0.49

Note: GJ = gigajoules; kL = kiloliters; T = metric tons.

Source: Thomson and Newman, 2017

Notes

Introduction: Urban Resilience: Cities of Fear and Hope

1. 100 Resilient Cities, http://www.100resilientcities.org/#/-_/.
2. Carbon Tracker Initiative, "Unburnable Carbon—Are the World's Financial Markets Carrying a Carbon Bubble?," 2012, http://www.carbontracker.org/wp-content /uploads/2014/09/Unburnable-Carbon-Full-rev2-1.pdf; Carbon Tracker Initiative, "Stranded Assets," 2014, accessed April 28, 2015, http://www.carbontracker.org/resources/; Tony Seba, "Clean Disruption of Energy and Transportation," accessed September 2, 2015, http://tonyseba.com/portfolio-item/clean-disruption-of-energy-and-transportation/; Tony Seba, *Clean Disruption of Energy and Transportation: How Silicon Valley Will Make Oil, Nuclear, Natural Gas, Coal, Electric Utilities, and Conventional Cars Obsolete by 2030* (Silicon Valley, CA: Clean Planet Ventures, 2014), http://www.tonyseba.com; *Economist*, "How to Lose Half a Trillion Euros: Europe's Electricity Providers Face an Existential Threat," October 12, 2013, http://www.economist.com/news/briefing/21587782 -europes-electricity-providers-face-existential-threat-how-lose-half-trillion-euros.
3. Carbon Tracker Initiative, "Stranded Assets"; Carbon Tracker Initiative, "Unburnable Carbon"; Seba, "Clean Disruption" (Web page); Seba, *Clean Disruption* (book); *Economist*, "How to Lose Half a Trillion Euros"; International Energy Agency, "World Energy Outlook 2015: Energy and Climate Change Special Report" (Paris: International Energy Agency, 2015).
4. Laura J. Nelson, "Los Angeles Area Can Claim the Worst Traffic in America. Again," *Los Angeles Times*, March 15, 2016, http://www.latimes.com/local/lanow/la-me-ln-la-worst -traffic-20160314-story.html.
5. Adam Nagourney, "The Capital of Car Culture, Los Angeles Warms to Mass Transit," *New York Times*, July 20, 2016, http://www.nytimes.com/2016/07/21/us/the-capital-of -car-culture-los-angeles-warms-to-mass-transit.html.
6. Jared M. Diamond, *Collapse: How Societies Choose to Fail or Succeed* (New York: Viking, 2005).
7. Nick Bostrom, "Existential Risk Prevention as Global Priority," *Global Policy* 4, no. 1 (February 2013): 15–31, doi:10.1111/1758-5899.12002. The Web site of Oxford

University's Future of Humanity Institute (http://www.existential-risk.org) lists, with links, the two dozen most important papers written on existential risk.

8. Nick Bostrom, "Existential Risks: Analyzing Human Extinction Scenarios and Related Hazards," *Journal of Evolution and Technology* 9, no. 1 (2002), http://www.nickbostrom.com/existential/risks.html.

9. United Nations Human Settlements Programme (UN-Habitat), "Energy," http://unhabitat.org/urban-themes/energy/.

10. United Nations Department of Economic and Social Affairs, Population Division, "Population 2030: Demographic Challenges and Opportunities for Sustainable Development Planning," ST/ESA/SER.A/389 (New York: United Nations, 2015), 37.

11. Peter Hall, *Cities in Civilisation: Culture, Innovation, and Urban Order* (London: Weidenfeld & Nicolson, 1998); Robert Friedel, *A Culture of Improvement: Technology and the Western Millennium* (Cambridge, MA: MIT Press, 2007); Lewis Mumford, *The City in History: Its Origins, Its Transformations, and Its Prospects* (Harmondsworth: Penguin Books, 1991); T. J. Gorringe, *A Theology of the Built Environment: Justice, Empowerment, Redemption* (Cambridge: Cambridge University Press, 2002), 140.

12. Ed Mazria, *Urban Land* 35 (November–December 2007).

13. Sarah Parsons, "Three Key Battlegrounds for Cities in the War against Climate Change," *GreenBiz*, July 21, 2016, https://www.greenbiz.com/article/3-key-battlegrounds-cities-war-against-climate-change.

14. Bruce Katz, "Devolution for an Urban Age: City Power and Problem-Solving," *Metropolitan Revolution* (blog), Brookings Institution, March 25, 2016, https://www.brookings.edu/blog/metropolitan-revolution/2016/03/25/devolution-for-an-urban-age-city-power-and-problem-solving/.

15. Laurie Mazur, "Bounce Forward: Urban Resilience in the Age of Climate Change," strategy paper from Island Press and the Kresge Foundation, 2015, https://islandpress.org/resources/KresgeBrochure-framing-doc.pdf.

16. "1.5 Degrees: Meeting the Challenges of the Paris Agreement," international conference, University of Oxford, September 20–22, 2016, http://www.1point5degrees.org.uk/.

17. Brian Walker and David Salt, with foreword by Walter Reid, *Resilience Thinking: Sustaining Ecosystems and People in a Changing World* (Washington, DC: Island Press, 2006), xiii; Tabatha J. Wallington, Richard J. Hobbs, and Susan A. Moore, "Implications of Current Ecological Thinking for Biodiversity Conservation: A Review of the Salient Issues," *Ecology and Society* 10, no. 1 (2005): 15.

18. This definition of sustainability for cities is from Peter Newman and Jeffrey Kenworthy, *Sustainability and Cities: Overcoming Automobile Dependence* (Washington, DC: Island Press, 1999). In other books, we have looked at the ecosystems and biodiversity that are part of city functions. See Peter Newman and Isabella Jennings, *Cities as Sustainable Ecosystems: Principles and Practices* (Washington, DC: Island Press, 2008); Timothy Beatley and Kristy Manning, *The Ecology of Place: Planning for Environment, Economy, and Community* (Washington, DC: Island Press, 1997); and Timothy Beatley and Peter Newman,

"Biophilic Cities Are Sustainable, Resilient Cities," *Sustainability* 5 (2013): 3328–3345, doi:10.3390/su5083328.

19. Data on fuel use in cities are from Peter Newman and Jeffrey Kenworthy, *The End of Automobile Dependence: How Cities Are Moving Beyond Car-Based Planning* (Washington, DC: Island Press, 2015); J. R. Kenworthy et al., *An International Sourcebook of Automobile Dependence in Cities, 1960–1990* (Boulder: University Press of Colorado, 1999); Peter Newman and Jeffrey Kenworthy, "Greening Urban Transportation," chap. 4 in *State of the World 2007: Our Urban Future*, by the Worldwatch Institute (New York: W. W. Norton & Company, 2007); and Reid Ewing et al., *Growing Cooler: The Evidence on Urban Development and Climate Change* (Washington, DC: Urban Land Institute, 2007).

20. Other books include Newman and Kenworthy, *Sustainability and Cities*; Newman and Jennings, *Cities as Sustainable Ecosystems*; and Timothy Beatley's *Green Urbanism: Learning from European Cities* (Washington, DC: Island Press, 1999) and *Biophilic Cities: Integrating Nature into Urban Design and Planning* (Washington, DC: Island Press, 2011). There are now too many books on the topic to include a full list. A good resource on the planning literature is http://www.planetizen.com.

21. In 1996, Lyle published *Regenerative Design for Sustainable Development* (Hoboken, NJ: John Wiley & Sons), the first comprehensive compendium of regenerative design.

22. For example, see Fiona Woo, *Regenerative Urban Development* (Hamburg: World Future Council, 2014); Chrisna du Plessis, "Towards a Regenerative Paradigm for the Built Environment," *Building Research & Information* 40, no. 1 (2012): 7–22, doi:10.1080 /09613218.2012.628548; Dominique Hes and Chrisna du Plessis, *Designing for Hope: Pathways to Regenerative Sustainability* (Boca Raton, FL: Taylor & Francis, 2014), and Herbert Girardet, "Regenerative Cities" (Hamburg: World Future Council, 2010), https://www.worldfuturecouncil.org/file/2016/01/WFC_2010_Regenerative_Cities.pdf, accessed October 17, 2016.

23. See Research & Degrowth, http://www.degrowth.org/.

24. United Nations Environment Programme, "Decoupling Natural Resource Use and Environmental Impacts from Economic Growth," Report of the Working Group on Decoupling to the International Resource Panel, by M. Fischer-Kowalski et al. (Nairobi: United Nations Environment Programme, 2011), http://www.unep.org/resourcepanel /decoupling/files/pdf/decoupling_report_english.pdf; United Nations Environment Programme, "City-Level Decoupling: Urban Resource Flows and the Governance of Infrastructure Transitions," Report of the Working Group on Cities of the International Resource Panel, by M. Swilling et al. (Nairobi: United Nations Environment Programme, 2013), http://unep.org/resourcepanel-old/portals/24102/pdfs/Cities-Full_Report.pdf; and Ernst Ulrich von Weizsäcker et al., *Factor Five: Transforming the Global Economy through 80% Improvements in Resource Productivity* (London: Earthscan, 2009), 277.

25. Tim Jackson, "The Myth of Decoupling," chap. 5 in *Prosperity without Growth: Economics for a Finite Planet* (London: Earthscan, 2009).

26. United Nations General Assembly, "The Road to Dignity by 2030: Ending Poverty,

Transforming All Lives, and Protecting the Planet," Synthesis Report of the Secretary-General on the Post-2015 Sustainable Development Agenda (New York: United Nations, December 4, 2014), 34, http://www.un.org/ga/search/view_doc.asp?symbol =A/69/700&Lang=E.

27. United Nations, "The Millennium Development Goals Report 2015." (New York: United Nations, 2015).

28. The notion of decoupling is based on the same idea as the economic theory of the Environmental Kondratieff Curve (EKC), which shows that as wealth grows, people increasingly choose environmental quality once their basic needs have been met. Decoupling is not only happening but happening earlier than expected in many parts of the world, indicating that there is more to this process than just simply getting wealthier. Perhaps one very key finding in a 2012 report by the Asian Development Bank, "Part 1—Special Chapter: Green Urbanization in Asia," in *Key Indicators for Asia and the Pacific 2012* (Mandaluyong City, Manila: Asian Development Bank, 2012), is that the EKC was related to how quickly urbanization is taking place, as it is in cities that the phenomenon is most easily observed.

29. World Economic Forum, Global Agenda Council on the Future of Cities, "Top Ten Urban Innovations" (Geneva: World Economic Forum, October 2015), http://www3 .weforum.org/docs/Top_10_Emerging_Urban_Innovations_report_2010_20.10.pdf.

Chapter 1: Invest in Renewable and Distributed Energy

1. Bloomberg New Energy Finance (BNEF), "New Energy Outlook 2015: Long-Term Projections of the Global Energy Sector" (New York: Bloomberg L.P., 2015); Bloomberg New Energy Finance (BNEF), "New Energy Outlook 2016: Powering a Changing World" (New York: Bloomberg L.P., 2016), https://www.bloomberg.com/company /new-energy-outlook.

2. Kari Alanne and Arto Saari, "Distributed Energy Generation and Sustainable Development," *Renewable and Sustainable Energy Reviews* 10, no. 6 (December 2006): 539–558, doi:10.1016/j.rser.2004.11.004.

3. BNEF, "New Energy Outlook 2015"; BNEF, "New Energy Outlook 2016."

4. U.S. Department of Energy, "Wind Vision: A New Era for Wind Power in the United States" (Washington, DC: U.S. Department of Energy, Office of Energy Efficiency and Renewable Energy, March 2015), http://energy.gov/eere/wind/wind-vision.

5. U.S. Department of Energy, "Unlocking Our Nation's Wind Potential" (Washington, DC: U.S. Department of Energy, Office of Energy Efficiency and Renewable Energy, May 19, 2015), http://energy.gov/eere/articles/unlocking-our-nation-s-wind-potential.

6. Björn Nykvist and Måns Nilsson, "Rapidly Falling Costs of Battery Packs for Electric Vehicles," *Nature Climate Change* 5 (2015): 329–332, doi:10.1038/nclimate2564.

7. Jemma Green and Peter Newman, "Citizen Utilities: The Emerging Power Paradigm, a Case Study in Perth, Australia," *Energy Policy* (2017), forthcoming.

8. Joseph L. Bower and Clayton M. Christensen, "Disruptive Technologies: Catching the

Wave," *Harvard Business Review* 73, no. 1 (January–February 1995): 43–54; Tony Seba, *Clean Disruption of Energy and Transportation: How Silicon Valley Will Make Oil, Nuclear, Natural Gas, Coal, Electric Utilities, and Conventional Cars Obsolete by 2030* (Silicon Valley, CA: Clean Planet Ventures, 2014), http://www.tonyseba.com; Tony Seba, "Clean Disruption of Energy and Transportation," accessed September 2, 2015, http://tonyseba .com/portfolio-item/clean-disruption-of-energy-and-transportation/; Jemma Green and Peter Newman, "Disruptive Innovation, Stranded Assets, and Forecasting: The Rise and Rise of Renewable Energy," *Journal of Sustainable Finance & Investment* (2016): 1–19, doi:10.1080/20430795.2016.1265410.

9. SolarQuotes, "Solar Battery Storage Comparison Table," http://www.solarquotes.com .au/battery-storage/comparison-table.

10. Galen Barbose et al., "Tracking the Sun VI: An Historical Summary of the Installed Price of Photovoltaics in the United States from 1998 to 2012," LBNL-6350E (Berkeley, CA: Lawrence Berkeley National Laboratory, July 2013), https://emp.lbl.gov/sites/all/files /lbnl-6350e.pdf.

11. J. Goldemberg, "Leapfrog Energy Technologies," *Energy Policy* 26, no. 10 (August 1998): 729–741; *Nature*, "Leapfrogging the Power Grid," editorial, *Nature* 427, no. 661 (February 19, 2004), doi:10.1038/427661a.

12. Moulton, "Perth Could Soon Be the First City to Be Completely Solar Powered," News.com.au, October 26, 2015, http://www.news.com.au/technology/environment /climate-change/perth-could-soon-be-the-first-city-to-be-completely-solar-powered /news-story/8fd36f41526e7619bd3db3b7f20fa0c4?csp=9920c057b85ae6a12fb a983c70c68e13.

13. Peter Bronski et al., "The Economics of Load Defection" (Boulder, CO: Rocky Mountain Institute, April 2015), http://www.rmi.org/cms/Download.aspx?id=11580 &file=2015-05_RMI-TheEconomicsOfLoadDefection-FullReport.pdf.

14. Fereidoon P. Sioshansi, *Distributed Generation and Its Implications for the Utility Industry* (Cambridge: Elsevier, Academic Press), 2014.

15. Damien P. Giurco, Stuart B. White, and Rodney A. Stewart, "Smart Metering and Water End-Use Data: Conservation Benefits and Privacy Risks," *Water* 2, no. 3 (2010): 461–467, doi:10.3390/w2030461.

16. B. Williams, "Hopetoun Infrastructure Study" (Perth: Landcorp, Government of Western Australia, 2008).

17. Bronski et al., "Economics of Load Defection"; Andrew Stock, Petra Stock, and Veena Sahajwalla, "Powerful Potential: Battery Storage for Renewable Energy and Electric Cars" (Sydney: Climate Council of Australia, 2015), https://www.climatecouncil.org .au/uploads/ebdfcdf89a6ce85c4c19a5f6a78989d7.pdf; World Bank, "Toward a Sustainable Energy Future for All: Directions for the World Bank's Energy Sector" (Washington, DC: World Bank Group, 2013), http://www-wds.worldbank.org/external/default /WDSContentServer/WDSP/IB/2013/07/17/000456286_20130717103746 /Rendered/PDF/795970SST0SecM00box377380B00PUBLIC0.pdf; Tim Flannery and Veena Sahajwalla, "The Critical Decade: Australia's Future—Solar Energy," Aus-

tralian Climate Commission, September 2, 2013, http://www.climatecouncil.org.au /uploads/497bcd1f058be45028e3df9d020ed561.pdf.

18. The Perth story is expanded in Green and Newman, "Disruptive Innovation," and Green and Newman, "Citizen Utilities."

19. Peter Newton and Peter Newman, "Critical Connections: The Role of the Built Environment Sector in Delivering Green Cities and a Green Economy," *Sustainability* 7 (2015): 9417–9443, doi:10.3390/su7079417.

20. Josh Byrne & Associates, Web site for Josh's House, http://joshshouse.com.au.

21. LandCorp, "Shared Solar Power on Trial in Australian First," Innovation WGV, September 9, 2015, http://www.landcorp.com.au/innovation/wgv/Latest/Shared-solar -power-on-trial-in-Australian-first/; Moulton, "Perth Could Soon Be the First."

22. Andy Extance, "The Future of Cryptocurrencies: Bitcoin and Beyond," *Nature* 526, no. 7571 (October 1, 2015): 21–23, doi:10.1038/526021a.

23. Aviva Rutkin, "Blockchain-Based Microgrid Gives Power to Consumers in New York," *New Scientist*, March 2, 2016, https://www.newscientist.com/article/2079334 -blockchain-based-microgrid-gives-power-to-consumers-in-new-york/?utm_source =NSNS&utm_medium=SOC&utm_campaign=hoot&cmpid=SOC%7CNSNS %7C2016-GLOBAL-hoot.

24. Özgür Yildiz et al., "Renewable Energy Cooperatives as Gatekeepers or Facilitators? Recent Developments in Germany and a Multidisciplinary Research Agenda," *Energy Research & Social Science* 6 (March 2015): 59–73, doi:10.1016/j.erss.2014.12.001.

25. Sustainable Built Environment National Research Centre, "Perth Airport Sustainability Research Project," Overview Report (Brisbane: Sustainable Built Environment National Research Centre, 2017), http://www.sbenrc.com.au.

26. Peter Fox-Penner, "Why Apple Is Getting into the Energy Business," *Harvard Business Review*, November 25, 2016, https://hbr.org/2016/11/why-apple-is-getting-into-the -energy-business.

27. Gerard Drew, "Zero Carbon Australia: Renewable Energy Superpower" (Melbourne: Beyond Zero Emissions, 2015), http://bze.org.au.

28. Gunter Pauli, *The Blue Economy: 10 Years, 100 Innovations, 100 Million Jobs* (Brookline, MA: Paradigm, 2010).

29. See Wang Wei and Gong Jinlong, "Methanation of Carbon Dioxide: An Overview," *Frontiers of Chemical Science and Engineering* 5, no. 1 (March 2011): 2–10, doi:10.1007/s11705-010-0528-3; Peter Newman and Jeffrey Kenworthy, *The End of Automobile Dependence: How Cities Are Moving Beyond Car-Based Planning* (Washington, DC: Island Press, 2015).

30. Drew, "Zero Carbon Australia."

31. EcoDistricts, http://www.ecodistricts.org.

32. Jan Scheurer and Peter Newman, "Vauban: A European Model Bridging the Green and Brown Agendas," unpublished case study prepared for *Planning Sustainable Cities: Global Report on Human Settlements 2009*, by the United Nations Human Settlements Programme (UN-Habitat) (London: Earthscan and United Nations Human Settlements Pro-

gramme, 2009), http://unhabitat.org/books/global-report-on-human-settlements-2009
-planning-sustainable-cities/; Isabelle de Pommereau, "New German Community Models
Car-Free Living," *Christian Science Monitor*, December 20, 2006.

33. Solar Austin, http://www.solaraustin.org/.

34. Sacramento Municipal Utility District, https://www.smud.org/en/index.htm.

35. Adelaide City Council, "Carbon Neutral Adelaide," http://www.adelaidecitycouncil
.com/city-living/sustainable-adelaide/carbon-neutral-adelaide/.

36. Laurie Guevara-Stone, "Barcelona: Spain's City of the Sun," RenewEconomy, August
12, 2014, http://reneweconomy.com.au/barcelona-spains-city-of-the-sun-54062/.

37. See Peter Newman and Isabella Jennings, *Cities as Sustainable Ecosystems: Principles and
Practices* (Washington, DC: Island Press, 2008).

38. See Vanessa Rauland and Peter Newman, *Decarbonising Cities: Mainstreaming Low Carbon Urban Development* (London: Springer, 2015).

39. Laurie Guevara-Stone, "How Malmö, Sweden Is Leading Way on Sustainability,"
RenewEconomy, September 24, 2014, http://reneweconomy.com.au/malmo-sweden
-leading-way-70597/.

40. Sacramento Municipal Utility District, https://www.smud.org/en/index.htm.

41. Bobby Magill, "We Could Put Utility-Scale Solar Plants in Our Cities," *Grist*, March 17,
2015, http://grist.org/business-technology/we-could-put-utility-scale-solar-plants-in
-our-cities/.

42. Instituto de Turismo de España, "The Island of El Hierro, a Model of Sustainable Tourism," http://www.spain.info/en/reportajes/el_hierro_modelo_de_turismosostenible.html.

43. Canada Solar Energy, *Toronto Citizens Take Control of Their Electricity Needs*, video, July 24, 2014, https://www.youtube.com/watch?v=8GpUBkb4Gh4; see also
C40 Cities Climate Leadership Group, "Case Study: Toronto's Eco-Roof Incentive
Program," January 16, 2015, http://www.c40.org/case_studies/toronto-s-eco-roof
-incentive-program.

44. "Brøset: Towards a Carbon Neutral Housing Settlement" (blog), https://brozed.wordpress
.com/project-examples/kronsberg-hannover/.

45. Peter Droege, *Urban Energy Transition: From Fossil Fuels to Renewable Power* (Oxford:
Elsevier, 2008).

46. Luke Sussams and James Leaton, "Expect the Unexpected: The Disruptive Power of Low-Carbon Technology," Carbon Tracker Initiative, February 2017, http://www.carbontracker.org
/wp-content/uploads/2017/02/Expect-the-Unexpected_CTI_Imperial.pdf.

Chapter 2: Create Sustainable Mobility Systems

1. EV-Volumes.com: The Electric Vehicle World Sales Database, http://www.ev
-volumes.com.

2. Kelly Carlin, Bodhi Rader, and Greg Rucks, "Interoperable Transit Data: Enabling a
Shift to Mobility as a Service" (Snowmass, CO: Rocky Mountain Institute, October
2015), http://www.rmi.org/mobility_itd.

3. Michael Kintner-Meyer, Kevin Schneider, and Robert Pratt, "Impacts Assessment of Plug-in Hybrid Vehicles on Electric Utilities and Regional U.S. Power Grids: Part 1: Technical Analysis," U.S. Department of Energy Contract no. DE-AC05-76RL01830 (Richland, WA: Pacific Northwest National Laboratory, November 2007).

4. International Energy Agency, "Global EV Outlook 2016: Beyond One Million Electric Cars" (Paris: International Energy Agency, 2016).

5. Lucy Wang, "Solar-Powered Totem Streetlight Makes Cities Smarter, Cleaner, and Better Connected," Inhabitat.com (blog), November 16, 2016, http://inhabitat.com/solar-powered-totem-wants-to-make-cities-smarter-cleaner-and-better-connected/.

6. City of Fremantle, Western Australia, "Policy: SG53—Parklets," https://www.fremantle.wa.gov.au/sites/default/files/sharepointdocs/Parklets-C-000081.pdf; "Wray Ave Solar Parklet," https://www.facebook.com/wrayavesolarparklet/.

7. See the discussion of the entrepreneur rail model later in the chapter.

8. Amela Ajanovic, "Biofuels versus Food Production: Does Biofuels Production Increase Food Prices?," *Energy* 36, no. 4 (April 2011): 2070–2076, doi:10.1016/j.energy.2010.05.019.

9. Lisa Mastny, ed. "Biofuels for Transportation: Global Potential and Implications for Sustainable Agriculture and Energy in the 21st Century," report prepared by the Worldwatch Institute for the German Federal Ministry of Food, Agriculture and Consumer Protection (BMELV), in cooperation with the Agency for Technical Cooperation (GTZ) and the Agency of Renewable Resources (FNR) (Washington, DC: Worldwatch Institute, 2006), http://www.worldwatch.org/system/files/EBF008_1.pdf.

10. Roberto Schaeffer et al., "Transport," chap. 8 in *Climate Change 2014: Mitigation of Climate Change. Contribution of Working Group III to the Fifth Assessment Report of the Intergovernmental Panel on Climate Change* (Cambridge: Cambridge University Press, 2015).

11. Richard Gilbert and Anthony Perl, *Transport Revolutions: Moving People and Freight without Oil* (London: Earthscan, 2007).

12. Danny Bradbury, "Airships Float Back to the Future," BusinessGreen.com, September 2, 2008.

13. Cadie Thompson, "It's Not Just Cars—Electric Airplanes Are Coming, Too," *Business Insider Australia*, June 20, 2016, http://www.businessinsider.com.au/its-not-just-cars-electric-airplanes-are-coming-too-2016-6.

14. Alan C. McKinnon, "Decoupling of Road Freight Transport and Economic Growth Trends in the UK: An Exploratory Analysis," *Transport Reviews* 27, no. 1 (2007): 37–64, doi:10.1080/01441640600825952.

15. Dora Marinova, Amzad Hossain, and Popie Hossain-Rhaman, "Sustaining Local Lifestyle through Self Reliance: Core Principles," chap. 40 in *Sharing Wisdom for Our Future: Environmental Education in Action: Proceedings of the 2006 Conference of the Australian Association of Environmental Education*, ed. Sandra Wooltorton and Dora Marinova. (Cotton Tree, Queensland: Australian Association of Environmental Education, 2006).

16. U.S. Department of Energy, Office of Energy Efficiency and Renewable Energy, Alternative Fuels Data Center, "Natural Gas Vehicles," http://www.afdc.energy.gov/vehicles/natural_gas.html.

17. Robert Salter, Subash Dhar, and Peter Newman, *Technologies for Climate Change Mitigation—Transport Sector*, TNA Guidebook Series (Roskilde, Denmark: UNEP Riso Centre on Energy, Climate and Sustainable Development, 2011).

18. Puregas Solutions, "Biogas Upgrading: Renewable Natural Gas," brochure, http://www.puregas-solutions.com/wp-content/uploads/2016/07/PUR-US-Brochure.pdf.

19. Wang Wei and Gong Jinlong, "Methanation of Carbon Dioxide: An Overview," *Frontiers of Chemical Science and Engineering* 5, no. 1 (March 2011): 2–10, doi:10.1007/s11705-010-0528-3.

20. Peter Calthorpe and Jerry Walters, "Autonomous Vehicles: Hype and Potential," *Public Square*, Congress for the New Urbanism, September 6, 2016.

21. Carmel DeAmicis, "Uber Says There Have Been Millions of Trips on UberPool, Its Carpool Option," *Recode*, April 16, 2015, http://www.recode.net/2015/4/16/11561556/.

22. Brendan Gogarty, "'Killer Robots' Hit the Road—and the Law Has Yet to Catch Up," *The Conversation*, November 8, 2015.

23. Peter Newman and Jeffrey Kenworthy, *The End of Automobile Dependence: How Cities Are Moving Beyond Car-Based Planning* (Washington, DC: Island Press, 2015).

24. Carlin, Rader, and Rucks, "Interoperable Transit Data." An example of a new shared mobility system is GoJek in Jakarta, which uses smart technology to enable a shared scooter system. Nick Wailes, "The Limits of Silicon Valley: How Indonesia's Go-Jek Is Beating Uber," *The Conversation*, November 24, 2016, https://theconversation.com/the-limits-of-silicon-valley-how-indonesias-gojek-is-beating-uber-69286?utm_medium=email&utm_campaign=The%20Weekend%20Conversation%20-%206162&utm_content=The%20Weekend%20Conversation%20-%206162+CID_fb74551f9c0a6dd07e3b16e3adb1059e&utm_source=campaign_monitor&utm_term=The%20limits%20of%20Silicon%20Valley%20how%20Indonesias%20GoJek%20is%20beating%20Uber.

25. Newman and Kenworthy, *End of Automobile Dependence*.

26. Peter Newman, Jeffrey Kenworthy, and Garry Glazebrook, "Peak Car Use and the Rise of Global Rail: Why This Is Happening and What It Means for Large and Small Cities," *Journal of Transportation Technologies* 3, no. 4 (October 2013): 272–287, doi:10.4236/jtts.2013.34029.

27. Newman and Kenworthy, *End of Automobile Dependence*.

28. John Pucher and Ralph Buehler, "Safer Cycling through Improved Infrastructure," editorial, *American Journal of Public Health* 106, no. 12 (December 2016): 2089–2091, doi:10.2105/AJPH.2016.303507; Jan Gehl, *Cities for People* (Washington, DC: Island Press, 2010); Annie Matan and Peter Newman, *People Cities: The Life and Legacy of Jan Gehl* (Washington, DC: Island Press, 2016).

29. Pucher and Buehler, "Safer Cycling."

30. Mikael Colville-Andersen, "Meteoric Rise in Bicycle Traffic in Copenhagen," Copenhag-

enize Design Co. (blog), November 4, 2016, http://www.copenhagenize.com/2016/11/meteoric-rise-in-bicycle-traffic-in.html.

31. Cesare Marchetti, "Anthropological Invariants in Travel Behavior," *Technological Forecasting and Social Change* 47, no. 1 (September 1994): 75–88, doi:10.1016/0040-1625(94)90041-8; Y. Zahavi and A. Talvitie, "Regularities in Travel Time and Money Expenditures," *Transportation Research Record* 750 (1980): 13–19.

32. Newman and Kenworthy, *End of Automobile Dependence.*

33. James McIntosh, Peter Newman, and Garry Glazebrook, "Why Fast Trains Work: An Assessment of a Fast Regional Rail System in Perth, Australia," *Journal of Transportation Technologies* 3, no. 2A (May 2013): 37–47.

34. See the Cheonggyecheon, Seoul, story in Newman and Kenworthy, *End of Automobile Dependence*, and more freeway destruction literature in Alana Semuels, "Highways Destroyed America's Cities: Can Tearing Them Down Bring Revitalization?," *Atlantic Monthly*, November 25, 2015.

35. Michael Patrick Kane, "Devising Public Transport Systems for Twenty-First Century Economically Productive Cities—the Proposed Knowledge Ring for Perth," *Australian Planner* 47, no. 2 (2010): 75–84, doi:10.1080/07293681003767777; Edward J. Malecki, "Cities and Regions Competing in the Global Economy: Knowledge and Local Development Policies," *Environment and Planning C: Government and Policy* 25, no. 5 (2007): 638–654, doi:10.1068/c0645; Tan Yigitcanlar, "Making Space and Place for the Knowledge Economy: Knowledge-Based Development of Australian Cities," *European Planning Studies* 18, no. 11 (2010): 1769–1786.

36. Jaison R. Abel, Ishita Dey, and Todd M. Gabe, "Productivity and the Density of Human Capital," *Journal of Regional Science* 52, no. 4 (October 2012): 562–586, doi:10.1111/j.1467-9787.2011.00742.x; Ash Amin and Patrick Cohendet, "Geographies of Knowledge Formation in Firms," *Industry and Innovation* 12, no. 4 (December 2005): 465–486, doi:10.1080/13662710500381658; Hans-Dieter Evers, Solvay Gerke, and Thomas Menkhoff, "Knowledge Clusters and Knowledge Hubs: Designing Epistemic Landscapes for Development," *Journal of Knowledge Management* 14, no. 5 (2010): 678–689, doi:10.1142/9789814343688_0002; Kevin Johnson, "The Geography of Melbourne's Knowledge Economy," in *Proceedings of the Third Knowledge Cities World Summit: From Theory to Practice*, ed. Tan Yigitcanlar, Peter Yates, and Klaus Kunzmann, 1055–1090 (Melbourne: World Capital Institute, City of Melbourne, and Office of Knowledge Capital, 2010).

37. Christopher B. Leinberger and Patrick Lynch, "Foot Traffic Ahead: Ranking Walkable Urbanism in America's Largest Metros" (Washington DC: George Washington University, School of Business, Center for Real Estate and Urban Analysis, 2014).

38. Richard Florida, *The Great Reset: How New Ways of Living and Working Drive Post-Crash Prosperity* (New York: HarperCollins, 2010).

39. Benjamin Davis, Tony Dutzik, and Phineas Baxandall, "Transportation and the New Generation: Why Young People Are Driving Less and What It Means for Transportation Policy" (San Francisco: Frontier Group and U.S. PIRG Education Fund, 2012).

40. Zlata Rodionova, "UberPool Gets More Than 1 Million Customers," *The Independent*, June 7, 2016.

41. Chuck Kooshian and Steve Winkelman, *Growing Wealthier: Smart Growth, Climate Change, and Prosperity* (Washington, DC: Center for Clean Air Policy, January 2011); Great Data, "CBSA Codes Database," http://greatdata.com/cbsa-data.

42. Newman and Kenworthy, *End of Automobile Dependence*.

43. McIntosh, Newman, and Glazebrook, "Why Fast Trains Work."

44. Peter Newman et al., "The Entrepreneur Rail Model: Tapping Private Investment for New Urban Rail" (Perth: Curtin University Sustainability Policy [CUSP] Institute, February 2016), http://www.curtin.edu.au/research/cusp/local/docs/Rail_Model _Report.pdf.

45. Peter Newman, "Australia Needs to Follow the US in Funding Urban Rail Projects," *The Conversation*, August 31, 2016.

46. Reid Ewing et al., "Testing Newman and Kenworthy's Theory of Density and Automobile Dependence," *Journal of Planning Education and Research* 52 (January 2017): 1–16, doi:10.1177/0739456X16688767.

47. Carey Curtis, John L. Renne, and Luca Bertolini, eds., *Transit Oriented Development: Making It Happen* (London: Ashgate, 2009).

48. Center for Transit-Oriented Development and Reconnecting America (CTODRA), "Hidden in Plain Sight: Capturing the Demand for Housing Near Transit," September 3, 2004, http://reconnectingamerica.org/assets/Uploads/2004Ctodreport.pdf; Jan Gehl and Lars Gemzøe, *Public Spaces, Public Life* (Copenhagen: Danish Architectural Press, 2004).

49. Curtis, Renne, and Bertolini, *Transit Oriented Development*.

50. James McIntosh, Roman Trubka, and Peter Newman, "Can Value Capture Work in a Car Dependent City? Willingness to Pay for Transit Access in Perth, Western Australia," *Transportation Research—Part A* 67 (2014): 320–339, doi:10.1016/j.tra.2014.07.008.

51. Shishir Mathur and Christopher E. Ferrell, "Effect of Suburban Transit Oriented Developments on Residential Property Values," MTI Report 08-07, June 2009, Mineta Transportation Institute and San Jose State University, http://www.reconnectingamerica.org /assets/Uploads/effectssuburbantransit2009.pdf.

52. Hank Dittmar and Gloria Ohland, eds., *The New Transit Town: Best Practices in Transit-Oriented Development* (Washington, DC: Island Press, 2003); CTODRA, "Hidden in Plain Sight"; Roman Trubka, Peter Newman, and Darren Bilsborough, "The Costs of Urban Sprawl—Greenhouse Gases," *Environment Design Guide* 84 (2010): 1–16.

53. Gehl and Gemzøe, *Public Spaces, Public Life*; Jan Gehl, *Life Between Buildings: Using Public Space*, trans. Jo Koch (New York: Van Nostrand Reinhold, 1987); Gehl, *Cities for People*; Jan Gehl and Lars Gemzøe, *New City Spaces* (Copenhagen: Danish Architectural Press, 2000); Jan Gehl et al., "Places for People: Study Report" (Melbourne and Copenhagen: City of Melbourne and Gehl Architects, 2004); Jan Gehl et al., "Perth 2009: Public Spaces and Public Life: Study Report" (Perth and Copenhagen: City of Perth and Gehl Architects, 2009).

54. Gerhard P. Metschies, *Fuel Prices and Vehicle Taxation* (Eschborn, Germany: Deutsche Gesellschaft für Technische Zusammenarbeit [GTZ] GmbH, 2001); Richard C. Porter, *Economics at the Wheel: The Costs of Cars and Drivers* (London: Academic Press, 2001).

55. Michael Sivak and Brandon Schoettle, "What Individual Americans Can Do to Assist in Meeting the Paris Agreement," UMTRI-2016-7 (Ann Arbor: University of Michigan, Transportation Research Institute, February 2016).

56. Todd Litman, "Changing Vehicle Travel Price Sensitivities: The Rebounding Rebound Effect" (Victoria, British Columbia: Victoria Transport Policy Institute, September 12, 2012), http://www.vtpi.org/VMT_Elasticities.pdf.

57. Randy Salzman, "Travel Smart: A Marketing Program Empowers Citizens to Be a Part of the Solution in Improving the Environment," *Mass Transit* 34, no. 2 (2008): 8–11; Randy Salzman, "Now That's What I Call Intelligent Transport . . . SmartTravel," *Thinking Highways*, 2008.

58. C. Ashton-Graham, "TravelSmart + TOD = Sustainability and Synergy," in Curtis, Renne, and Bertolini, *Transit Oriented Development*.

59. I. Ker, "North Brisbane Household TravelSmart: Peer Review and Evaluation, for Brisbane City Council" (Brisbane: Queensland Transport and Australian Greenhouse Office, 2008).

60. Western Australia Department of Transport, "TravelSmart Household Final Evaluation Report Murdoch Station Catchment (City of Melville 2007)" (Perth: Socialdata Australia, September 2009).

61. C. Ashton-Graham, "TravelSmart and LivingSmart Case Study—Western Australia," in *The Garnaut Climate Change Review*, ed. Ross Garnaut (Cambridge: Cambridge University Press, 2008), http://www.garnautreview.org.au/2008-review.html.

62. David Wake, "Reducing Car Commuting through Employer-Based Travel Planning in Perth, Australia," *TDM Review* 15, no. 1 (2007): 11–13.

63. Davis, Dutzik, and Baxandall, "Transportation and the New Generation."

Chapter 3: Foster Inclusive and Healthy Cities

1. United Nations Human Settlements Programme (UN-Habitat), *World Cities Report 2016: Urbanization and Development: Emerging Futures* (Nairobi: United Nations Human Settlements Programme, 2016), http://wcr.unhabitat.org/, 17.

2. World Health Organization, "Air Pollution Levels Rising in Many of the World's Poorest Cities," news release, May 12, 2016, http://www.who.int/mediacentre/news/releases/2016/air-pollution-rising/en/.

3. Todd Litman, "Truly Responsive and Inclusive Planning," *Planetizen* (blog), November 15, 2016, http://www.planetizen.com/node/89718.

4. Peter Newman and Jeffrey Kenworthy, *The End of Automobile Dependence: How Cities Are Moving Beyond Car-Based Planning* (Washington, DC: Island Press, 2015); Annie Matan et al., "Health, Transport, and Urban Planning: Quantifying the Links between Urban Assessment Models and Human Health," *Urban Policy and Research*

33, no. 2 (2015): 145–159, doi:10.1080/08111146.2014.990626; Roman Trubka, Peter Newman, and Darren Bilsborough, "The Costs of Urban Sprawl—Physical Activity Links to Healthcare Costs and Productivity," *Environment Design Guide* 85 (2010): 1–13.

5. UNESCO and UN Water, "Water Cooperation 2013," http://www.unwater.org /water-cooperation-2013/water-cooperation/facts-and-figures/en/.

6. Charles D. Ellison, "Infrastructure Failures, Like Flint, Are a Crisis for Black America," *The Root*, January 27, 2016, http://www.theroot.com/infrastructure-failures-like-flint -are-a-crisis-for-b-1790854028.

7. Franziska Schreiber and Alexander Carius, "The Inclusive City: Urban Planning for Diversity and Social Cohesion," chap. 18 in *Can a City Be Sustainable? (State of the World)* by Worldwatch Institute (Washington, DC: Island Press, 2016), 319.

8. National Equity Atlas, "Data Summaries: United States," http://nationalequityatlas.org /data-summaries.

9. Ibid.

10. Richard Jackson, preface to *Making Healthy Places: Designing and Building for Health, Well-being, and Sustainability*, ed. Andrew L. Dannenberg, Howard Frumkin, and Richard Jackson (Washington, DC: Island Press, 2011), xv.

11. John Mickey, "Six Health Benefits of Public Transportation," TransLoc, June 25, 2013, http://transloc.com/6-health-benefits-of-public-transportation/.

12. United Nations Department of Economic and Social Affairs, Population Division (ESCAP), "World Urbanization Prospects: The 2014 Revision, Highlights," ST/ESA /SER.A/352 (New York: United Nations, 2014).

13. Kirk Johnson, "Targeting Inequality, This Time on Public Transit," *New York Times*, February 28, 2015, http://mobile.nytimes.com/2015/03/01/us/targeting-inequality -this-time-on-public-transit.html.

14. Ibid.

15. Emma G. Fitzsimmons, "Advocates for New York's Working Poor Push for Discounted Transit Fares," *New York Times*, November 11, 2016, http://www.nytimes .com/2016/11/12/nyregion/advocates-for-new-yorks-working-poor-push-for -discounted-transit-fares.html.

16. Dennis Normile, "China Rethinks Cities," *Science* 352, no. 6288 (May 20, 2016): 916–918, doi:10.1126/science.352.6288.916.

17. National Association of City Transportation Officials (NACTO), "High-Quality Bike Facilities Increase Ridership and Make Biking Safer," July 20, 2016, http://nacto .org/2016/07/20/high-quality-bike-facilities-increase-ridership-make-biking-safer/.

18. Ibid.

19. Trubka, Newman, and Bilsborough, "Costs of Urban Sprawl—Physical Activity"; and a series of *The Lancet*, "Urban Design, Transport, and Health," September 23, 2016, http://www.thelancet.com/series/urban-design.

20. Neil B. Oldridge, "Economic Burden of Physical Inactivity: Healthcare Costs Associated with Cardiovascular Disease," *European Journal of Preventive Cardiology* (formerly *Euro-*

pean Journal of Cardiovascular Prevention and Rehabilitation) 15, no. 2 (2008): 130–139, doi:10.1097/HJR.0b013e3282f19d42.

21. Trubka, Newman, and Bilsborough, "Costs of Urban Sprawl—Physical Activity."

22. Vision Zero Network, http://visionzeronetwork.org/.

23. Annie Matan and Peter Newman, *People Cities: The Life and Legacy of Jan Gehl* (Washington, DC: Island Press, 2016), 131.

24. Gehl Studio NY and J. Max Bond Center on Design for the Just City, "Public Life & Urban Justice in NYC's Plazas" (New York: Gehl Studio NY and J. Max Bond Center on Design for the Just City, November 14, 2015), https://issuu.com/gehlarchitects/docs/nycplazastudy/c/smf4qso.

25. The study shows the value of groups such as New York City's Neighborhood Plaza Partnership; see http://neighborhoodplazapartnership.org/about/.

26. Cecil C. Konijnendijk et al., "Benefits of Urban Parks: A Systematic Review" (Copenhagen: International Federation of Parks and Recreation Administration, January 2013), http://www.worldurbanparks.org/images/Newsletters/IfpraBenefitsOfUrbanParks.pdf.

27. Ronald Sturm and Deborah Cohen, "Proximity to Urban Parks and Mental Health," *Journal of Mental Health Policy and Economics* 17, no. 1 (March 2014): 19–24, https://www.ncbi.nlm.nih.gov/pmc/articles/PMC4049158/.

28. City Parks Alliance, "Why Are Parks Important to Cities?," http://www.cityparksalliance.org/mayors-for-parks/why-are-parks-and-lwcf-important.

29. Matthew Desmond, *Evicted: Poverty and Profit in the American City* (New York: Crown, 2016), 300.

30. Ibid., 303.

31. Neil Smith, "There's No Such Thing as a Natural Disaster," *Understanding Katrina* (blog), Social Science Research Council, June 11, 2006, http://understandingkatrina.ssrc.org/Smith/.

32. For more on the Enterprise Green Communities program, see http://www.enterprisecommunity.org/solutions-and-innovation/green-communities.

33. Desmond, *Evicted*, 303.

34. Parul Sehgal, interview by Rachel Martin, *NPR Weekend Edition Sunday*, December 6, 2015, "How 'Resilience' Is Misunderstood When Talking about Racism," http://www.npr.org/2015/12/06/458662021/how-resilience-is-misunderstood-when-talking-about-racism.

35. Josh Feldman, "MSNBC Guest: Stop Using the Word 'Resilient' to Describe Katrina Victims," Mediaite, August 29, 2015, http://www.mediaite.com/tv/msnbc-guest-stop-using-the-word-resilient-to-describe-katrina-victims/.

36. David Uberti, "Ten Years after the Storm: Has New Orleans Learned the Lessons of Hurricane Katrina?," *The Guardian*, July 27, 2015, https://www.theguardian.com/cities/2015/jul/27/new-orleans-hurricane-katrina-10-years-lessons.

37. Smith, "No Such Thing as a Natural Disaster."

38. Ibid.

39. Ibid.

40. Garrett Jacobs, quoted in Meg Miller, "What Designers Should Do Now," *Fast Company*, November 10, 2016, https://www.fastcodesign.com/3065502/what-designers-should-do-now.

41. James Svara et al., "Advancing Social Equity as an Integral Dimension of Sustainability in Local Communities," *Cityscape: A Journal of Policy Development and Research* 17, no. 2 (2015): 140, https://www.huduser.gov/portal/periodicals/cityscpe/vol17num2/ch5.pdf.

42. Litman, "Truly Responsive and Inclusive Planning."

43. Jen Kinney, "Boston Resilience Blueprint Leads with Discussions of Race, Equity," Next City, November 21, 2016, https://nextcity.org/daily/entry/boston-resilience-plan-race-equity.

44. United Nations Human Settlements Programme (UN-Habitat), *State of the World's Cities 2012/2013: Prosperity of Cities* (Nairobi: United Nations Human Settlements Programme, 2013), https://sustainabledevelopment.un.org/content/documents/745habitat.pdf.

45. Stuart Merkel and Jane Otai, "Meeting the Health Needs of the Urban Poor in African Informal Settlements: Best Practices and Lessons Learned" (Nairobi: Jhpiego, June 2007).

46. United Nations Human Settlements Programme (UN-Habitat), *Planning Sustainable Cities: Global Report on Human Settlements 2009* (London: Earthscan and United Nations Human Settlements Programme, 2009), http://unhabitat.org/books/global-report-on-human-settlements-2009-planning-sustainable-cities/.

47. Peter Newman and Jeffrey Kenworthy, *Sustainability and Cities: Overcoming Automobile Dependence* (Washington DC: Island Press, 1999).

48. Peter Newman, "Bridging the Green and Brown Agendas," chap. 6 in UN-Habitat, *Planning Sustainable Cities.*

49. United Nations Environment Programme (UNEP), "City-Level Decoupling: Urban Resource Flows and the Governance of Infrastructure Transitions," report of the Working Group on Cities of the International Resource Panel, by M. Swilling et al. (Nairobi: United Nations Environment Programme, 2013), http://unep.org/resourcepanel-old/portals/24102/pdfs/Cities-Full_Report.pdf.

50. Newman and Kenworthy, *Sustainability and Cities.*

51. Zafu Teferi, Peter Newman, and Annie Matan, "Applying a Sustainable Development Model to Informal Settlements in Addis Ababa," chap. 8 in *Indian Ocean Futures: Communities, Sustainability, and Security*, ed. Thor Kerr and John Stephens (Newcastle upon Tyne: Cambridge Scholars Publishing, 2016).

52. Joo Wha Philip Bay has many designs in Singapore that retain traditional community facilities in high-rise form. See Joo Hwa Bay, "Singapore High-Rise with Traditional Qualities," *Nova Terra* 2, no. 4 (December 2002); Joo Hwa Bay and B. L. Ong, eds., *Tropical Sustainable Architecture: Social and Environmental Dimensions* (London: Architectural Press, 2006); Joo Hwa Bay, "Sustainable Community and Environment in Tropical Singapore High-Rise Housing: The Case of Bedok Court Condominium," *Architectural Research Quarterly* 8, nos. 3–4 (2004).

53. Diana Budds, "How Urban Design Perpetuates Racial Inequality—and What We Can Do About It," *Fast Company*, July 18, 2016, https://www.fastcodesign.com/3061873 /slicker-city/how-urban-design-perpetuates-racial-inequality-and-what-we-can-do -about-it.

Chapter 4: Shape Disaster Recovery for the Future

1. Arthur T. Bradley, *The Disaster Preparedness Handbook: A Guide for Families*, 2nd ed. (New York: Skyhorse Publishing, 2012).
2. Doug Peeples, "Want a Truly Resilient Smart City? Then Let's Talk Microgrids," Smart Cities Council, November 17, 2016, http://smartcitiescouncil.com/article/want-truly -resilient-smart-city-then-lets-talk-microgrids.
3. See John L. Renne, "Evacuation Planning for Vulnerable Populations: Lessons from the New Orleans City Assisted Evacuation Plan," chap. 8 in *Resilience and Opportunity: Lessons from the U.S. Gulf Coast after Katrina and Rita*, ed. Amy Liu et al. (Washington, DC: Brookings Institution Press, 2011).
4. John L. Renne and Billy Fields, "Introduction: Moving from Disaster to Opportunity: Transitioning the Transportation Sector from Oil Dependence," in *Transport Beyond Oil: Policy Choices for a Multimodal Future*, ed. John L. Renne and Billy Fields, 1–8 (Washington, DC: Island Press, 2013).
5. Peter Newman, Tim Beatley, and Linda Blagg, *Christchurch: Resilient City*, a Curtin University Sustainability Policy (CUSP) Institute video, posted March 30, 2014, https://www.youtube.com/watch?v=otv4JwjrznI.
6. Barnaby Bennett et al., eds., *Once in a Lifetime: City-Building after Disaster in Christchurch* (Christchurch, New Zealand: Freerange Press, 2014).
7. See Gap Filler's Web site, http://www.gapfiller.org.nz/.
8. Peter Newman, "How Christchurch Can Build Light Rail—and Create the Centres It Needs in the Process," in Bennett et al., *Once in a Lifetime*, 401–405.
9. See the Lyttelton Harbour TimeBank's Web site, http://www.lyttelton.net.nz/timebank.
10. See American Rivers, "The Impacts of Climate Change on Rivers," http://www.american rivers.org/threats-solutions/clean-water/impacts-rivers/.
11. David Brown, "Saving the Mekong Delta," *Saturday Extra with Geraldine Doogue*, ABC Radio National, November 19, 2016, http://www.abc.net.au/radionational/programs /saturdayextra/mekong/8038260.
12. Tim Flannery, *The Weather Makers: The History and Future Impact of Climate Change* (Melbourne: Text Publishing Company, 2005); *Tim Flannery: One Man and a Vision*, video posted October 9, 2008, http://www.abc.net.au/tv/bigideas /stories/2008/10/09/2384652.htm.
13. Don McFarlane, quoted in Peter Newman, "The Story of Perth's Water Resilience Turnaround," *Water: Journal of the Australian Water Association* 41, no. 7 (November 2014): 24, http://digitaledition.awa.asn.au/default.aspx?iid=105088&startpage=page0000026 #folio=26.

14. Water Corporation of Western Australia, "Water Forever: Towards Climate Resilience" (Perth: Water Corporation of Western Australia, October 2009), https://www.water corporation.com.au/-/media/files/about-us/planning-for-the-future/water-forever -50-year-plan.pdf.

15. LandCorp, Innovation WGV, https://www.landcorp.com.au/Residential/White-Gum -Valley/; Josh Byrne & Associates, Josh's House, http://.joshshouse.com.au.

16. Karissa Rosenfeld, "Animated Film Envisions BIG's Manhattan 'Dry Line,'" Arch-Daily, February 17, 2015, http://www.archdaily.com/599775/animated-film -envisions-big-s-manhattan-dry-line/.

17. Sustainable Built Environment National Research Centre, "A Stakeholder Engagement Approach to Enhancing Transport Network Resilience in Australia: A Sustainable Built Environment National Research Centre (SBEnrc) Transport Resilience Industry Report," Report 1.35 (Brisbane: Sustainable Built Environment National Research Centre, 2016).

Chapter 5: Build Biophilic Urbanism in the City and Its Bioregion

1. Robert L. Thayer Jr., *LifePlace: Bioregional Thought and Practice* (Berkeley: University of California Press), 2003; Timothy Beatley, *Native to Nowhere: Sustaining Home and Community in a Global Age* (Washington, DC: Island Press, 2004).

2. Tom Daniels and Katherine Daniels, *The Environmental Planning Handbook for Sustainable Communities and Regions* (Chicago: Planners Press, 2003).

3. Erich Fromm, *The Heart of Man: Its Genius for Good and Evil* (New York: Harper & Row, 1964); Jana Söderlund and Peter Newman, "Biophilic Architecture: A Review of the Rationale and Outcomes," *AIMS Environmental Science* 2, no. 4 (2015): 950–969, doi:10.3934/environsci.2015.4.950.

4. Edward O. Wilson, *Biophilia: The Human Bond with Other Species* (Cambridge, MA: Harvard University Press, 1984).

5. Stephen R. Kellert, Judith Heerwagen, and Martin Mador, eds., *Biophilic Design: The Theory, Science, and Practice of Bringing Buildings to Life* (Hoboken, NJ: John Wiley & Sons, 2008); Timothy Beatley, *Biophilic Cities: Integrating Nature into Urban Design and Planning* (Washington, DC: Island Press, 2011).

6. See Biophilic Cities, http://biophiliccities.org.

7. For example, see National Lifestyle Villages, http://www.nlv.com.au/, which has recently developed a series of carbon-positive villages for retirees.

8. For example, see Australian Wildlife Conservancy, "Karakamia," http://www .australianwildlife.org/sanctuaries/karakamia-sanctuary.aspx.

9. Beatley, *Biophilic Cities*; Alex Tan and Kelly Chiang, *Vertical Greenery for the Tropics* (Singapore: Centre for Urban Greenery and Ecology, 2009).

10. Jana Söderlund, "Biophilic Design: A Social Movement Journey," PhD diss., Curtin University, Curtin University Sustainability Policy (CUSP) Institute, 2015.

11. Söderlund and Newman, "Biophilic Architecture."

12. Söderlund, "Biophilic Design."
13. Peter Newman, "Biophilic Urbanism: A Case Study on Singapore," *Australian Planner* 51, no. 1 (2014): 47–65, doi:10.1080/07293682.2013.790832.
14. Isabelle Lomholt, "Living Wall Biofilter," *e-architect* (blog), April 22, 2014, http://www.e-architect.co.uk/toronto/living-wall-biofilter.
15. M. Burchett et al., "Greening the Great Indoors for Human Health and Wellbeing" (Sydney: University of Technology Sydney, 2010).
16. Peter Newman and Jeffrey Kenworthy, *The End of Automobile Dependence: How Cities Are Moving Beyond Car-Based Planning* (Washington, DC: Island Press, 2015).
17. H. Akbari, "Shade Trees Reduce Building Energy Use and CO_2 Emissions from Power Plants," *Environmental Pollution* 116, Supplement 1 (March 2002): S119–S126, doi:10.1016/S0269-7491(01)00264-0; Dennis Y. Leung et al., "Effects of Urban Vegetation on Urban Air Quality," *Landscape Research* 36, no. 2 (2011): 173–188; Samar Sheweka and Nourhan Magdy Mohamed, "The Living Walls as an Approach for a Healthy Urban Environment," *Energy Procedia* 6 (2011): 592–599, doi:10.1016/j.egypro.2011.05.068.
18. Nyuk Hien Wong et al., "Thermal Evaluation of Vertical Greenery Systems for Building Walls," *Building and Environment* 45, no. 3 (March 2010): 663–672, doi:10.1016/j.buildenv.2009.08.005; K. J. Kontoleon and E. A. Eumorfopoulou, "The Effect of the Orientation and Proportion of a Plant-Covered Wall Layer on the Thermal Performance of a Building Zone," *Building and Environment* 45 (2010): 1287–1303, doi:10.1016/j.buildenv.2009.11.013.
19. Samar Sheweka and Nourhan Magdy Mohamed, "Green Facades as a New Sustainable Approach Towards Climate Change," *Energy Procedia* 18 (2012): 507–520, doi:10.1016/j.egypro.2012.05.062; Tiziana Susca, Stuart R. Gaffin, and G. R. Dell'Osso, "Positive Effects of Vegetation: Urban Heat Island and Green Roofs," *Environmental Pollution* 159, nos. 8–9 (August 2011): 2119–2126, doi:10.1016/j.envpol.2011.03.007; C. Y. Cheng, Ken K. S. Cheung, and L. M. Chu, "Thermal Performance of a Vegetated Cladding System on Facade Walls," *Building and Environment* 45 (2010): 1779–1787, doi:10.1016/j.buildenv.2010.02.005; Issa Jaffal, Salah-Eddine Ouldboukhitine, and Rafik Belarbi, "A Comprehensive Study of the Impact of Green Roofs on Building Energy Performance," *Renewable Energy* 43 (July 2012): 157–164, doi:10.1016/j.renene.2011.12.004.
20. Robert M. Anders and J. B. Walker, "Green Roof Stormwater Performance in a Southeastern U.S. Climate," paper presented at Cities Alive: Ninth Annual Green Roofs and Green Walls Conference, Philadelphia, November 30–December 3, 2011; Jeroen Mentens, Dirk Raes, and Martin Hermy, "Green Roofs as a Tool for Solving the Rainwater Runoff Problem in the Urbanized 21st Century?," *Landscape and Urban Planning* 77 (2006): 217–226, doi:10.1016/j.landurbplan.2005.02.010; Erin Schroll et al., "The Role of Vegetation in Regulating Stormwater Runoff from Green Roofs in a Winter Rainfall Climate," *Ecological Engineering* 37, no. 4 (April 2011): 595–600, doi:10.1016/j.ecoleng.2010.12.020; Bruce G. Gregoire and John C. Clausen, "Effect of

a Modular Extensive Green Roof on Stormwater Runoff and Water Quality," *Ecological Engineering* 37 (2011): 963–969, doi:10.1016/j.ecoleng.2011.02.004; J. Y. Lee et al., "Quantitative Analysis on the Urban Flood Mitigation Effect by the Extensive Green Roof System," *Environmental Pollution* 181 (October 2013): 257–261, doi:10.1016 /j.envpol.2013.06.039; M. Ostendorf et al., "Storm Water Runoff from Green Retaining Wall Systems," paper presented at Cities Alive: Ninth Annual Green Roofs and Green Walls Conference, Philadelphia, November 30–December 3, 2011; R. M. Burrows and M. A. Corragio, "Living Walls: Integration of Water Re-use Systems," paper presented at Cities Alive: Ninth Annual Green Roofs and Green Walls Conference, Philadelphia, November 30–December 3, 2011.

21. Steven J. Burian et al., "Urban Wastewater Management in the United States: Past, Present, and Future," *Journal of Urban Technology* 7, no. 3 (2000): 33–62, doi:10.1080/713684134; D. Bradley Rowe, "Green Roofs as a Means of Pollution Abatement," *Environmental Pollution* 159, nos. 8–9 (August–September 2011): 2100–2110, doi:10.1016/j.envpol.2010.10.029; Ranran Wang, Matthew J. Eckelman, and Julie B. Zimmerman, "Consequential Environmental and Economic Life Cycle Assessment of Green and Gray Stormwater Infrastructures for Combined Sewer Systems," *Environmental Science & Technology* 47, no. 19 (October 2013): 11189–11198, doi:10.1021 /es4026547; Anacostia Watershed Society, "RiverSmart Rooftops," 2015, http://www .anacostiaws.org/green-roofs; Martin Seidl et al., "Effect of Substrate Depth and Rain-Event History on the Pollutant Abatement of Green Roofs," *Environmental Pollution* 183 (December 2013): 195–203, doi:10.1016/j.envpol.2013.05.026; Akbari, "Shade Trees"; Leung et al., "Effects of Urban Vegetation"; Sheweka and Mohamed, "The Living Walls"; Plains CO_2 Reduction (PCOR) Partnership, "Regional Storage Potential," http://www.undeerc.org/pcor/region/.

22. Patrick Carey, "A Guide to Phytoremediation: A Symbiotic Relationship with Plants, Water, and Living Architecture," Greenroofs.com, February 12, 2013, http://www .greenroofs.com/content/Phytoremediation-A-Symbiotic-Relationship-with-Plants -Water-and-Living-Architecture.htm; Akira Miyawaki, "Restoration of Urban Green Environments Based on the Theories of Vegetation Ecology," *Ecological Engineering* 11, nos. 1–4 (October 1998): 157–165, doi:10.1016/S0925-8574(98)00033-0; Marc Ottelé et al., "Comparative Life Cycle Analysis for Green Façades and Living Wall Systems," *Energy and Buildings* 43, no. 12 (December 2011): 3419–3429, doi:10.1016 /j.enbuild.2011.09.010; Thomas A. M. Pugh et al., "Effectiveness of Green Infrastructure for Improvement of Air Quality in Urban Street Canyons," *Environmental Science & Technology* 46, no. 14 (2012): 7692–7699, doi:10.1021/es300826w; Marc Ottelé, Hein D. van Bohemen, and Alex L. A. Fraaij, "Quantifying the Deposition of Particulate Matter on Climber Vegetation on Living Walls," *Ecological Engineering* 36, no. 2 (February 2010): 154–162, doi:10.1016/j.ecoleng.2009.02.007; B. C. Wolverton, Rebecca C. McDonald, and E. A. Watkins Jr., "Foliage Plants for Removing Indoor Air Pollutants from Energy-Efficient Homes," *Economic Botany* 38, no. 2 (April–June 1984): 224–228, doi:10.1007/BF02858837; Priscilla Nascimento Pegas et al., "Could Houseplants

Improve Indoor Air Quality in Schools?," *Journal of Toxicology and Environmental Health, Part A* 75, nos. 22–23 (2012): 1371–1380, doi:10.1080/15287394.2012.721 169; Hal Levin, "Can House Plants Solve Indoor Air Quality Problems?," *Indoor Air Bulletin* 2, no. 2 (February 1992).

23. Lomholt, "Living Wall Biofilter."
24. Stephan Brenneisan, "Space for Urban Wildlife: Designing Green Roofs as Habitats in Switzerland," *Urban Habitats* 4, no. 1 (2006): 27–36; Nathalie Baumann, "Ground-Nesting Birds on Green Roofs in Switzerland: Preliminary Observations," *Urban Habitats* 4 (December 2006): 37–50, http://www.urbanhabitats.org/v04n01/birds_full.html; Frédéric Madre et al., "Green Roofs as Habitats for Wild Plant Species in Urban Landscapes: First Insights from a Large-Scale Sampling," *Landscape and Urban Planning* 122 (2014): 100–107, doi:10.1016/j.landurbplan.2013.11.012.
25. Peter Newman, "Biophilic Urbanism: A Case Study on Singapore," *Australian Planner* 51, no. 1 (2014): 47–65, doi:10.1080/07293682.2013.790832.
26. Roger S. Ulrich et al., "Stress Recovery During Exposure to Natural and Urban Environments," *Journal of Environmental Psychology* 11, no. 3 (September 1991): 201–230, doi:10.1016/S0272-4944(05)80184-7.
27. Liisa Tyrväinen et al., "The Influence of Urban Green Environments on Stress Relief Measures: A Field Experiment," *Journal of Environmental Psychology* 38 (June 2014): 1–9, doi:10.1016/j.jenvp.2013.12.005.
28. Richard Louv, *Last Child in the Woods: Saving Our Children from Nature-Deficit Disorder* (New York: Algonquin Books, 2006).
29. See the Web site for Nature Play, http://www.natureplay.org.au.
30. Marlon Nieuwenhuis et al., "The Relative Benefits of Green versus Lean Office Space: Three Field Experiments," *Journal of Experimental Psychology: Applied* 20, no. 3 (2014): 199–214, doi:10.1037/xap0000024; Tom DeMarco and Tim Lister, *Peopleware: Productive Projects and Teams*, 3rd ed. (Boston: Addison-Wesley, 2013).
31. Harumi Ikei et al., "The Physiological and Psychological Relaxing Effects of Viewing Rose Flowers in Office Workers," *Journal of Physiological Anthropology* 33, no. 6 (2014): 1–5, doi:10.1186/1880-6805-33-6.
32. Roger S. Ulrich, "View through a Window May Influence Recovery from Surgery," *Science* 224, no. 4647 (April 27, 1984): 420–421; Seong-Hyun Park and Richard H. Mattson, "Effects of Flowering and Foliage Plants in Hospital Rooms on Patients Recovering from Abdominal Surgery," *HortTechnology* 18, no. 4 (December 2008): 563–568; E. O. Moore, "A Prison Environment's Effect on Health Care Service Demands," *Journal of Environmental Systems* 11 (1981): 17–34; Qing Li et al., "Acute Effects of Walking in Forest Environments on Cardiovascular and Metabolic Parameters," *European Journal of Applied Physiology* 111, no. 11 (November 2011): 2845–2853, doi:10.1007/s00421-011-1918-z; Marc G. Berman et al., "Interacting with Nature Improves Cognition and Affect for Individuals with Depression," *Journal of Affective Disorders* 140, no. 3 (November 2012): 300–305, doi:10.1016/j.jad.2012.03.012; K. Matsunaga et al., "Physiologically Relaxing Effect of a Hospital Rooftop Forest on Older Women Re-

quiring Care," *Journal of the American Geriatrics Society* 59, no. 11 (November 2011): 2162–2163, doi:10.1111/j.1532-5415.2011.03651.x; Bum Jin Park et al., "The Physiological Effects of *Shinrin-Yoku* (Taking In the Forest Atmosphere or Forest Bathing): Evidence from Field Experiments in 24 Forests across Japan," *Environmental Health and Preventive Medicine* 15 (2010): 18–26, doi:10.1007/s12199-009-0086-9; Tyrväinen et al., "Influence of Urban Green Environments"; Marc G. Berman, John Jonides, and Stephen Kaplan, "The Cognitive Benefits of Interacting with Nature," *Psychological Science* 19, no. 12 (2008): 1207–1212, doi:10.1111/j.1467-9280.2008.02225.x.

33. N. Guéguen and J. Stefan, "'Green Altruism': Short Immersion in Natural Green Environments and Helping Behavior," *Environment and Behavior* 48, no. 2 (2016): 324–342 (first published July 1, 2014), doi:10.1177/0013916514536576; Nikos Salingaros and Kenneth Masden, "Neuroscience, the Natural Environment, and Building Design," chap. 5 in Kellert, Heerwagen, and Mador, *Biophilic Design*; Terry Hartig, Tina Bringslimark, and Grete Grindal Patil, "Restorative Environmental Design: What, When, Where, and for Whom," chap. 9 in Kellert, Heerwagen, and Mador, *Biophilic Design*; Upali Nanda et al., "Lessons from Neuroscience: Form Follows Function, Emotions Follow Form," *Intelligent Buildings International* 5, no. S1 (2013): 61–78, doi:10.1080/17508975.2013.807767; Frances E. Kuo and William C. Sullivan, "Environment and Crime in the Inner City: Does Vegetation Reduce Crime?," *Environment and Behavior* 33, no. 3 (May 2001): 343–367.

34. J. Jasper, "Social Movements," in *The Blackwell Encyclopedia of Sociology*, ed. George Ritzer (Malden, MA: Blackwell, 2007); Söderlund, "Biophilic Design."

35. See Barbara Schaffer, "Green Visions: Nature as Infrastructure," *Landscape Architecture Australia* 146 (May 2015), http://landscapeaustralia.com/articles/green-visions-nature-as-infrastructure/.

36. For more information about these biophilic city initiatives, see Timothy Beatley, *Handbook of Biophilic City Planning & Design* (Washington, DC: Island Press, 2017).

37. City of Vancouver, British Columbia, "Greenest City 2020 Action Plan, Part 2: 2015–2020," http://vancouver.ca/files/cov/greenest-city-2020-action-plan-2015-2020.pdf.

38. "Sustainability DC: Sustainable DC Plan," http://sustainable.dc.gov/sites/default/files/dc/sites/sustainable/page_content/attachments/DCS-008%20Report%20508.3j.pdf.

39. Philadelphia Water Department, "Green City, Clean Waters," http://www.phillywatersheds.org/what_were_doing/documents_and_data/cso_long_term_control_plan.

40. Ibid.

41. Eric Jaffe, "Trees Can Make Waiting for the Bus Feel Shorter," *CityLab*, August 13, 2015, http://www.citylab.com/commute/2015/08/trees-can-make-waiting-for-the-bus-feel-shorter/401135/.

42. See Beatley, *Biophilic Cities*, for a more extensive discussion of Jane Martin and her work.

43. Singapore's biophilic urbanism is set out in Newman, "Biophilic Urbanism"; Peter Newman and Annie Matan, *Green Urbanism in Asia: The Emerging Green Tigers* (Singapore: World Scientific, 2013); and a popular YouTube film by Peter Newman, Tim Beatley, and Linda Blagg, *Singapore: Biophilic City*, a Curtin University Sustainability Policy (CUSP) Institute

video posted May 7, 2012, https://www.youtube.com/watch?v=XMWOu9xIM_k. Other details can be found in Lena Chan and Ahmed Djoghlaf, "Invitation to Help Compile an Index of Biodiversity in Cities," *Nature* 460, no. 33 (July 2, 2009), doi:10.1038/460033a; and Lena Chan, "Singapore Index on Cities' Biodiversity," paper presented at World Cities Summit, Singapore, July 3, 2012.

44. See the Web site for Portland's Depave, http://depave.org.

Chapter 6: Produce a More Cyclical and Regenerative Metabolism

1. Johan Rockström et al., "A Safe Operating Space for Humanity," *Nature* 461 (September 24, 2009): 472–475, doi 10.1038/461472a; Johan Rockström et al., "Planetary Boundaries: Exploring the Safe Operating Space for Humanity," *Ecology and Society* 14, no. 2 (2009): art. 32, http://www.ecologyandsociety.org/vol14/iss2/art32/; Will Steffen et al., "Planetary Boundaries: Guiding Human Development on a Changing Planet," *Science* 347, no. 6223 (February 13, 2015), doi:10.1126/science.1259855.

2. Paul J. Crutzen, "Geology of Mankind," *Nature* 415, no. 6867 (January 3, 2002): 23, doi:10.1038/415023a; Will Steffen et al., "The Anthropocene: From Global Change to Planetary Stewardship," *Ambio* 40, no. 7 (November 2011): 739–761, doi:10.1007 /s13280-011-0185-x; Colin N. Waters et al., "The Anthropocene Is Functionally and Stratigraphically Distinct from the Holocene," *Science* 351, no. 6269 (January 8, 2016): 137–147, doi:10.1126/science.aad2622.

3. Intergovernmental Panel on Climate Change (IPCC), *Climate Change 2014: Mitigation of Climate Change. Contribution of Working Group III to the Fifth Assessment Report of the Intergovernmental Panel on Climate Change*, ed. Omar Edenhofer et al. (Cambridge: Cambridge University Press, 2014), http://www.ipcc.ch/pdf/assessment-report/ar5 /wg3/ipcc_wg3_ar5_full.pdf.

4. See the literature on sustainable development and eco-economics.

5. Gerhard Petschel-Held et al., "The Tolerable Windows Approach: Theoretical and Methodological Foundations," *Climatic Change* 41, no. 3 (March 1999): 303–331, doi:10.1023/A:1005487123751; Paul Ekins et al., "A Framework for the Practical Application of the Concepts of Critical Natural Capital and Strong Sustainability," *Ecological Economics* 44, nos. 2–3 (March 2003): 165–185, doi:10.1016/S0921-8009(02)00272 -0; German Advisory Council on Global Change, "Human Progress within Planetary Guard Rails: A Contribution to the SDG Debate," Policy Paper no. 8 (Berlin: German Advisory Council on Global Change, June 2014), https://www.die-gdi.de/uploads /media/wbgu_pp8_en.pdf.

6. Karl-Henrik Robèrt, Göran I. Broman, and George Basile, "Analyzing the Concept of Planetary Boundaries from a Strategic Sustainability Perspective: How Does Humanity Avoid Tipping the Planet?," *Ecology and Society* 18, no. 2 (2013): art. 5, doi:10.5751/ES 05336-180205; Göran I. Broman, John Holmberg, and Karl-Henrik Robèrt, "Simplicity without Reduction: Thinking Upstream Towards the Sustainable Society," *Interfaces* 30, no. 3 (2000): 13–25, doi:10.1287/inte.30.3.13.11662; Herman E. Daly, "Toward

Some Operational Principles of Sustainable Development," *Ecological Economics* 2, no. 1 (April 1990): 1–6, doi:10.1016/0921-8009(90)90010-R; Christian Azar, John Holmberg, and Kristian Lindgren, "Socio-ecological Indicators for Sustainability," *Ecological Economics* 18, no. 2 (August 1996): 89–112, doi:10.1016/0921-8009(96)00028-6.

7. John Holmberg et al., "The Ecological Footprint from a Systems Perspective of Sustainability," *International Journal of Sustainable Development and World Ecology* 6, no. 1 (1999): 17–33, doi:10.1080/13504509.1999.9728469.

8. Andrea Collins et al., "The Environmental Impacts of Consumption at a Subnational Level," *Journal of Industrial Ecology* 10, no. 3 (July 2006): 9–24, doi:10.1162/jiec.2006.10.3.9; Peter Newman and Isabella Jennings, *Cities as Sustainable Ecosystems: Principles and Practices* (Washington, DC: Island Press, 2008).

9. Reed F. Noss and Allen Y. Cooperrider, *Saving Nature's Legacy: Protecting and Restoring Biodiversity* (Washington, DC: Island Press, 1994).

10. Detlef P. van Vuuren et al., "Horses for Courses: Analytical Tools to Explore Planetary Boundaries," *Earth System Dynamics* 7, no. 1 (2016): 267–279, doi:10.5194/esd-7-267-2016.

11. Steffen et al., "The Anthropocene."

12. Rockström et al., "Planetary Boundaries"; Steffen et al., "Planetary Boundaries."

13. Steve Bass, "Planetary Boundaries: Keep Off the Grass," *Nature Reports Climate Change* 3 (October 2009): 113–114, doi:10.1038/climate.2009.94; David Molden, "Planetary Boundaries: The Devil Is in the Detail," *Nature Reports Climate Change* 3 (October 2009): 116–117, doi:10.1038/climate.2009.97.

14. Sustainable Development Solutions Network, "An Action Agenda for Sustainable Development," Report for the UN Secretary-General (Paris: Sustainable Development Solutions Network, June 6, 2013), http://unstats.un.org/unsd/broaderprogress/pdf/130613-SDSN-An-Action-Agenda-for-Sustainable-Development-FINAL.pdf; David Griggs et al., "Policy: Sustainable Development Goals for People and Planet," *Nature* 495, no. 7441 (March 21, 2013): 305–307, doi:10.1038/495305a; Umberto Pisano and Gerald Berger, "Planetary Boundaries for SD: From an International Perspective to National Applications," ESDN Quarterly Report no. 30 (Vienna: European Sustainable Development Network, October 2013), http://www.sd-network.eu/quarterly%20reports/report%20files/pdf/2013-October-Planetary_Boundaries_for_SD.pdf.

15. House of Commons Science and Technology Committee, "The Regulation of Geoengineering: Fifth Report of Session 2009–10" (London: House of Commons Science and Technology Committee, March 2010), 54, http://www.publications.parliament.uk/pa/cm200910/cmselect/cmsctech/221/221.pdf; National Research Council of the National Academies, *Climate Intervention: Reflecting Sunlight to Cool Earth* (Washington, DC: National Academies Press, 2015); University of Oxford, Oxford Martin School, "'Oxford Principles' Vital for Geoengineering Research," press release, September 14, 2011, http://www.oxfordmartin.ox.ac.uk/news/201109-oxfordprinciples.

16. IPCC, *Climate Change 2014*; National Research Council of the National Academies, *Cli-*

mate Intervention: Carbon Dioxide Removal and Reliable Sequestration (Washington, DC: National Academies Press, 2015); United Nations Environment Programme, Secretariat of the Convention on Biological Diversity (SCBD), "UN Biodiversity Report Identifies Risks and Uncertainties of Novel Strategies to Tackle Climate Change," press release, October 31, 2016, https://www.cbd.int/doc/press/2016/pr-2016-10-31-ts84-en.pdf.

17. Jonathan H. Fink, "Geoengineering Cities to Stabilise Climate," *Proceedings of the Institution of Civil Engineers—Engineering Sustainability* 166, no. 5 (October 2013): 242–248, doi:10.1680/ensu.13.00002; Tim Flannery, *Atmosphere of Hope: Solutions to the Climate Crisis* (London: Penguin, 2015).

18. See William McDonough, "Carbon Is Not the Enemy," *Nature* 539, no. 7629 (November 14, 2016): 349–351, doi:10.1038/539349a.

19. See http://www.nature.com/news/circular-economy-1.19546.

20. Peter Newman and Jeffrey Kenworthy, *Sustainability and Cities: Overcoming Automobile Dependence* (Washington, DC: Island Press, 1999).

21. Peter Newton and Peter Newman, "Critical Connections: The Role of the Built Environment Sector in Delivering Green Cities and a Green Economy," *Sustainability* 7, no. 7 (2015): 9417–9443, doi:10.3390/su7079417.

22. Peter Newton and Peter Newman, "Low Carbon Green Growth: Tracking Progress in Australia's Built Environment Industry Towards a Green Economy" (Melbourne and Perth: Swinburne University of Technology and Curtin University, September 2013), https://www.gbca.org.au/gbc_scripts/js/tiny_mce/plugins/filemanager/Low_Carbon_Green_Growth_BE_Report_16Sept.pdf; Jemma Green and Peter Newman, "Citizen Utilities: The Emerging Power Paradigm, a Case Study in Perth, Australia," *Energy Policy* (2017), forthcoming; Giles Thomson and Peter Newman, "Urban Fabrics and Urban Metabolism: From Sustainable to Regenerative Cities," *Resources, Conservation, and Recycling* (online February 13, 2017), doi:10.1016/j.resconrec.2017.01.010; University of California, Davis, "UC Davis West Village Energy Initiative Annual Report 2013–2014" (Davis: University of California, Davis, 2014), http://sustainability.ucdavis.edu/local_resources/docs/wvei_annual_report_2013_14.pdf.

23. Peter Newman and Jeffrey Kenworthy, *The End of Automobile Dependence: How Cities Are Moving Beyond Car-Based Planning* (Washington, DC: Island Press, 2015).

24. David Brownstone and Thomas F. Golob, "The Impact of Residential Density on Vehicle Usage and Energy Consumption," *Journal of Urban Economics* 65, no. 1 (January 2009): 91–98, doi:10.1016/j.jue.2008.09.002; Chao Liu and Qing Shen, "An Empirical Analysis of the Influence of Urban Form on Household Travel and Energy Consumption," *Computers, Environment, and Urban Systems* 35, no. 5 (September 2011): 347–357, doi:10.1016/j.compenvurbsys.2011.05.006.

25. Hugh Gardner and Peter Newman, "Reducing the Materials and Resource Intensity of the Built Form in the Perth and Peel Regions" (Perth: Arup and Curtin University Sustainability Policy [CUSP] Institute, June 2013), https://www.environment.gov.au/system/files/resources/012e6df0-dce8-4bb2-9861-dad1dfc0f779/files/built-form.pdf.

26. Newman and Jennings, *Cities as Sustainable Ecosystems.*

Conclusion: Growing Regeneratively

1. For examples of agglomeration economics, see Marius Brülhart and Federica Sbergami, "Agglomeration and Growth: Cross-Country Evidence," *Journal of Urban Economics* 65, no. 1 (January 2009): 48–63, doi:10.1016/j.jue.2008.08.003; Satyajit Chatterjee, "A Quantitative Assessment of the Role of Agglomeration Economies in the Spatial Concentration of U.S. Employment," FRB Working Paper no. 06-20 (Philadelphia, PA: Federal Reserve Bank of Philadelphia, November 2006); Masahisa Fujita and Jacques-François Thisse, *Economics of Agglomeration: Cities, Industrial Location, and Regional Growth* (Cambridge: Cambridge University Press, 2002); Edward L. Glaeser, "Growth: The Death and Life of Cities," in *Making Cities Work: Prospects and Policies for Urban America*, ed. Robert P. Inman, 22–62 (Princeton, NJ: Princeton University Press, 2009); Börje Johansson and John M. Quigley, "Agglomeration and Networks in Spatial Economics," *Papers in Regional Science* 83, no. 1 (January 2004): 165–176, doi:10.1007/s10110-003-0181-z.

2. For examples of urban impact analysis, see David Brownstone and Thomas F. Golob, "The Impact of Residential Density on Vehicle Usage and Energy Consumption," *Journal of Urban Economics* 65, no. 1 (January 2009): 91–98, doi:10.1016/j.jue.2008.09.002; Chao Liu and Qing Shen, "An Empirical Analysis of the Influence of Urban Form on Household Travel and Energy Consumption," *Computers, Environment, and Urban Systems* 35, no. 5 (September 2011): 347–357.

3. Peter Newman, "Perth as a 'Big' City: Reflections on Urban Growth," *Thesis Eleven* 135, no. 1 (July 4, 2016): 139–151, doi:10.1177/0725513616657906.

4. Mark Girouard, *Cities and People: A Social and Architectural History* (New Haven, CT: Yale University Press, 1985); Spiro Kostoff, *The City Assembled: The Elements of Urban Form through History* (London: Thames & Hudson, 1992).

5. United Nations Department of Economic and Social Affairs, Population Division, "World Urbanization Prospects: The 2014 Revision, Highlights," ST/ESA/SER.A/352 (New York: United Nations, 2014), https://esa.un.org/unpd/wup/Publications/Files/WUP2014-Highlights.pdf.

6. For example, Calthorpe Analytics (see note 7) has a precinct design scenario tool; others are summarized in Vanessa Rauland and Peter Newman, *Decarbonising Cities: Mainstreaming Low Carbon Urban Development* (London: Springer, 2015). A new public tool called the Envision Scenario Planner (ESP) has been developed by the CRC for Spatial Information; see Chris J. Pettit et al., "A Co-design Prototyping Approach for Building a Precinct Planning Tool," *ISPRS Annals of the Photogrammetry, Remote Sensing, and Spatial Information Sciences* II-2 (2014): 47–53, doi:10.5194/isprsannals-II-2-47-2014.

7. See Calthorpe Analytics, http://calthorpeanalytics.com/.

8. Roman Trubka et al., "A Web-Based 3D Visualisation and Assessment System for Urban Precinct Scenario Modelling," *ISPRS Journal of Photogrammetry and Remote Sensing* 117 (July 2016): 175–186.

9. Margaret Gollagher and Janette Hartz-Karp, "The Role of Deliberative Collaborative

Governance in Achieving Sustainable Cities," *Sustainability* 5, no. 6 (2013): 2343–2366, doi:10.3390/su5062343; Janette Hartz-Karp and Peter Newman, "The Participative Route to Sustainability," in *Communities Doing It for Themselves: Creating Space for Sustainability*, ed. S. Paulin, 28–42 (Perth: University of Western Australia Press, 2006).

10. See the Participatory Budgeting Project, https://www.participatorybudgeting.org; Janette Hartz-Karp, "Laying the Groundwork for Participatory Budgeting—Developing a Deliberative Community and Collaborative Governance: Greater Geraldton, Western Australia," *Journal of Public Deliberation* 8, no. 2 (2012): art. 6, http://www.publicdeliberation.net/jpd/vol8/iss2/art6/.

11. Satya Sai Kumar Jillella and Peter Newman, "Participatory Sustainability Approach to Value Capture-Based Urban Rail Financing in India through Deliberated Stakeholder Engagement," *Sustainability* 7, no. 7 (2015): 8091–8115, doi:10.3390/su7078091. A film was made of this project in India; see Peter Newman, Janette Hartz-Karp, and Linda Blagg, *Taming Streets: Design, Deliberation, and Delivery in Indian Cities*, a Curtin University Sustainability Policy (CUSP) Institute video, posted December 5, 2015, https://www.youtube.com/watch?v=NxXDNtcaMno.

12. Peter Newman et al., "The Entrepreneur Rail Model: Tapping Private Investment for New Urban Rail" (Perth: Curtin University Sustainability Policy [CUSP] Institute, February 2016), http://www.curtin.edu.au/research/cusp/local/docs/Rail_Model_Report.pdf.

Bibliography

Abel, Jaison R., Ishita Dey, and Todd M. Gabe. "Productivity and the Density of Human Capital." *Journal of Regional Science* 52, no. 4 (October 2012): 562–586. doi:10.1111/j.1467-9787.2011.00742.x.

Ajanovic, Amela. "Biofuels versus Food Production: Does Biofuels Production Increase Food Prices?" *Energy* 36, no. 4 (April 2011): 2070–2076. doi:10.1016/j.energy.2010.05.019.

Akbari, H. "Shade Trees Reduce Building Energy Use and CO_2 Emissions from Power Plants." *Environmental Pollution* 116, Supplement 1 (March 2002): S119–S126. doi:10.1016/S0269-7491(01)00264-0.

Alanne, Kari, and Arto Saari. "Distributed Energy Generation and Sustainable Development." *Renewable and Sustainable Energy Reviews* 10, no. 6 (December 2006): 539–558. doi:10.1016/j.rser.2004.11.004.

Amin, Ash, and Patrick Cohendet. "Geographies of Knowledge Formation in Firms." *Industry and Innovation* 12, no. 4 (December 2005): 465–486. doi:10.1080/13662710500381658.

Anacostia Watershed Society. "RiverSmart Rooftops." 2015. http://www.anacostiaws.org/green-roofs.

Anders, Robert M., and J. B. Walker. "Green Roof Stormwater Performance in a Southeastern U.S. Climate." Paper presented at Cities Alive: Ninth Annual Green Roofs and Green Walls Conference, Philadelphia, November 30–December 3, 2011.

Ashton-Graham, C. "TravelSmart and LivingSmart Case Study—Western Australia." In *The Garnaut Climate Change Review*, edited by Ross Garnaut. Cambridge: Cambridge University Press, 2008. http://www.garnautreview.org.au/2008-review.html.

Asian Development Bank. "Part 1—Special Chapter: Green Urbanization in Asia," in *Key Indicators for Asia and the Pacific 2012*. Mandaluyong City, Manila: Asian Development Bank, 2012.

Azar, Christian, John Holmberg, and Kristian Lindgren. "Socio-ecological Indicators for Sustainability." *Ecological Economics* 18, no. 2 (August 1996): 89–112. doi:10.1016/0921-8009(96)00028-6.

Banister, David. "The Sustainable Mobility Paradigm." *Transport Policy* 15, no. 2 (March 2008): 73–80. doi:10.1016/j.tranpol.2007.10.005.

Barbose, Galen, Naïm Darghouth, Samantha Weaver, and Ryan Wiser. "Tracking the Sun

VI: An Historical Summary of the Installed Price of Photovoltaics in the United States from 1998 to 2012." LBNL-6350E. Berkeley, CA: Lawrence Berkeley National Laboratory, July 2013. https://emp.lbl.gov/sites/all/files/lbnl-6350e.pdf.

Bass, Steve. "Planetary Boundaries: Keep Off the Grass." *Nature Reports Climate Change* 3 (October 2009): 113–114. doi:10.1038/climate.2009.94.

Baumann, Nathalie. "Ground-Nesting Birds on Green Roofs in Switzerland: Preliminary Observations." *Urban Habitats* 4 (December 2006): 37–50. http://www.urbanhabitats.org/v04n01/birds_full.html.

Bay, Joo Hwa. "Singapore High-Rise with Traditional Qualities." *Nova Terra* 2, no. 4 (December 2002).

———. "Sustainable Community and Environment in Tropical Singapore High-Rise Housing: The Case of Bedok Court Condominium." *Architectural Research Quarterly* 8, nos. 3–4 (2004).

Bay, Joo Hwa, and B. L. Ong, eds. *Tropical Sustainable Architecture: Social and Environmental Dimensions*. London: Architectural Press, 2006.

Beatley, Timothy. *Biophilic Cities: Integrating Nature into Urban Design and Planning*. Washington, DC: Island Press, 2011.

———. *Native to Nowhere: Sustaining Home and Community in a Global Age*. Washington, DC: Island Press, 2004.

Beatley, Timothy, and Kristy Manning. *The Ecology of Place: Planning for Environment, Economy, and Community*. Washington, DC: Island Press, 1997.

Beatley, Timothy, and Peter Newman. "Biophilic Cities Are Sustainable, Resilient Cities." *Sustainability* 5 (2013): 3328–3345. doi:10.3390/su5083328.

Bennett, Barnaby, James Dann, Emma Johnson, and Ryan Reynolds, eds. *Once in a Lifetime: City-Building after Disaster in Christchurch*. Christchurch, New Zealand: Freerange Press, 2014.

Berman, Marc G., John Jonides, and Stephen Kaplan. "The Cognitive Benefits of Interacting with Nature." *Psychological Science* 19, no. 12 (2008): 1207–1212. doi:10.1111/j.1467-9280.2008.02225.x.

Berman, Marc G., Ethan Kross, Katherine M. Krpan, Mary K. Askren, Aleah Burson, Patricia J. Deldin, Stephen Kaplan, Lindsey Sherdell, Ian H. Gotlib, and John Jonides. "Interacting with Nature Improves Cognition and Affect for Individuals with Depression." *Journal of Affective Disorders* 140, no. 3 (November 2012): 300–305. doi:10.1016/j.jad.2012.03.012.

Bloomberg New Energy Finance. "New Energy Outlook 2015: Long-Term Projections of the Global Energy Sector." New York: Bloomberg L.P., 2015.

———. "New Energy Outlook 2016: Powering a Changing World." New York: Bloomberg L.P., 2016. https://www.bloomberg.com/company/new-energy-outlook/.

Bower, Joseph L., and Clayton M. Christensen. "Disruptive Technologies: Catching the Wave." *Harvard Business Review* 73, no. 1 (January–February 1995): 43–54.

Bradbury, Danny. "Airships Float Back to the Future." BusinessGreen.com, September 2, 2008.

Bradley, Arthur T. *The Disaster Preparedness Handbook: A Guide for Families.* 2nd ed. New York: Skyhorse Publishing, 2012.

Brenneisen, Stephan. "Space for Urban Wildlife: Designing Green Roofs as Habitats in Switzerland." *Urban Habitats* 4, no. 1 (2006): 27–36.

Broman, Göran I., John Holmberg, and Karl-Henrik Robèrt. "Simplicity without Reduction: Thinking Upstream Towards the Sustainable Society." *Interfaces* 30, no. 3 (2000): 13–25. doi:10.1287/inte.30.3.13.11662.

Bronski, Peter, Jon Creyts, Mark Crowdis, Stephen Doig, John Glassmire, Leia Guccione, Peter Lilienthal, et al. "The Economics of Load Defection." Boulder, CO: Rocky Mountain Institute, April 2015. http://www.rmi.org/cms /Download.aspx?id=11580&file=2015-05_RMI-TheEconomicsOfLoad Defection-FullReport.pdf.

Brown, David. "Saving the Mekong Delta." *Saturday Extra with Geraldine Doogue.* ABC Radio National, November 19, 2016. http://www.abc.net.au/radionational/programs /saturdayextra/mekong/8038260.

Browning, Bill, C. Garvin, C. Ryan, et al. "The Economics of Biophilia: Why Designing with Nature in Mind Makes Financial Sense." Washington, DC: Terrapin Bright Green, 2012. http://www.terrapinbrightgreen.com/report/economics-of-biophilia/.

Brownstone, David, and Thomas F. Golob. "The Impact of Residential Density on Vehicle Usage and Energy Consumption." *Journal of Urban Economics* 65, no. 1 (January 2009): 91–98. doi:10.1016/j.jue.2008.09.002.

Brülhart, Marius, and Federica Sbergami. "Agglomeration and Growth: Cross-Country Evidence." *Journal of Urban Economics* 65, no. 1 (January 2009): 48–63. doi:10.1016/j .jue.2008.08.003.

Burchett, M., et al. "Greening the Great Indoors for Human Health and Wellbeing." Sydney: University of Technology, Sydney, 2010.

Burian, Steven J., Stephan J. Nix, Robert E. Pitt, and S. Rocky Durrans. "Urban Wastewater Management in the United States: Past, Present, and Future." *Journal of Urban Technology* 7, no. 3 (2000): 33–62. doi:10.1080/713684134.

Burrows, R. M., and M. A. Corragio. "Living Walls: Integration of Water Re-use Systems." Paper presented at Cities Alive: Ninth Annual Green Roofs and Green Walls Conference, Philadelphia, November 30–December 3, 2011.

Calthorpe, Peter, and Jerry Walters. "Autonomous Vehicles: Hype and Potential." *Public Square*, Congress of New Urbanism, September 6, 2016.

Carbon Tracker Initiative. "Unburnable Carbon—Are the World's Financial Markets Carrying a Carbon Bubble?," 2012. http://www.carbontracker.org/wp-content/uploads /2014/09/Unburnable-Carbon-Full-rev2-1.pdf.

Carey, Patrick. "A Guide to Phytoremediation: A Symbiotic Relationship with Plants, Water, and Living Architecture." February 12, 2013. http://www.greenroofs.com /content/Phytoremediation-A-Symbiotic-Relationship-with-Plants-Water-and -Living-Architecture.htm.

Carlin, Kelly, Bodhi Rader, and Greg Rucks. "Interoperable Transit Data: Enabling a Shift to Mobility as a Service." Snowmass, CO: Rocky Mountain Institute, October 2015. http://www.rmi.org/mobility_itd.

Center for Transit-Oriented Development and Reconnecting America (CTODRA). "Hidden in Plain Sight: Capturing the Demand for Housing Near Transit." September 3, 2004. http://reconnectingamerica.org/assets/Uploads/2004Ctodreport.pdf.

Chan, Lena. "Singapore Index on Cities' Biodiversity." Paper presented at World Cities Summit, Singapore, July 3, 2012. http://www.worldcitiessummit.com.sg/sites/sites2.globalsignin.com.2.wcs-2014/files/Dr_Lena_Chan.pdf.

Chan, Lena, and Ahmed Djoghlaf. "Invitation to Help Compile an Index of Biodiversity in Cities." Nature 460, no. 33 (July 2, 2009). doi:10.1038/460033a.

Chatterjee, Satyajit. "A Quantitative Assessment of the Role of Agglomeration Economies in the Spatial Concentration of U.S. Employment." FRB Working Paper no. 06-20. Philadelphia, PA: Federal Reserve Bank of Philadelphia, November 2006.

Cheng, C. Y., Ken K. S. Cheung, and L. M. Chu. "Thermal Performance of a Vegetated Cladding System on Facade Walls." Building and Environment 45 (2010): 1779–1787. doi:10.1016/j.buildenv.2010.02.005.

Cole, M. J., R. M. Bailey, and M. G. New. "Tracking Sustainable Development with a National Barometer for South Africa Using a Downscaled 'Safe and Just Space' Framework." Proceedings of the National Academy of Sciences 111, no. 42 (2014): E4399–E4408.

Collins, Andrea, Andrew Flynn, Thomas Wiedmann, and John Barrett. "The Environmental Impacts of Consumption at a Subnational Level." Journal of Industrial Ecology 10, no. 3 (July 2006): 9–24. doi:10.1162/jiec.2006.10.3.9.

Colville-Andersen, Mikael. "Meteoric Rise in Bicycle Traffic in Copenhagen." Copenhagenize Design Co. (blog), November 4, 2016. http://www.copenhagenize.com/2016/11/meteoric-rise-in-bicycle-traffic-in.html.

Crutzen, Paul J. "Geology of Mankind." Nature 415, no. 6867 (January 3, 2002): 23. doi:10.1038/415023a.

Curtis, Carey, John L. Renne, and Luca Bertolini, eds. Transit Oriented Development: Making It Happen. London: Ashgate, 2009.

Daly, Herman E. "Toward Some Operational Principles of Sustainable Development." Ecological Economics 2, no. 1 (April 1990): 1–6. doi:10.1016/0921-8009(90)90010-R.

Daniels, Tom, and Katherine Daniels. The Environmental Planning Handbook for Sustainable Communities and Regions. Chicago: Planners Press, 2003.

Dannenberg, Andrew L., Howard Frumkin, and Richard Jackson, eds. Making Healthy Places: Designing and Building for Health, Well-being, and Sustainability. Washington, DC: Island Press, 2011.

Dao, H., D. Friot, P. Peduzzi, B. Chatenoux, A. De Bono, and S. Schwarzer. "Environmental Limits and Swiss Footprints Based on Planetary Boundaries." Geneva: United Nations Environment Programme and GRID-Geneva, 2015.

Davis, Benjamin, Tony Dutzik, and Phineas Baxandall. "Transportation and the New Generation: Why Young People Are Driving Less and What It Means for Transportation Policy." San Francisco: Frontier Group and U.S. PIRG Education Fund, 2012.

de Pommereau, Isabelle. "New German Community Models Car-Free Living." *Christian Science Monitor*, December 20, 2006.

Desmond, Matthew. *Evicted: Poverty and Profit in the American City*. New York: Crown, 2016.

Diamond, Jared M. *Collapse: How Societies Choose to Fail or Succeed*. New York: Viking, 2005.

Dittmar, Hank, and Gloria Ohland, eds. *The New Transit Town: Best Practices in Transit-Oriented Development*. Washington, DC: Island Press, 2003.

Drew, Gerard. "Zero Carbon Australia: Renewable Energy Superpower." Melbourne: Beyond Zero Emissions, October 2015. http://media.bze.org.au/resp/bze_superpower_plan.pdf.

Droege, Peter. *Urban Energy Transition: From Fossil Fuels to Renewable Power*. Oxford: Elsevier, 2008.

du Plessis, Chrisna. "Towards a Regenerative Paradigm for the Built Environment." *Building Research & Information* 40, no. 1 (2012): 7–22. doi:10.1080/09613218.2012.628548.

Ekins, Paul, Sandrine Simon, Lisa Deutsch, Carl Folke, and Rudolf De Groot. "A Framework for the Practical Application of the Concepts of Critical Natural Capital and Strong Sustainability." *Ecological Economics* 44, nos. 2–3 (March 2003): 165–185. doi:10.1016/S0921-8009(02)00272-0.

Ellison, Charles D. "Infrastructure Failures, Like Flint, Are a Crisis for Black America." *The Root*, January 27, 2016. http://www.theroot.com/infrastructure-failures-like-flint-are-a-crisis-for-b-1790854028.

Erwine, B., and L. Heschong. "Daylight: Healthy, Wealthy, and Wise." *Architectural Lighting* 15 (April–May 2000): 98.

Evers, Hans-Dieter, Solvay Gerke, and Thomas Menkhoff. "Knowledge Clusters and Knowledge Hubs: Designing Epistemic Landscapes for Development." *Journal of Knowledge Management* 14, no. 5 (2010): 678–689. doi:10.1142/9789814343688_0002.

Ewing, Reid, Keith Bartholomew, Steve Winkelman, Jerry Walters, and Don Chen. *Growing Cooler: The Evidence on Urban Development and Climate Change*. Washington, DC: Urban Land Institute, 2007.

Extance, Andy. "The Future of Cryptocurrencies: Bitcoin and Beyond." *Nature* 526, no. 7571 (October 1, 2015): 21–23. doi:10.1038/526021a.

Fink, Jonathan H. "Geoengineering Cities to Stabilise Climate." *Proceedings of the Institution of Civil Engineers—Engineering Sustainability* 166, no. 5 (October 2013): 242–248. doi:10.1680/ensu.13.00002.

Fitzsimmons, Emma G. "Advocates for New York's Working Poor Push for Discounted Transit Fares." *New York Times*, November 11, 2016. http://www.nytimes.com/2016/11/12/nyregion/advocates-for-new-yorks-working-poor-push-for-discounted-transit-fares.html.

Flannery, Tim. *Atmosphere of Hope: Solutions to the Climate Crisis*. London: Penguin, 2015.

Flannery, Tim, and Veena Sahajwalla. "The Critical Decade: Australia's Future—Solar En-

ergy." Australian Climate Commission, September 2, 2013. http://www.climatecouncil
.org.au/uploads/497bcd1f058be45028e3df9d020ed561.pdf.

Florida, Richard. *The Great Reset: How New Ways of Living and Working Drive Post-Crash Prosperity.* New York: HarperCollins, 2010.

Friedel, Robert. *A Culture of Improvement: Technology and the Western Millennium.* Cambridge, MA: MIT Press, 2007.

Fromm, Erich. *The Heart of Man: Its Genius for Good and Evil.* New York: Harper & Row, 1964.

Fujita, Masahisa, and Jacques-François Thisse. *Economics of Agglomeration: Cities, Industrial Location, and Regional Growth.* Cambridge: Cambridge University Press, 2002.

Gardner, Hugh, and Peter Newman. "Reducing the Materials and Resource Intensity of the Built Form in the Perth and Peel Regions." Perth: Arup and Curtin University Sustainability Policy (CUSP) Institute, June 2013. https://www.environment.gov.au/system /files/resources/012e6df0-dce8-4bb2-9861-dad1dfc0f779/files/built-form.pdf.

Gehl, Jan. *Cities for People.* Washington, DC: Island Press, 2010.

———. *Life Between Buildings: Using Public Space.* Washington, DC: Island Press, 2011.

Gehl, Jan, and Lars Gemzøe. *New City Spaces.* Copenhagen: Danish Architectural Press, 2000.

———. *Public Spaces, Public Life.* Copenhagen: Danish Architectural Press, 2004.

Gehl, Jan, A. Modin, J. Wittenmark, L. Grassow, A. Matan, E. Hagströmer, L. Bernado, and J. Enhörning. "Perth 2009: Public Spaces and Public Life: Study Report." Perth and Copenhagen: City of Perth and Gehl Architects, 2009.

Gehl, Jan, H. Mortensen, P. Ducourtial, I. S. Duckett, L. H. Nielsen, J. M. R. Nielsen, R. Adams, et al. "Places for People: Study Report." Melbourne and Copenhagen: City of Melbourne and Gehl Architects, 2004.

Gehl Studio NY and J. Max Bond Center on Design for the Just City. "Public Life and Urban Justice in NYC's Plazas." New York: Gehl Studio NY and J. Max Bond Center on Design for the Just City, November 14, 2015. https://issuu.com/gehlarchitects/docs /nycplazastudy/c/smf4qso.

German Advisory Council on Global Change (GACGC). "Human Progress within Planetary Guard Rails: A Contribution to the SDG Debate." Policy Paper no. 8. Berlin: German Advisory Council on Global Change, June 2014. https://www.die-gdi.de/uploads /media/wbgu_pp8_en.pdf.

Gilbert, Richard, and Anthony Perl. *Transport Revolutions: Moving People and Freight without Oil.* London: Earthscan, 2007.

Girardet, Herbert. "Regenerative Cities." Hamburg: World Future Council, 2010. https://www.worldfuturecouncil.org/file/2016/01/WFC_2010_Regenerative_Cities.pdf.

Girouard, Mark. *Cities and People: A Social and Architectural History.* New Haven, CT: Yale University Press, 1985.

Giurco, Damien P., Stuart B. White, and Rodney A. Stewart. "Smart Metering and Water End-Use Data: Conservation Benefits and Privacy Risks." *Water* 2, no. 3 (2010): 461–467. doi:10.3390/w2030461.

Gladwell, Malcolm. *The Tipping Point: How Little Things Can Make a Big Difference*. New York: Little, Brown, 2000.

Glaeser, Edward L. "Growth: The Death and Life of Cities." In *Making Cities Work: Prospects and Policies for Urban America*, edited by Robert P. Inman, 22–62. Princeton, NJ: Princeton University Press, 2009.

Gogarty, Brendan. "'Killer Robots' Hit the Road—and the Law Has Yet to Catch Up." *The Conversation*, November 8, 2015.

Goldemberg, J. "Leapfrog Energy Technologies." *Energy Policy* 26, no. 10 (August 1998): 729–741.

Gollagher, Margaret, and Janette Hartz-Karp. "The Role of Deliberative Collaborative Governance in Achieving Sustainable Cities." *Sustainability* 5, no. 6 (2013): 2343–2366. doi:10.3390/su5062343.

Gorringe, T. J. *A Theology of the Built Environment: Justice, Empowerment, Redemption*. Cambridge: Cambridge University Press, 2002.

Green, Jemma, and Peter Newman. "Citizen Utilities: The Emerging Power Paradigm. A Case Study in Perth, Australia." *Energy Policy* (2017), forthcoming.

———. "Demand Drivers for Medium Density Housing and the Relative Importance of Sustainability Attributes." *Urban Policy and Research* (2017), forthcoming.

———. "Disruptive Innovation, Stranded Assets, and Forecasting: The Rise and Rise of Renewable Energy." *Journal of Sustainable Finance & Investment* (2016): 1–19. doi:10.1080/20430795.2016.1265410.

Gregoire, Bruce G., and John C. Clausen. "Effect of a Modular Extensive Green Roof on Stormwater Runoff and Water Quality." *Ecological Engineering* 37 (2011): 963–969. doi:10.1016/j.ecoleng.2011.02.004.

Griggs, David, Mark Stafford-Smith, Owen Gaffney, Johan Rockström, Marcus C. Öhman, Priya Shyamsundar, Will Steffen, Gisbert Glaser, Norichika Kanie, and Ian Noble. "Policy: Sustainable Development Goals for People and Planet." *Nature* 495, no. 7441 (March 21, 2013): 305–307. doi:10.1038/495305a.

Guéguen, N., and J. Stefan. "'Green Altruism': Short Immersion in Natural Green Environments and Helping Behavior." *Environment and Behavior* 48, no. 2 (2016): 324–342. (First published July 1, 2014.) doi:10.1177/0013916514536576.

Hall, Peter. *Cities in Civilisation: Culture, Innovation, and Urban Order*. London: Weidenfeld & Nicolson, 1998.

Hartz-Karp, Janette. "Laying the Groundwork for Participatory Budgeting—Developing a Deliberative Community and Collaborative Governance: Greater Geraldton, Western Australia." *Journal of Public Deliberation* 8, no. 2 (2012): art. 6. http://www.public deliberation.net/jpd/vol8/iss2/art6/.

Hartz-Karp, Janette, and Peter Newman. "The Participative Route to Sustainability." In *Communities Doing It for Themselves: Creating Space for Sustainability*, edited by S. Paulin, 28–42. Perth: University of Western Australia Press, 2006.

Heerwagen, Judith. "Green Buildings, Organizational Success, and Occupant Productivity." *Building Research and Information* 28, no. 5 (2000): 353–367.

Hes, Dominique, and Chrisna du Plessis. *Designing for Hope: Pathways to Regenerative Sustainability*. Boca Raton, FL: Taylor & Francis, 2014.

Holmberg, John, Ulrika Lundqvist, Karl-Henrik Robèrt, and Mathis Wackernagel. "The Ecological Footprint from a Systems Perspective of Sustainability." *International Journal of Sustainable Development and World Ecology* 6, no. 1 (1999): 17–33. doi:10.1080 /13504509.1999.9728469.

House of Commons Science and Technology Committee (HCSTC). "The Regulation of Geoengineering: Fifth Report of Session 2009–10." London: House of Commons Science and Technology Committee, March 2010. http://www.publications.parliament .uk/pa/cm200910/cmselect/cmsctech/221/221.pdf.

Ikei, Harumi, Misako Komatsu, Chorong Song, Eri Himoro, and Yoshifumi Miyazaki. "The Physiological and Psychological Relaxing Effects of Viewing Rose Flowers in Office Workers." *Journal of Physiological Anthropology* 33, no. 6 (2014): 1–5. doi:10.1186/1880-6805-33-6.

Intergovernmental Panel on Climate Change (IPCC). *Climate Change 2014: Mitigation of Climate Change. Contribution of Working Group III to the Fifth Assessment Report of the Intergovernmental Panel on Climate Change*, ed. Ottmar Edenhofer, Ramón Pichs-Madruga, Youba Sokona, Ellie Farahani, Susanne Kadner, Kristin Seyboth, Anna Adler, et al. Cambridge: Cambridge University Press, 2014. http://www.ipcc.ch/pdf/assessment -report/ar5/wg3/ipcc_wg3_ar5_full.pdf.

International Energy Agency. "Global EV Outlook 2016: Beyond One Million Electric Cars." Paris: International Energy Agency, 2016.

———. "World Energy Outlook 2015: Energy and Climate Change Special Report." Paris: International Energy Agency, 2015.

Jackson, Tim. *Prosperity without Growth: Economics for a Finite Planet*. London: Routledge, 2011.

Jaffal, Issa, Salah-Eddine Ouldboukhitine, and Rafik Belarbi. "A Comprehensive Study of the Impact of Green Roofs on Building Energy Performance." *Renewable Energy* 43 (July 2012): 157–164. doi:10.1016/j.renene.2011.12.004.

Jasper, J. "Social Movements." In *The Blackwell Encyclopedia of Sociology*, edited by George Ritzer. Malden, MA: Blackwell, 2007.

Jillella, Satya Sai Kumar, Annie Matan, and Peter Newman. "Participatory Sustainability Approach to Value Capture-Based Urban Rail Financing in India through Deliberated Stakeholder Engagement." *Sustainability* 7, no. 7 (2015): 8091–8115. doi:10.3390 /su7078091.

Johansson, Börje, and John M. Quigley. "Agglomeration and Networks in Spatial Economics." *Papers in Regional Science* 83, no. 1 (January 2004): 165–176. doi:10.1007 /s10110-003-0181-z.

Johnson, Kevin. "The Geography of Melbourne's Knowledge Economy." In *Proceedings of the Third Knowledge Cities World Summit: From Theory to Practice*, edited by Tan Yigitcanlar, Peter Yates, and Klaus Kunzmann, 1055–1090. Melbourne: World Capital Institute, City of Melbourne, and Office of Knowledge Capital, 2010.

Johnson, Kirk. "Targeting Inequality, This Time on Public Transit." *New York Times*, February 28, 2015. http://mobile.nytimes.com/2015/03/01/us/targeting-inequality -this-time-on-public-transit.html.

Kane, Michael Patrick. "Devising Public Transport Systems for Twenty-First Century Economically Productive Cities—the Proposed Knowledge Ring for Perth." *Australian Planner* 47, no. 2 (2010): 75–84. doi:10.1080/07293681003767777.

Kellert, Stephen R., Judith Heerwagen, and Martin Mador. *Biophilic Design: The Theory, Science, and Practice of Bringing Buildings to Life*. Hoboken, NJ: John Wiley & Sons, 2008.

Kenworthy, J. R., F. B. Laube, P. Newman, P. Barter, T. Raad, C. Poboon, and B. Guia Jr. *An International Sourcebook of Automobile Dependence in Cities, 1960–1990*. Boulder: University Press of Colorado, 1999.

Ker, I. "North Brisbane Household TravelSmart: Peer Review and Evaluation, for Brisbane City Council." Brisbane: Queensland Transport and Australian Greenhouse Office, 2008.

Kintner-Meyer, Michael, Kevin Schneider, and Robert Pratt. "Impacts Assessment of Plug-in Hybrid Vehicles on Electric Utilities and Regional U.S. Power Grids: Part 1: Technical Analysis." U.S. Department of Energy Contract no. DE-AC05-76RL01830. Richland, WA: Pacific Northwest National Laboratory, November 2007.

Kontoleon, K. J., and E. A. Eumorfopoulou. "The Effect of the Orientation and Proportion of a Plant-Covered Wall Layer on the Thermal Performance of a Building Zone." *Building and Environment* 45 (2010): 1287–1303. doi:10.1016/j.buildenv.2009.11.013.

Kooshian, Chuck, and Steve Winkelman. *Growing Wealthier: Smart Growth, Climate Change, and Prosperity*. Washington, DC: Center for Clean Air Policy, January 2011.

Kostoff, Spiro. *The City Assembled: The Elements of Urban Form through History*. London: Thames & Hudson, 1992.

Kuo, Frances E., and William C. Sullivan. "Environment and Crime in the Inner City: Does Vegetation Reduce Crime?" *Environment and Behavior* 33, no. 3 (May 2001): 343–367.

The Lancet. Series. "Urban Design, Transport, and Health." September 23, 2016. http://www.thelancet.com/series/urban-design.

LandCorp. "Shared Solar Power on Trial in Australian First." Innovation WGV, September 9, 2015. http://www.landcorp.com.au/innovation/wgv/Latest/Shared-solar-power -on-trial-in-Australian-first/.

Lee, J. Y., H. J. Moon, T. I. Kim, H. W. Kim, and M. Y. Han. "Quantitative Analysis on the Urban Flood Mitigation Effect by the Extensive Green Roof System." *Environmental Pollution* 181 (October 2013): 257–261. doi:10.1016/j.envpol.2013.06.039.

Leinberger, Christopher B., and Patrick Lynch. "Foot Traffic Ahead: Ranking Walkable Urbanism in America's Largest Metros." Washington, DC: George Washington University School of Business, Center for Real Estate and Urban Analysis, 2014.

Leung, Dennis Y. C., Jeanie K. Y. Tsui, Feng Chen, Wing-Kin Yip, Lilian L. P. Vrijmoed, and Chun-Ho Liu. "Effects of Urban Vegetation on Urban Air Quality." *Landscape Research* 36, no. 2 (2011): 173–188.

Levin, Hal. "Can House Plants Solve Indoor Air Quality Problems?" *Indoor Air Bulletin* 2, no. 2 (February 1992).

Li, Qing, T. Otsuka, M. Kobayashi, Y. Wakayama, H. Inagaki, M. Katsumata, Y. Hirata, et al. "Acute Effects of Walking in Forest Environments on Cardiovascular and Metabolic Parameters." *European Journal of Applied Physiology* 111, no. 11 (November 2011): 2845–2853. doi:10.1007/s00421-011-1918-z.

Litman, Todd. "Changing Vehicle Travel Price Sensitivities: The Rebounding Rebound Effect." Victoria, British Columbia: Victoria Transport Policy Institute, September 12, 2012. http://www.vtpi.org/VMT_Elasticities.pdf.

———. "Truly Responsive and Inclusive Planning." *Planetizen* (blog), November 15, 2016. http://www.planetizen.com/node/89718.

Liu, Amy, Roland V. Anglin, Richard M. Mizelle, and Allison Plyer, eds. *Resilience and Opportunity: Lessons from the U.S. Gulf Coast after Katrina and Rita*. Washington, DC: Brookings Institution Press, 2011.

Liu, Chao, and Qing Shen. "An Empirical Analysis of the Influence of Urban Form on Household Travel and Energy Consumption." *Computers, Environment, and Urban Systems* 35, no. 5 (September 2011): 347–357. doi:http://dx.doi.org/10.1016/j.compenvurbsys.2011.05.006.

Lomholt, Isabelle. "Living Wall Biofilter." *e-architect* (blog), April 22, 2014. http://www.e-architect.co.uk/toronto/living-wall-biofilter.

Louv, Richard. *Last Child in the Woods: Saving Our Children from Nature-Deficit Disorder.* New York: Algonquin Books, 2006.

Lyle, John Tillman. *Regenerative Design for Sustainable Development.* Hoboken, NJ: John Wiley & Sons, 1996.

Madre, Frédéric, Alan Vergnes, Nathalie Machon, and Philippe Clergeau. "Green Roofs as Habitats for Wild Plant Species in Urban Landscapes: First Insights from a Large-Scale Sampling." *Landscape and Urban Planning* 122 (2014): 100–107. doi:10.1016/j.landurbplan.2013.11.012.

Malecki, Edward J. "Cities and Regions Competing in the Global Economy: Knowledge and Local Development Policies." *Environment and Planning C: Government and Policy* 25, no. 5 (2007): 638–654. doi:10.1068/c0645.

Marchetti, Cesare. "Anthropological Invariants in Travel Behavior." *Technological Forecasting and Social Change* 47, no. 1 (September 1994): 75–88. doi:10.1016/0040-1625(94)90041-8.

Marinova, Dora, Amzad Hossain, and Popie Hossain-Rhaman. "Sustaining Local Lifestyle through Self Reliance: Core Principles." Chap. 40 in *Sharing Wisdom for Our Future: Environmental Education in Action: Proceedings of the 2006 Conference of the Australian Association of Environmental Education,* edited by Sandra Wooltorton and Dora Marinova. Cotton Tree, Queensland: Australian Association of Environmental Education, 2006.

Mastny, Lisa, ed. "Biofuels for Transportation: Global Potential and Implications for Sustainable Agriculture and Energy in the 21st Century." Report prepared by the Worldwatch Institute for the German Federal Ministry of Food, Agriculture and Consumer

Protection (BMELV), in cooperation with the Agency for Technical Cooperation (GTZ) and the Agency of Renewable Resources (FNR). Washington, DC: Worldwatch Institute, 2006. http://www.worldwatch.org/system/files/EBF008_1.pdf.

Matan, Annie, and Peter Newman. *People Cities: The Life and Legacy of Jan Gehl.* Washington, DC: Island Press, 2016.

Matan, Annie, Peter Newman, Roman Trubka, Colin Beattie, and Linda Anne Selvey. "Health, Transport, and Urban Planning: Quantifying the Links between Urban Assessment Models and Human Health." *Urban Policy and Research* 33, no. 2 (2015): 145–159. doi:10.1080/08111146.2014.990626.

Matsunaga, K., B.-J. Park, H. Kobayashi, and Y. Miyazaki. "Physiologically Relaxing Effect of a Hospital Rooftop Forest on Older Women Requiring Care." *Journal of the American Geriatrics Society* 59, no. 11 (November 2011): 2162–2163. doi:10.1111/j.1532-5415.2011.03651.x.

Mazria, Ed. *Urban Land* 35 (November–December 2007).

Mazur, Laurie. "Bounce Forward: Urban Resilience in the Age of Climate Change." Strategy paper from Island Press and the Kresge Foundation, 2015. https://islandpress.org/resources/KresgeBrochure-framing-doc.pdf.

McIntosh, James, Peter Newman, and Garry Glazebrook. "Why Fast Trains Work: An Assessment of a Fast Regional Rail System in Perth, Australia." *Journal of Transportation Technologies* 3, no. 2A (May 2013): 37–47. doi:10.4236/jtts.2013.32A005.

McIntosh, James, Roman Trubka, and Peter Newman. "Can Value Capture Work in a Car Dependent City? Willingness to Pay for Transit Access in Perth, Western Australia." *Transportation Research Part A* 67 (2014): 320–339. doi:10.1016/j.tra.2014.07.008.

McKinnon, Alan C. "Decoupling of Road Freight Transport and Economic Growth Trends in the UK: An Exploratory Analysis." *Transport Reviews* 27, no. 1 (2007): 37–64. doi:10.1080/01441640600825952.

Mentens, Jeroen, Dirk Raes, and Martin Hermy. "Green Roofs as a Tool for Solving the Rainwater Runoff Problem in the Urbanized 21st Century?" *Landscape and Urban Planning* 77 (2006): 217–226. doi:10.1016/j.landurbplan.2005.02.010.

Metschies, Gerhard P. *Fuel Prices and Vehicle Taxation.* Eschborn, Germany: Deutsche Gesellschaft für Technische Zusammenarbeit (GTZ) GmbH, 2001.

Mickey, John. "Six Health Benefits of Public Transportation." TransLoc, June 25, 2013. http://transloc.com/6-health-benefits-of-public-transportation/.

Miyawaki, Akira. "Restoration of Urban Green Environments Based on the Theories of Vegetation Ecology." *Ecological Engineering* 11, nos. 1–4 (October 1998): 157–165. doi:10.1016/S0925-8574(98)00033-0.

Molden, David. "Planetary Boundaries: The Devil Is in the Detail." *Nature Reports Climate Change* 3 (October 2009): 116–117. doi:10.1038/climate.2009.97.

Moore, E. O. "A Prison Environment's Effect on Health Care Service Demands." *Journal of Environmental Systems* 11 (1981): 17–34.

Moulton, Emily. "Perth Could Soon Be the First City to Be Completely Solar Powered." News.com.au, October 26, 2015. http://www.news.com.au/technology/environment

/climate-change/perth-could-soon-be-the-first-city-to-be-completely-solar-powered
/news-story/8fd36f41526e7619bd3db3b7f20fa0c4?csp=9920c057b85ae6a12fba
983c70c68e13.

Mumford, Lewis. *The City in History: Its Origins, Its Transformations, and Its Prospects*. Harmondsworth: Penguin Books, 1991.

Nagourney, Adam. "The Capital of Car Culture, Los Angeles Warms to Mass Transit." *New York Times*, July 20, 2016. http://www.nytimes.com/2016/07/21/us/the-capital-of-car-culture-los-angeles-warms-to-mass-transit.html.

Nanda, Upali, Debajyoti Pati, Hessam Ghamari, and Robyn Bajema. "Lessons from Neuroscience: Form Follows Function, Emotions Follow Form." *Intelligent Buildings International* 5, no. S1 (2013): 61–78. doi:10.1080/17508975.2013.807767.

National Research Council of the National Academies. *Climate Intervention: Reflecting Sunlight to Cool Earth*. Washington, DC: National Academies Press, 2015.

Nature. "Leapfrogging the Power Grid." Editorial. *Nature* 427, no. 661 (February 19, 2004). doi:10.1038/427661a.

Nelson, Laura J. "Los Angeles Area Can Claim the Worst Traffic in America. Again." *Los Angeles Times*, March 15, 2016. http://www.latimes.com/local/lanow/la-me-ln-la-worst-traffic-20160314-story.html.

Newman, Peter. "Australia Needs to Follow the US in Funding Urban Rail Projects." *The Conversation*, August 31, 2016.

———. "Biophilic Urbanism: A Case Study on Singapore." *Australian Planner* 51, no. 1 (2014): 47–65. doi:10.1080/07293682.2013.790832.

———. "Bridging the Green and Brown Agendas." Chap. 6 in *Planning Sustainable Cities: Global Report on Human Settlements 2009*, by the United Nations Human Settlements Programme (UN-Habitat). London: Earthscan and United Nations Human Settlements Programme, 2009. http://unhabitat.org/books/global-report-on-human-settlements-2009-planning-sustainable-cities/.

———. "Perth as a 'Big' City: Reflections on Urban Growth." *Thesis Eleven* 135, no. 1 (July 4, 2016): 139–151. doi:10.1177/0725513616657906.

———. "The Story of Perth's Water Resilience Turnaround." *Water: Journal of the Australian Water Association* 41, no. 7 (November 2014): 24–26. http://digitaledition.awa.asn.au/default.aspx?iid=105088&startpage=page0000026#folio=26.

Newman, Peter, Tim Beatley, and Linda Blagg. *Christchurch: Resilient City*. A Curtin University Sustainability Policy (CUSP) Institute video. Posted March 30, 2014. https://www.youtube.com/watch?v=otv4JwjrznI.

———. *Singapore: Biophilic City*. A Curtin University Sustainability Policy (CUSP) Institute video. Posted May 7, 2012. https://www.youtube.com/watch?v=XMWOu9xIM_k.

Newman, Peter, Janette Hartz-Karp, and Linda Blagg. *Taming Streets: Design, Deliberation, and Delivery in Indian Cities*. A Curtin University Sustainability Policy (CUSP) Institute video. Posted December 5, 2015. https://www.youtube.com/watch?v=NxXDNtcaMno.

Newman, Peter, and Isabella Jennings. *Cities as Sustainable Ecosystems: Principles and Practices*. Washington, DC: Island Press, 2008.

Newman, Peter, Evan Jones, Jemma Green, and Sebastian Davies-Slate. "The Entrepreneur Rail Model: Tapping Private Investment for New Urban Rail." Perth: Curtin University Sustainability Policy (CUSP) Institute, February 2016. http://www.curtin.edu.au /research/cusp/local/docs/Rail_Model_Report.pdf.

Newman, Peter, and Jeffrey Kenworthy. *The End of Automobile Dependence: How Cities Are Moving Beyond Car-Based Planning.* Washington, DC: Island Press, 2015.

———. "Greening Urban Transportation." Chap. 4 in *State of the World 2007: Our Urban Future,* by the Worldwatch Institute. New York: W. W. Norton & Company, 2007.

———. *Sustainability and Cities: Overcoming Automobile Dependence.* Washington, DC: Island Press, 1999.

Newman, Peter, Jeffrey Kenworthy, and Garry Glazebrook. "Peak Car Use and the Rise of Global Rail: Why This Is Happening and What It Means for Large and Small Cities." *Journal of Transportation Technologies* 3, no. 4 (October 2013): 272–287. doi:10.4236 /jtts.2013.34029.

Newman, Peter, Leo Kosonen, and Jeff Kenworthy. "Theory of Urban Fabrics: Planning the Walking, Transit/Public Transport, and Automobile/Motor Car Cities for Reduced Car Dependency." *Town Planning Review* 87, no. 4 (2016): 429–458. doi:10.3828/tpr.2016.28.

Newman, Peter, and Annie Matan. *Green Urbanism in Asia: The Emerging Green Tigers.* Singapore: World Scientific, 2013.

Newton, Peter, and Peter Newman. "Critical Connections: The Role of the Built Environment Sector in Delivering Green Cities and a Green Economy." *Sustainability* 7, no. 7 (2015): 9417–9443. doi:10.3390/su7079417.

———. "Low Carbon Green Growth: Tracking Progress in Australia's Built Environment Industry Towards a Green Economy." Melbourne and Perth: Swinburne University of Technology and Curtin University, September 2013. https://www.gbca.org.au /gbc_scripts/js/tiny_mce/plugins/filemanager/Low_Carbon_Green_Growth_BE _Report_16Sept.pdf.

Nieuwenhuis, Marlon, Craig Knight, Tom Postmes, and S. Alexander Haslam. "The Relative Benefits of Green versus Lean Office Space: Three Field Experiments." *Journal of Experimental Psychology: Applied* 20, no. 3 (2014): 199–214. doi:10.1037/xap0000024.

Normile, Dennis. "China Rethinks Cities." *Science* 352, no. 6288 (May 20, 2016): 916–918. doi:10.1126/science.352.6288.916.

Noss, Reed F., and Allen Y. Cooperrider. *Saving Nature's Legacy: Protecting and Restoring Biodiversity.* Washington, DC: Island Press, 1994.

Nykvist, Björn, and Måns Nilsson. "Rapidly Falling Costs of Battery Packs for Electric Vehicles." *Nature Climate Change* 5 (2015): 329–332. doi:10.1038/nclimate2564.

Oldridge, Neil B. "Economic Burden of Physical Inactivity: Healthcare Costs Associated with Cardiovascular Disease." *European Journal of Preventive Cardiology* (formerly *European Journal of Cardiovascular Prevention and Rehabilitation*) 15, no. 2 (2008): 130–139. doi:10.1097/HJR.0b013e3282f19d42.

Ostendorf, M., W. Retzlaff, K. Thompson, M. Woolbright, S. Morgan, and S. Celik. "Storm Water Runoff from Green Retaining Wall Systems." Paper presented at Cities

Alive: Ninth Annual Green Roofs and Green Walls Conference, Philadelphia, November 30–December 3, 2011.

Ottelé, Marc, Katia Perini, A. L. A. Fraaij, E. M. Haas, and R. Raiteri. "Comparative Life Cycle Analysis for Green Façades and Living Wall Systems." *Energy and Buildings* 43, no. 12 (December 2011): 3419–3429. doi:10.1016/j.enbuild.2011.09.010.

Ottelé, Marc, Hein D. van Bohemen, and Alex L. A. Fraaij. "Quantifying the Deposition of Particulate Matter on Climber Vegetation on Living Walls." *Ecological Engineering* 36, no. 2 (February 2010): 154–162. doi:10.1016/j.ecoleng.2009.02.007.

Park, Bum Jin, Yuko Tsunetsugu, Tamami Kasetani, Takahide Kagawa, and Yoshifumi Miyazaki. "The Physiological Effects of *Shinrin-Yoku* (Taking In the Forest Atmosphere or Forest Bathing): Evidence from Field Experiments in 24 Forests across Japan." *Environmental Health and Preventive Medicine* 15 (2010): 18–26. doi:10.1007/s12199-009-0086-9.

Park, Seong-Hyun, and Richard H. Mattson. "Effects of Flowering and Foliage Plants in Hospital Rooms on Patients Recovering from Abdominal Surgery." *HortTechnology* 18, no. 4 (December 2008): 563–568.

Pauli, Gunter. *The Blue Economy: 10 Years, 100 Innovations, 100 Million Jobs.* Brookline, MA: Paradigm, 2010.

Peeples, Doug. "Want a Truly Resilient Smart City? Then Let's Talk Microgrids." Smart Cities Council, November 17, 2016. http://smartcitiescouncil.com/article/want-truly-resilient-smart-city-then-lets-talk-microgrids.

Pegas, Priscilla Nascimento, Célia Alves, Teresa Nunes, E. F. Bate-Epey, M. Evtyugina, and Casimiro Adrião Pio. "Could Houseplants Improve Indoor Air Quality in Schools?" *Journal of Toxicology and Environmental Health, Part A* 75, nos. 22–23 (2012): 1371–1380. doi:10.1080/15287394.2012.721169.

Petschel-Held, Gerhard, Hans-Joachim Schellnhuber, Thomas Bruckner, Ferenc L. Tóth, and Klaus Hasselmann. "The Tolerable Windows Approach: Theoretical and Methodological Foundations." *Climatic Change* 41, no. 3 (March 1999): 303–331. doi:10.1023/A:1005487123751.

Pettit, Chris J., Stephen Glackin, Roman Trubka, Tuan Ngo, Oliver Lade, Peter Newton, and Peter Newman. "A Co-design Prototyping Approach for Building a Precinct Planning Tool." *ISPRS Annals of the Photogrammetry, Remote Sensing, and Spatial Information Sciences* II-2 (2014): 47–53. doi:10.5194/isprsannals-II-2-47-2014.

Pisano, Umberto, and Gerald Berger. "Planetary Boundaries for SD: From an International Perspective to National Applications." ESDN Quarterly Report no. 30 (Vienna: European Sustainable Development Network, October 2013). http://www.sd-network.eu/quarterly%20reports/report%20files/pdf/2013-October-Planetary_Boundaries_for_SD.pdf.

Plains CO_2 Reduction (PCOR) Partnership. "Regional Storage Potential." http://www.undeerc.org/pcor/region/.

Porter, Richard C. *Economics at the Wheel: The Costs of Cars and Drivers.* London: Academic Press, 1999.

Pucher, John, and Ralph Buehler. "Safer Cycling through Improved Infrastructure." Editorial. *American Journal of Public Health* 106, no. 12 (December 2016): 2089–2091. doi:10.2105/AJPH.2016.303507.

Pugh, Thomas A. M., A. Robert MacKenzie, J. Duncan Whyatt, and C. Nicholas Hewitt. "Effectiveness of Green Infrastructure for Improvement of Air Quality in Urban Street Canyons." *Environmental Science & Technology* 46, no. 14 (2012): 7692–7699. doi:10.1021/es300826w.

Rauland, Vanessa, and Peter Newman. *Decarbonising Cities: Mainstreaming Low Carbon Urban Development.* London: Springer, 2015.

Renne, John L., and Billy Fields, eds. *Transport Beyond Oil: Policy Choices for a Multimodal Future.* Washington, DC: Island Press, 2013.

Robèrt, Karl-Henrik, Göran I. Broman, and George Basile. "Analyzing the Concept of Planetary Boundaries from a Strategic Sustainability Perspective: How Does Humanity Avoid Tipping the Planet?" *Ecology and Society* 18, no. 2 (2013): art. 5. doi:10.5751/ES-05336-180205.

Rockström, Johan, Will Steffen, Kevin Noone, Åsa Persson, F. Stuart Chapin III, Eric F. Lambin, Timothy M. Lenton, et al. "A Safe Operating Space for Humanity." *Nature* 461 (September 24, 2009): 472–475. doi:10.1038/461472a.

Rockström, Johan, Will Steffen, Kevin Noone, Åsa Persson, F. Stuart Chapin III, Eric F. Lambin, Timothy M. Lenton, et al. "Planetary Boundaries: Exploring the Safe Operating Space for Humanity." *Ecology and Society* 14, no. 2 (2009): art. 32. http://www.ecologyandsociety.org/vol14/iss2/art32/.

Rodionova, Zlata. "UberPOOL Gets More Than 1 Million Customers." *The Independent,* June 7, 2016.

Rowe, D. Bradley. "Green Roofs as a Means of Pollution Abatement." *Environmental Pollution* 159, nos. 8–9 (August–September 2011): 2100–2110. doi:10.1016/j.envpol.2010.10.029.

Rutkin, Aviva. "Blockchain-Based Microgrid Gives Power to Consumers in New York." *New Scientist,* March 2, 2016. https://www.newscientist.com/article/2079334-blockchain-based-microgrid-gives-power-to-consumers-in-new-york/?utm_source=NSNS&utm_medium=SOC&utm_campaign=hoot&cmpid=SOC%7CNSNS%7C2016-GLOBAL-hoot.

Salter, Robert, Subash Dhar, and Peter Newman. *Technologies for Climate Change Mitigation—Transport Sector.* TNA Guidebook Series. Roskilde, Denmark: UNEP Riso Centre on Energy, Climate and Sustainable Development, 2011.

Salzman, Randy. "Now That's What I Call Intelligent Transport . . . SmartTravel." *Thinking Highways,* 2008.

———. "Travel Smart: A Marketing Program Empowers Citizens to Be a Part of the Solution in Improving the Environment." *Mass Transit* 34, no. 2 (2008): 8–11.

Scheurer, Jan, and Peter Newman. "Vauban: A European Model Bridging the Green and Brown Agendas." Unpublished case study prepared for *Planning Sustainable Cities: Global Report on Human Settlements 2009,* by the United Nations Human Settlements Programme (UN-Habitat). London: Earthscan and United Nations Human Settlements Programme,

2009. http://unhabitat.org/books/global-report-on-human-settlements-2009-planning-sustainable-cities/.

Schreiber, Franziska, and Alexander Carius. "The Inclusive City: Urban Planning for Diversity and Social Cohesion." Chap. 18 in *Can a City Be Sustainable? (State of the World)* by Worldwatch Institute. Washington, DC: Island Press, 2016.

Schroll, Erin, John Lambrinos, Tim Righetti, and David Sandrock. "The Role of Vegetation in Regulating Stormwater Runoff from Green Roofs in a Winter Rainfall Climate." *Ecological Engineering* 37, no. 4 (April 2011): 595–600. doi:10.1016/j.ecoleng.2010.12.020.

Seba, Tony. *Clean Disruption of Energy and Transportation: How Silicon Valley Will Make Oil, Nuclear, Natural Gas, Coal, Electric Utilities, and Conventional Cars Obsolete by 2030.* Silicon Valley, CA: Clean Planet Ventures, 2014. http://www.tonyseba.com.

Seidl, Martin, Marie-Christine Gromaire, Mohamed Saad, and Bernard De Gouvello. "Effect of Substrate Depth and Rain-Event History on the Pollutant Abatement of Green Roofs." *Environmental Pollution* 183 (December 2013): 195–203. doi:10.1016/j.envpol.2013.05.026.

Semuels, Alana. "Highways Destroyed America's Cities: Can Tearing Them Down Bring Revitalization?" *Atlantic Monthly*, November 25, 2015.

Sheweka, Samar, and Nourhan Magdy Mohamed. "Green Facades as a New Sustainable Approach Towards Climate Change." *Energy Procedia* 18 (2012): 507–520. doi:10.1016/j.egypro.2012.05.062.

———. "The Living Walls as an Approach for a Healthy Urban Environment." *Energy Procedia* 6 (2011): 592–599. doi:10.1016/j.egypro.2011.05.068.

Sioshansi, Fereidoon P. *Distributed Generation and Its Implications for the Utility Industry.* Cambridge: Elsevier, Academic Press, 2014.

Sivak, Michael, and Brandon Schoettle. "What Individual Americans Can Do to Assist in Meeting the Paris Agreement." UMTRI-2016-7. Ann Arbor: University of Michigan, Transportation Research Institute, February 2016.

Söderlund, Jana. "Biophilic Design: A Social Movement Journey." PhD diss., Curtin University, Curtin University Sustainability Policy (CUSP) Institute, 2015.

Söderlund, Jana, and Peter Newman. "Biophilic Architecture: A Review of the Rationale and Outcomes." *AIMS Environmental Science* 2, no. 4 (2015): 950–969. doi:10.3934/environsci.2015.4.950.

Steffen, Will, Åsa Persson, Lisa Deutsch, Jan Zalasiewicz, Mark Williams, Katherine Richardson, Carole Crumley, et al. "The Anthropocene: From Global Change to Planetary Stewardship." *Ambio* 40, no. 7 (November 2011): 739–761. doi:10.1007/s13280-011-0185-x.

Steffen, Will, Katherine Richardson, Johan Rockström, Sarah E. Cornell, Ingo Fetzer, Elena M. Bennett, Reinette Biggs, et al. "Planetary Boundaries: Guiding Human Development on a Changing Planet." *Science* 347, no. 6223 (February 13, 2015). doi:10.1126/science.1259855.

Stock, Andrew, Petra Stock, and Veena Sahajwalla. "Powerful Potential: Battery Storage for Renewable Energy and Electric Cars." Sydney: Climate Council of Australia, 2015. https://www.climatecouncil.org.au/uploads/ebdfcdf89a6ce85c4c19a5f6a78989d7.pdf.

Susca, Tiziana, Stuart R. Gaffin, and G. R. Dell'Osso. "Positive Effects of Vegetation: Urban Heat Island and Green Roofs." *Environmental Pollution* 159, nos. 8–9 (August 2011): 2119–2126. doi:10.1016/j.envpol.2011.03.007.

Sustainable Built Environment National Research Centre. "Perth Airport Sustainability Research Project." Overview Report. Brisbane: Sustainable Built Environment National Research Centre, 2017. http://www.sbenrc.com.au.

———. "A Stakeholder Engagement Approach to Enhancing Transport Network Resilience in Australia: A Sustainable Built Environment National Research Centre (SBEnrc) Industry Report." Report no. 1.35. Brisbane: Sustainable Built Environment National Research Centre, 2016.

Sustainable Development Solutions Network (SDSN). "An Action Agenda for Sustainable Development." Report for the UN Secretary-General. Paris: Sustainable Development Solutions Network, June 6, 2013. http://unstats.un.org/unsd/broaderprogress/pdf/130613-SDSN-An-Action-Agenda-for-Sustainable-Development-FINAL.pdf.

Tan, Alex, and Kelly Chiang. *Vertical Greenery for the Tropics.* Singapore: Centre for Urban Greenery and Ecology, 2009.

Teferi, Zafu, Peter Newman, and Annie Matan. "Applying a Sustainable Development Model to Informal Settlements in Addis Ababa." Chap. 8 in *Indian Ocean Futures: Communities, Sustainability, and Security,* edited by Thor Kerr and John Stephens. Newcastle upon Tyne: Cambridge Scholars Publishing, 2016.

Thayer, Robert L. Jr. *LifePlace: Bioregional Thought and Practice.* Berkeley: University of California Press, 2003.

Thomson, Giles, and Peter Newman. "Urban Fabrics and Urban Metabolism: From Sustainable to Regenerative Cities." *Resources, Conservation, and Recycling* (online February 2017). doi:10.1016/j.resconrec.2017.01.010.

Trubka, Roman, Peter Newman, and Darren Bilsborough. "The Costs of Urban Sprawl—Physical Activity Links to Healthcare Costs and Productivity." *Environment Design Guide* 85 (2010): 1–13.

Tyrväinen, Liisa, Ann Ojala, Kalevi Korpela, Timo Lanki, Yuko Tsunetsugu, and Takahide Kagawa. "The Influence of Urban Green Environments on Stress Relief Measures: A Field Experiment." *Journal of Environmental Psychology* 38 (June 2014): 1–9. doi:10.1016/j.jenvp.2013.12.005.

Ulrich, Roger S. "View through a Window May Influence Recovery from Surgery." *Science* 224, no. 4647 (April 27, 1984): 420–421.

Ulrich, Roger S., Robert F. Simons, Barbara D. Losito, Evelyn Fiorito, Mark A. Miles, and Michael Zelson. "Stress Recovery During Exposure to Natural and Urban Environments." *Journal of Environmental Psychology* 11, no. 3 (September 1991): 201–230. doi:10.1016/S0272-4944(05)80184-7.

United Nations. "The Millennium Development Goals Report 2015." New York: United Nations, 2015.

United Nations Department of Economic and Social Affairs, Population Division. "World Urbanization Prospects: The 2014 Revision, Highlights." ST/ESA/SER.A/352.

New York: United Nations, 2014. https://esa.un.org/unpd/wup/Publications/Files /WUP2014-Highlights.pdf.

United Nations Environment Programme (UNEP). "City-Level Decoupling: Urban Resource Flows and the Governance of Infrastructure Transitions." Report of the Working Group on Cities of the International Resource Panel, by M. Swilling, B. Robinson, S. Marvin, and M. Hodson. Nairobi: United Nations Environment Programme, 2013. http://unep.org/resourcepanel-old/portals/24102/pdfs/Cities-Full_Report.pdf.

———. "Decoupling Natural Resource Use and Environmental Impacts from Economic Growth." Report of the Working Group on Decoupling to the International Resource Panel, by M. Fischer-Kowalski, M. Swilling, E. U. von Weizsäcker, Y. Ren, Y. Moriguchi, W. Crane, F. Krausmann, et al. Nairobi: United Nations Environment Programme, 2011. http://www.unep.org/resourcepanel/decoupling/files/pdf/decoupling_report_english.pdf.

United Nations Human Settlements Programme (UN-Habitat). *Planning Sustainable Cities: Global Report on Human Settlements 2009*. London: Earthscan and United Nations Human Settlements Programme, 2009. http://unhabitat.org/books/global-report-on -human-settlements-2009-planning-sustainable-cities/.

———. *State of the World's Cities 2012/2013: Prosperity of Cities*. Nairobi: United Nations Human Settlements Programme, 2013. https://sustainabledevelopment.un.org /content/documents/745habitat.pdf.

———. *World Cities Report 2016: Urbanization and Development: Emerging Futures*. Nairobi: United Nations Human Settlements Programme, 2016. http://wcr.unhabitat.org/.

University of California, Davis. "UC Davis West Village Energy Initiative Annual Report 2013–2014." Davis: University of California, Davis, 2014. http://sustainability.ucdavis .edu/local_resources/docs/wvei_annual_report_2013_14.pdf.

University of Oxford, Oxford Martin School. "'Oxford Principles' Vital for Geoengineering Research." Press release, September 14, 2011. http://www.oxfordmartin.ox.ac.uk /news/201109-oxfordprinciples.

van Vuuren, Detlef P., Paul L. Lucas, Tiina Häyhä, Sarah E. Cornell, and Mark Stafford-Smith. "Horses for Courses: Analytical Tools to Explore Planetary Boundaries." *Earth System Dynamics* 7, no. 1 (2016): 267–279. doi:10.5194/esd-7-267-2016.

von Weizsäcker, Ernst Ulrich, Karlson "Charlie" Hargroves, Michael H. Smith, Cheryl Desha, and Peter Stasinopoulos. *Factor Five: Transforming the Global Economy through 80% Improvements in Resource Productivity*. London: Earthscan, 2009.

Wake, David. "Reducing Car Commuting through Employer-Based Travel Planning in Perth, Australia." *TDM Review* 15, no. 1 (2007): 11–13.

Walker, Brian, and David Salt, with foreword by Walter Reid. *Resilience Thinking: Sustaining Ecosystems and People in a Changing World*. Washington, DC: Island Press, 2006.

Wallington, Tabatha J., Richard J. Hobbs, and Susan A. Moore. "Implications of Current Ecological Thinking for Biodiversity Conservation: A Review of the Salient Issues." *Ecology and Society* 10, no. 1 (2005): 15-1–15-15.

Wang, Ranran, Matthew J. Eckelman, and Julie B. Zimmerman. "Consequential Environmental and Economic Life Cycle Assessment of Green and Gray Stormwater Infrastructures for Combined Sewer Systems." *Environmental Science & Technology* 47, no. 19 (October 2013): 11189–11198. doi:10.1021/es4026547.

Water Corporation of Western Australia. "Water Forever: Towards Climate Resilience." Perth: Water Corporation of Western Australia, October 2009. https://www.water corporation.com.au/-/media/files/about-us/planning-for-the-future/water-forever-50 -year-plan.pdf.

Waters, Colin N., Jan Zalasiewicz, Colin Summerhayes, Anthony Barnosky, Clément Poir-ier, Agnieszka Gałuszka, Alejandro Cearreta, et al. "The Anthropocene Is Functionally and Stratigraphically Distinct from the Holocene." *Science* 351, no. 6269 (January 8, 2016): 137–147. doi:10.1126/science.aad2622.

Wei, Wang, and Gong Jinlong. "Methanation of Carbon Dioxide: An Overview." *Frontiers of Chemical Science and Engineering* 5, no. 1 (March 2011): 2–10. doi:10.1007/s11705 -010-0528-3.

Western Australia Department of Transport. "TravelSmart Household Final Evaluation Re-port Murdoch Station Catchment (City of Melville 2007)." Perth: Socialdata Australia, September 2009.

Williams, B. "Hopetoun Infrastructure Study." Perth: Landcorp, Government of Western Australia, 2008.

Wilson, Edward O. *Biophilia: The Human Bond with Other Species.* Cambridge, MA: Harvard University Press, 1984.

Wolf, Kathleen L. "Trees in the Small City Retail Business District: Comparing Resident and Visitor Perceptions." *Journal of Forestry* 103, no. 8 (December 2005): 390–395.

Wolman, Abel. "The Metabolism of Cities." *Scientific American* 213, no. 3 (1965): 179–190.

Wolverton, B. C., Rebecca C. McDonald, and E. A. Watkins Jr. "Foliage Plants for Remov-ing Indoor Air Pollutants from Energy-Efficient Homes." *Economic Botany* 38, no. 2 (April–June 1984): 224–228. doi:10.1007/BF02858837.

Wong, Nyuk Hien, Alex Yong Kwang Tan, Yu Chen, Kannagi Sekar, Puay Yok Tan, Derek Chan, Kelly Chiang, and Ngian Chung Wong. "Thermal Evaluation of Vertical Green-ery Systems for Building Walls." *Building and Environment* 45, no. 3 (March 2010): 663–672. doi:10.1016/j.buildenv.2009.08.005.

Woo, Fiona. *Regenerative Urban Development.* Hamburg: World Future Council, 2014.

World Bank. "Toward a Sustainable Energy Future for All: Directions for the World Bank Group's Energy Sector." Washington, DC: World Bank Group, 2013. http://www-wds .worldbank.org/external/default/WDSContentServer/WDSP/IB/2013/07/17/000456286 _20130717103746/Rendered/PDF/795970SST0SecM00box377380B00PUBLIC0.pdf.

Yigitcanlar, Tan. "Making Space and Place for the Knowledge Economy: Knowl-edge-Based Development of Australian Cities." *European Planning Studies* 18, no. 11 (2010): 1769–1786.

Yildiz, Özgür, Jens Rommel, Sarah Debor, Lars Holstenkamp, Franziska Mey, Jakob R. Müller, Jörg Radtke, and Judith Rognli. "Renewable Energy Cooperatives as Gatekeepers or Facilitators? Recent Developments in Germany and a Multidisciplinary Research

Agenda." *Energy Research & Social Science* 6 (March 2015): 59–73. doi:10.1016 /j.erss.2014.12.001.

Zahavi, Y., and A. Talvitie. "Regularities in Travel Time and Money Expenditures." *Transportation Research Record* 750 (1980): 13–19.

Index